CHILD ABUSE AND NEGLECT – A MULTIDIMENSIONAL APPROACH

Edited by **Alexander Muela**

Child Abuse and Neglect – A Multidimensional Approach
http://dx.doi.org/10.5772/3035
Edited by Alexander Muela

Contributors

Alexander Muela, Elena López de Arana, Alexander Barandiaran, Iñaki Larrea, José Ramón Vitoria, Essam Al-Shail, Ahmed Hassan, Abdullah Aldowaish, Hoda Kattan, Anne Lazenbatt, Chantal Cyr, Karine Dubois-Comtois, Geneviève Michel, Caroline Poulin, Katherine Pascuzzo, Valérie Losier, Marilyne Dumais, Diane St-Laurent, Ellen Moss, Thozama Mandisa Lutya, Thais H. Bannwart, Lúcia C. A. Williams, Eduardo Martín, Euichul Jung and Joonbin Im

Published by InTech

Janeza Trdine 9, 51000 Rijeka, Croatia

Publishing Process Manager Martina Durovic
Technical Editor InTech Prepress, Novi Sad
Cover InTech Design team

Additional hard copies can be obtained from orders@intechopen.com

Child Abuse and Neglect – A Multidimensional Approach, Edited by Alexander Muela
p. cm.
ISBN 978-953-51-0671-5

For EU product safety concerns:
IN TECH d.o.o., Prolaz Marije Krucifikse Kozulić 3, 51000 Rijeka, Croatia,
info@intechopen.com or visit our website at intechopen.com.

Meet the editor

Dr Alexander Muela is a Professor and a Researcher of Psychology at the University of Mondragon, Spain. He received his Doctorate (Ph.D.) in Psychology from the University of the Basque Country, Spain where he worked from 2004 until 2010 as a Professor of Psychology. Dr Muela also works as a psychotherapist in the clinical field with abused children and adolescents, while his research interests include prevention programs for mistreated children, new interventions to promote positive parenting, and programs to improve the social integration and mental health of maltreated children. He has also published several articles related to this field of work and research in various Spanish publishing houses recognized internationally.

Contents

Preface

Child maltreatment constitutes a social problem that affects all societies of the world. A recent study by the World Health Organisation points out that millions of children suffer some form of maltreatment and require medical and social attention. It should be noted that around 53,000 children are murdered every year; the prevalence of sexual abuse is 73 million (7%) and 150 million (14%) in boys and girls, respectively, under 18 years of age; and between 25% and 50% of the children inform that they have been physically abused.

Child maltreatment in childhood and adolescence is recognized as an important psychopathological risk factor and is associated with poor psychological function in childhood and adolescence and adulthood. The aim of this book is to address the issue of child abuse and neglect from a multidimensional perspective. The reader will find a selection of internationally recognized works addressing the issue of child maltreatment both from theoretical and applied view.

In the opening chapter, Dr Muela, Dr López de Arana, Dr Barandiaran, Dr Larrea, and Dr Vitoria tackle the difficulties present in adequately conceptualizing child abuse and neglect, provide data on its incidence and describe the main psychopathological consequences associated with each type of child maltreatment. Thus, Dr Muela and colleagues focus on the heterogeneity of the phenomenon and on the complexity that gives rise to that heterogeneity to define the child abuse and neglect. In respect to negative impact of child maltreatment, they emphasize that it is wrong to believe that current knowledge has enabled the identification of clearly differentiated consequences for each type of child maltreatment. There is a high degree of co-morbidity among the different types, in such a way that many children experience more than one form of maltreatment and display common consequences. Moreover, it still needs to be clarified whether child abuse and neglect produce a general vulnerability towards psychopathology, in such a way that other factors would be responsible for the form finally adopted by psychopathology.

In the second chapter, Prof Al-Shail Essam, Dr Kattan Hoda, Dr Aldowaish Abdullah, and Dr Hassan Ahmed, focusing on Saudi Arabia, examine cultural factors that contribute to child abuse and neglect. Saudi Arabia is a country occupying most of the Arabian Peninsula with a population of about 27 million who are entirely Muslims. The country is governed according to the Islamic Sharia law whereby the Islamic orthodoxy and conservatism generally dominate the social and cultural characteristics and mechanisms of the Saudi society. Traditional tribal principles and customs, however, have significant influence over a wide range of cultural, behavioral, and attitudinal manifestations in the society. Children are usually well taken care of in terms of basic needs, and are expected to show almost total subordination and obedience to their parents. Corporal punishment by parents is a common practice, especially in less modernized portions of the society. The authors analyze the Saudi Arabian experience in the realm of child abuse that is in its conception stage.

In the third chapter, Dr Lazenbatt examines how domestic maltreatment can have an impact early in an infant's life, even as early as pregnancy and the postpartum period and can affect infants' physical and emotional health, their learning and their capacity to form positive relationships throughout their lives. The chapter is divided into sections that cover the issues of domestic abuse as a child protection issue; the co-occurrence of domestic and child abuse; understanding the impact that both domestic and child abuse have on both mother and child in the perinatal period; the impact of foetal abuse; and the role of health professionals especially midwives in recognizing and reporting the co-occurrence of domestic and child maltreatment.

In the fourth chapter, Dr Cyr, Dr Dubois-Comtois, Dr Michel, Dr Poulin, Dr Pascuzzo, Dr Losier, Dr St-Laurent, Dr Moss, and Dr Dumais inform on how attachment theory may be useful to assess and promote parental competency in child protection cases. Child attachment is predictive of short- and long-term child psychosocial adaptation and cognitive functioning in normative as well as clinical groups. According to the ecological-transactional perspective and related empirical studies, child attachment has even shown to be an important protective factor for the development of children with a history of abuse and neglect. Hence, attachment theory provides a solid foundation for both understanding the risk and resiliency factors involved in the development of maltreated children, and guiding the development of assessment and intervention protocols for this multiple-risk population. Attachment-based intervention aims at increasing maternal sensitivity to decrease child maltreatment and increase child attachment security and socioemotional and cognitive functioning. Cyr and colleagues describe the attachment-based treatment programs that have been specifically developed for maltreated children and their parents reported to Child Protection Services, and scientifically tested using state-of-the-art randomized control trials. They also present an innovative project that uses the short-term video-feedback intervention strategy to assess parents' capacity to change.

In the fifth chapter, Prof Mandisa Lutya provides a background theoretical context to the occurrence of human trafficking of young women and girls for sexual exploitation in South Africa. Although forms of human trafficking for the purposes of muti murder, child labour, criminal activities and adoption are acknowledged, this work presents a literature review that focuses on young women and girls trafficked in South Africa, of whom 79% are trafficked to be sexually exploited. The socio-cultural and socio-economic context within which human trafficking occurs is analysed, and South African responses to human trafficking are described. Although some sections of existing legislation are already used to prosecute human trafficking, legal practitioners face some challenges in prosecuting such cases. The politics of legal reform that hinder the Prevention and Combating of Trafficking in Persons Bill from coming into effect in South Africa are also discussed. Finally, a more effective policy that could assist in the reduction of human trafficking of young women and girls for sexual exploitation is proposed.

In the sixth chapter, Prof Bannwart and Prof Williams examine health professionals difficulties in identifying and reporting child maltreatment. These difficulties are related to a gap in their professional training on child abuse and neglect, to the reproduction of cultural patterns of non-involvement in matters concerning the family, the disbelief in the effectiveness of Child Protection Services, negative past experiences, and other personal issues. The authors present a case study whose goal was to raise awareness among Brazilian Family Health Professionals on the need to report child abuse and neglect, by evaluating a training course to identify and report child maltreatment. They conclude that the training of health professionals to identify and report cases of child abuse is an efficient way to maximize reporting behavior.

In the seventh chapter, Dr Martín analyzes the role played by residential care within the childhood welfare systems, acknowledging its strengths, but also its weaknesses. The historical evolution and changes undergone by the model to adapt it to current legislations are briefly analyzed. The model is contextualized in the Spanish reality, where it is still more relevant than in other European countries, in which other alternatives of solutions for children and adolescents who must be separated from their biological families-such as placement with foster families-are more developed. Data are presented about the number of children who live in residential care in comparison to other protective measures, as well as the principles of quality criteria of the care of the children within these resources that the people who are in charge attempt to apply.

Finally, in the last chapter, Prof Euichul Jung and Prof Joonbin Im analyze current technologies used to prevent crimes against children. The chapter is focused on discussing various examples and features of the current interaction designs based on diversified examination on designed products, services and social systems. It also aims to understand and analyze characteristics of crimes against children from designer's perspectives and suggest a new direction for design while discussing basic suggestions on crimes against children and examining various methods on designs with regard to crimes against children.

I want to thank all the professionals who have made this book possible. I hope that it will be a humble contribution that will enrich all of those who want to learn more about child maltreatment.

Dr Alexander Muela
University of Mondragon (MU)
Spain

Chapter 1

Definition, Incidence and Psychopathological Consequences of Child Abuse and Neglect

Alexander Muela, Elena López de Arana,
Alexander Barandiaran, Iñaki Larrea and José Ramón Vitoria

Additional information is available at the end of the chapter

http://dx.doi.org/10.5772/46135

1. Introduction

In this paper we tackle the difficulties present in adequately conceptualising child abuse and neglect, we provide data on its incidence and we describe the main psychopathological consequences associated with each type of child maltreatment.

Thus, we focus on the heterogeneity of the phenomenon (heterogeneity of the notion of "child maltreatment", heterogeneity of the classification criteria, heterogeneity of the different approaches that are related to maltreatment and the heterogeneity of the causes and consequences) and on the complexity that gives rise to that heterogeneity to define the child abuse and neglect.

In children and adolescents, child abuse and neglect can produce a decline in their biological, psychological and social functions. Child maltreatment in childhood and adolescence is recognised as an important psychopathological risk factor and is associated with poor psychological function in childhood and adolescence and adulthood. In this respect, we emphasise that it is wrong to believe that current knowledge has enabled the identification of clearly differentiated consequences for each type of child maltreatment. There is a high degree of co-morbidity among the different types, in such a way that many children experience more than one form of maltreatment and display common consequences. Moreover, it still needs to be clarified whether child abuse and neglect produces a general vulnerability towards psychopathology, in such a way that other factors would be responsible for the form finally adopted by psychopathology.

2. Definition of child abuse

The first problem we encounter when studying child abuse and neglect is that of its definition [1-9].

Historically, the definition of child abuse has passed through different stages. At first, it was the academics and professionals attending the cases of child maltreatment who tried to define child abuse and neglect by focusing on the characteristics of the maltreated children [10]. At the beginning of the 1990's, there was still a lack of consensus from the scientific community on a common definition of child abuse and neglect [11]. Despite vigorous debates on this matter, little has been achieved to provide a clear, reliable, valid and useful definition of child abuse and neglect [13].

Problems in proposing effective operational definitions include factors such as the lack of social consensus on unacceptable or dangerous parenting styles or actions; the lack of certainty on the appropriateness of defining child abuse and neglect according to the adults' behaviour, to its effect on the children, or to a combination of both; the controversy over whether damage criteria should be included in the definition of maltreatment, and the confusion over whether similar definitions should be used for scientific, legal and clinical purposes [13].

Based on ideas set out by Aber and Zigler [1], Cicchetti and Barnett [3] and Zuravin [9], Palacios, Moreno and Jiménez [7] consider that main difficulty in defining child abuse lies in the *heterogeneity* of the phenomenon. They consider the following dimensions: heterogeneity of the notion of "child maltreatment", heterogeneity of the classification criteria, heterogeneity of the different approaches related to the maltreatment and heterogeneity of the causes and consequences. In our review of the conceptualisation of child abuse and neglect we will follow the proposal made by these authors.

2.1. Heterogeneity of the notion of "child maltreatment"

The generic label of maltreatment includes a significant variety of types (physical abuse, child neglect, sexual abuse, etc.) and subtypes (e.g. physical abuse would have subtypes like burns, blows with injuries, drowning, etc.) on which no unanimity exists between researchers [14,7].

Various authors [15-17] postulate that child abuse and neglect can be conceptualised as a continuum. Thus, in its most restricted form, we would encounter definitions of child abuse and neglect that only include intentional and severe physical abuse and, in its broadest form, we would have the definitions that include everything that could interfere in the child's optimum development [18,19].

Initially, the concept of child maltreatment was restricted to the "severe physical harm generally caused by one of the parents or caregivers" [20]. This definition excluded other forms of maltreatment such as sexual abuse, cases of child neglect and emotional maltreatment, except when they led to physical injuries. This early research led to an increase in the scientific community's interest in child abuse and neglect as a focus of study and concern. In a short time, the definition of abuse was extended to include emotional deprivation, malnutrition, child neglect and sexual abuse, and the consequences derived from physical and emotional abandonment were evaluated. This extension of the definition of child abuse and neglect contributed to consolidating the idea that not all abusive parents wanted to destroy their descendents and considered the social factors as determining factors in explaining the etiology of child maltreatment [3,21].

Based on research and studies carried out in the 1980's, broader conceptualisation of child abuse and neglect has progressively been constructed [1,22, 23], defining it as all actions carried out by the caregivers, which significantly interfere in the child's optimum development and do not adhere to social standards. This conceptualisation contemplates aspects such as neglecting the physical-biological, cognitive, emotional and social needs, and the different types of child maltreatment are also classified.

The heterogeneity of the phenomenon is not only related to the conceptualisation of the different types of child maltreatment, but also to the areas in which it takes place. Thus, we speak of child abuse and neglect in the family context, in the social context or in development contexts outside of the family microsystem and in the institutional area, as is the case of the context of schools or residential care centres, etc. [14].

2.2. Heterogeneity of the identification criteria

Important discrepancies exist between the criteria on which the identification of child abuse and neglect should be based. According to Palacios, Moreno and Jiménez [7], "the presence of child maltreatment can be decided by considering the intentions or consequences; it may require evidence or be based on suspicions; it may or may not establish strict frequency of occurrence criteria, distinguishing between isolated episodes and recurrent behaviour; it may or may not be set against dominant social perceptions, which tend to establish borders between discipline and physical abuse, for example". The use of one criteria or another would lead to essential modifications in the statistics, the conclusions on the etiology, the prevention models and the intervention guidelines in cases of child maltreatment [14].

An adequate approach to the definition of child abuse and neglect should take into consideration the concept of intentionality [21]. Kempe, Silverman, Steele, Droegemueller, & Silver [20] recognise the importance of this aspect in their definition of abuse ("... any child who receives non-accidental physical harm as a result of actions or omissions by their parents or caregivers"). Another significant aspect of the criteria to be considered when defining child abuse is the aspect regarding the consequences that the child maltreatment would have on the child. According to De Paúl [24], we would have to consider three basic issues when defining child abuse:

1. *The developmental perspective*: the child's age may be the difference between an abusive action or omission or normal behaviour. It is not the same to leave a 3-month-old baby alone for a few hours as it is a 10-year-old child. Thus, both the limit of what can be considered maltreatment and its severity can depend on the child's developmental moment.
2. *The child's vulnerability*: The same parental behaviour may not be harmful for a healthy child; however, it may be abusive or negligent if the child has a serious chronic illness or some type of disability.

3. *The consequences for the child*: When assessing the consequences of the maltreatment we must take into account that, on a high percentage of occasions, the harm or injuries do not appear on the child immediately and, except in exceptional circumstances, the psychological consequences are more serious than the physical ones. On the other hand, we must assess the potential harm that the child could eventually suffer if this parental behaviour is continued for a certain amount of time at the same level of severity.

The frequency of abusive behaviour and the chronicity of such conduct are important factors when considering behaviour to be abusive or not, as well as their severity [25]. Moreover, as it is a phenomenon that is defined in the community, an adequate definition of child abuse and neglect must implicitly recognise the importance of community and cultural standards [26-27]. It is impossible to discriminate between abusive and non-abusive parents, if you do not take into account the standard community values or the social representation of the abuse. For this purpose, it is necessary to consider that cultures are substantially different from each other in the guidelines for bringing up children, the degree in which childhood is recognised as a stage of development that deserves special attention, the conditions considered necessary for healthy development and the rights recognised to children [28].

2.3. Heterogeneity of professional approaches related to the abuse phenomenon

Five approaches or perspectives are distinguished, which have had a notable influence on the definition of child abuse and neglect: The medical approach, the legal approach, the sociological approach, the research perspective, the subjective approach and the ecological perspective. Table 1 combines the determining factors and the essential objective of each of these approaches.

The *medical perspective* defines maltreatment as the action that causes physical harm to the child [29]. It focuses on the diagnosis, and therefore, a cardinal aspect of this perspective is the notion that child abuse and neglect is the symptom of a medical pathology and pursues the objective of establishing a system to classify potentially abusive parents. The medical approach asks the question: Is this parent potentially abusive?

The definition of the medical approach on child abuse and neglect is closed and essentially limited to the most severe cases of abuse, documented with x-rays that provide proof of injuries such as multiple fractures and subdural haematomas. From this perspective, the treatment of the disorder from which the abusive parents are believed to suffer takes on great importance. According to Barnett, Manly, & Cicchetti [31], by grouping child abuse with other children's illnesses, the medical community releases society from any responsibility in the etiology of the abuse and provides an optimistic view of the problem which is conceived as a phenomenon that can be resolved through research and treatment focused on the abusive parents.

In the *sociological perspective,* which emerged partly as a reaction and criticism to the pathological model of child abuse and neglect, the actions of abuse are defined by the cultural standards of a specific society [1,30]. The sociological definition focuses on the very fact of the abuse and not on the characteristics of the abusers. The sociological approach asks the question: How serious is this type of maltreatment? What is needed to control it? [30,21,5].

The theorists of the sociological perspective stress the importance of counting on public opinion and the professionals' opinion when defining what unacceptable parental behaviour should be and they emphasise the importance of knowing society's role in the perpetuation of child maltreatment. Furthermore, the sociological perspective proclaims a more open definition of child abuse and neglect which includes a wide range of parental actions that have negative consequences on the child, such as child neglect in all its forms.

Epistemological Priorities		
Perspective	*Determining Factor*	*Aim*
Medical	• Parents' characteristics, adjustment of the parents or caregivers.	• To identify and cure the abuser's psychopathology.
Sociological	• Actions of the parents or caregivers.	• To label and control the social deviation.
Legal	• Evidence of physical and psychological harm on the child.	• To create a legal child protection system.
Research	• Environment.	• To guide the research on multilevel processes that determine the child's development and promote social programmes and policies that favour adaptive human development.
Subjective	• Perception of the actions.	• To discover the subjective experience of the victims of maltreatment and promote the necessary therapeutic actions for their treatment.

Table 1. Professional Approaches Related to the Abuse Phenomenon[1]

In the *legal approach* the definitions focus on demonstrating the harm, not necessarily physical, that has been caused to the child. The definition of what maltreatment is or is not is based on the State's initiative to create a legal child protection system. From this perspective, hardly any doubts and contradictions arise when it is a case of demonstrating physical abuse, as the evidence is usually tangible and conclusive. However, psychological

[1] Sources: [1,31,4,32].

maltreatment, for example, was questioned by the legal system until very recently, due to the difficulties in proving its occurrence.

From the *research approach or ecological perspective* numerous efforts have been made to define child maltreatment, its nature, causes and effects, programmes for intervention, control and prevention of the problem, etc. In this way, numerous definitions, etiological models and contradictions have arisen. We must point out that with the objective of discovering the characteristics of abusive parents, the actions of abuse, the consequences in the children and the environmental conditions in which the maltreatment is produced, the research approach has aimed to open up the concept of child abuse and neglect by focusing on the ecology of human development [33-35], in the studies of family/environment transaction and in the role of the community support systems.

Lastly, from the *subjective approach,* maltreatment is defined by oneself. That is to say, the subjective experience of abuse is defined by the victim through their own perception, language and considerations. From this perspective, the main aim of the child protection system is to discover the subjective experience of maltreatment in the victim and promote the necessary therapeutic actions for their treatment [32].

Taking into account the number of approaches that exist, it is not surprising that different professionals access the problem of maltreatment along different routes, either by using their own classification criteria and/or their own detection procedures and placing more emphasis on some aspects rather than others [1,4,36]. In this way, the researchers, social workers, health workers, educators and the Child Protection Services frequently have different and often contradictory views about the diverse aspects regarding abuse, which substantially respond to their own objectives. Thus, the child abuse and neglect can be considered as a medical problem, which needs to be diagnosed and treated; as criminal conduct that needs to be defined in legal terms and punished; as a social problem that needs to be analysed as a social phenomenon; as a problem of child protection, which requires the resources and intervention of the Child Protection Services; and as a family problem, which needs to be understood in the context of the family dynamics [37-38].

Zuravin [9] suggests that, insofar as research is concerned, the studies that focus on specific acts that harm the child may be the most appropriate. The challenge of researchers is to develop a precise operational definition that minimises the lack of agreement among professionals. This lack of consensus on what constitutes maltreatment greatly obstructs the communication and collaboration between the respective fields of intervention.

According to Zigler and Hall [18], the absence of a consensus on the definition of child abuse and neglect could be explained, at least in part, by the lack of agreement to accept that one single definition is not capable of meeting all the aspects that the social scientists and the social services professionals consider relevant in order to conceptualise the maltreatment. Aber and Zigler [1] propose the development of three different categories of definitions: legal definitions, definitions for the management of cases and definitions for research. In any case, the way in which child maltreatment is defined can affect factors such as the classification of the cases and their severity, decision-making regarding the legal and social actions that must be undertaken (by whom, how and at what time) and even the perception of who is maltreating, who is maltreated, either by themselves or by others [18]. According to Giovannoni and Becerra [5], the lack of definition can lead to the situation of some children and adolescents who require protection not being detected, whilst other children or adolescents, who have not been maltreated, are inadequately classified and subjected to unnecessary treatment and intervention.

2.4. Heterogeneity of the causes and the consequences

Early research developed to clarify the etiology of child abuse focused on the abusive parents. Thus, numerous authors have suggested that child abuse and neglect is produced as a result of the actions of perverse parents with mental health problems [39-41]. Other authors have emphasised the importance of the stressful interactive role between the environment, the abuser and the abused child [30,42-44]. Several authors have focused on the children's characteristics (age, physical health, behaviour, etc.) as factors that can provoke the maltreatment from caregivers [45]. Multi-factor models have also been developed, such as the Integrative-Ecological Model [33], the Transactional Model [25] and the Ecological-Transactional Model [13] which represented a considerable advance in knowledge on the etiology of child abuse and neglect.

As regards the consequences of child abuse and neglect, it is not surprising that, depending on the perspective adopted for its definition, the professional approach and the explicative model on the causes of the maltreatment, the results found are also diverging.

Based on this context, the following definition of child abuse and negelct is proposed:

Definition of Child Abuse and Neglect: Any physical and/or psychological harm, which parents or caregivers inflict on children who are in their care or custody or for whom they are responsible, as the result of physical, sexual or emotional actions, of omission or commission, which interfere or threaten the adequate development of the child and violate the community demands concerning the good treatment of children.

2.5. Some myths and false beliefs about child abuse and neglect

One of the most important aspects in the detection and prevention of maltreatment is the social representation that the members of a particular society have regarding this problem. The social representation of child abuse and neglect has also experienced an evolution in which ideas, beliefs and distortions have gradually been ruled out which would explain seminal aspects of child abuse and neglect. We will now take a look at them:

- *Child abuse is infrequent.* A recent study by the World Health Organisation [46] points out that millions of children suffer some form of abuse and require medical and social attention. It should be noted that around 53,000 children are murdered every year; the prevalence of sexual abuse is 73 million (7%) and 150 million (14%) in boys and girls, respectively, under 18 years of age; and between 25% and 50% of the children inform that they have been physically abused. The strong belief that the family is a place where people can find affection and support makes it harder to believe that a high number of people are involved in family violence [15].

- *Child maltreatment is a consequence of psychological traits and psychopathological problems of the parents.* Various research studies focusing on abusive parents, in comparison with non-abusive parents, have found a greater presence of symptoms like depression, anxiety, low levels of personal self-esteem [47-49], lack of skills to adequately handle situations of stress [50], antisocial behaviour [49], personality disorders [51], dissociative symptoms [52] schizophrenia [49] impulsive tendencies [53,40] and difficulties controlling reactions of tension [54]. However, there is a low frequency of psychiatric diagnoses among the perpetrators of child maltreatment. At present, the authors accept that in 10% to 15% of the cases of maltreatment the parents show some kind of mental disorder [50,55].
- *Child abuse and neglect is limited to the lowest social classes.* It is a mistaken belief to think that child maltreatment is only a question of educational or economic deficiencies. The data shows that child abuse and neglect exists in all countries and, although it is not distributed proportionally, it occurs in all social classes [56,41].
- *Child abuse and neglect is understood as an extension and generalisation of the physical abuse.* At present, different forms of child maltreatment have been recognised (emotional maltreatment, child neglect, etc.) which go beyond physical abuse. An adequate understanding of the different forms of maltreatment is necessary in order to encourage good detection and prevention of ill-treatment.
- *Child abuse and neglect is transmitted from parents to children and so on.* The notion of intergenerational transmission of child abuse and neglect upholds that all children who are maltreated will maltreat their children in the future or, on the contrary, all parents who maltreat their children were maltreated in their childhood. The current accepted rate of intergenerational transmission of child abuse and neglect among researchers is around 25% (+/- 5) of the cases. Most of the people who were maltreated as a child (around 70%) do not reproduce this problem with their children [57].

3. Incidence of the problem

Children in a situation of vulnerability constitute a social problem that affects all societies of the world. Throughout history, violence against children has been practiced in many ways: physically and emotionally, through sexual and labour exploitation. Therefore, child maltreatment is not a new phenomenon; it has been around since the beginning of time. History documents that the problem of child abuse and neglect is present from the start of civilisation and that, despite this, abusive conducts have for a long time gone "unnoticed" for families and for communities [58-60].

From the social discovery of the abuse phenomenon, different governments and societies have aimed to carry out research to discover the real scope of the problem.

The most contrasted data on this matter comes from the United States and Great Britain. For instance, according to the governmental statistics published in the United States [12,61], it is estimated that 1.8 million U.S. children may be the victims of child maltreatment every year, of which around 800,000 are cases that are actually confirmed. This data was collected from the Child Protection Services, to which we should add the cases that are not detected by these sources and/or are not reported.

In the United States, the rate of victimisation for every 1000 children is 12.4, whereby it is children under three who display the highest rates of victimisation; that is to say, 16 children are maltreated per 1000 [62]. In Great Britain, the rate of child abuse and neglect, in children under 18 years of age is 2.8 children per 1000, whereby the highest percentages are found in children under one (7.1 per 1000) [63].

Besides the negative consequences it has on the victim, child abuse and neglect also has important consequences for society. The price paid for child maltreatment is very high; it has a direct cost (e.g. hospitalisations, social and judicial action, victim support programmes, child protection measures, etc.) and an indirect cost (pain, decrease in the quality of life, a less healthy and positive society, etc.). For instance, it is estimated that in the United States, child maltreatment annually generates costs to the value of 56 billion dollars [12].

4. Psychopathological consequences of the child abuse and neglect

Child maltreatment can produce a decline in biological, psychological and social function in children and adolescents. Maltreatment in childhood and adolescence is recognised as an important psychopathological risk factor and is associated with poor psychological function in *childhood* [64-71] and in *adolescence* [68,72-75] and in *adulthood* [76-78].

As we have already mentioned, many different difficulties exist to adequately classify the phenomenon of child abuse and neglect. In this respect, it would be wrong to think that current knowledge has allowed us to identify clearly differentiated consequences for each type of child maltreatment. There is a high degree of co-morbidity between the different types, to the extent that many children experience more than one form of maltreatment and demonstrate common consequences [79-80]. Furthermore, it still needs to be clarified whether child maltreatment produces psychopathology in children or whether it generates general vulnerability towards psychopathology in such a way that other factors would be responsible for the type of psychopathological deviation eventually adopted.

Despite these limitations, many studies have found an association between different types of child maltreatment and various psychopathological symptoms in adolescence and at the beginning of adulthood. We will now briefly focus on the psychopathological consequences associated with each type of maltreatment.

4.1. Psychopathological consequences of physical abuse

Being physically abused in childhood is a risk factor associated with psychopathological problems in adolescence and adulthood. Numerous research studies have demonstrated that physically abused adolescents and adults who were subjected to physical abuse in childhood have a high risk of displaying mental health problems [81-88].

By way of example, various studies have found that children and young people who are the victims of physical abuse and children and young people who are part of a violent family context, in comparison with children and young people who do not display these characteristics, display more emotional problems [69,84,89-91]. The research reveals that physical abuse is associated with a variety of emotional problems such as somatisation, depression, anxiety, hostility, paranoid ideation, psychosis, posttraumatic symptoms and dissociative disorder. This relationship is moderated by aspects such as the presence of multiple types of abuse and the gender of the perpetrator. The data obtained in the various research studies indicates that the combination of physical and sexual abuse has greater emotional consequences for the victims, generating above all, depression and anxiety [92-94].

An important association exists between being physically abused in childhood and an increase in the manifestation of self-harming behaviour and suicides in adolescence and adulthood [94-101]. However, different research studies have demonstrated that this correlation varies depending on the victim's gender, the type of abuse and the level of parental conflict. For instance, it has been suggested that physical abuse in itself does not produce suicidal behaviour; however, when physical and sexual abuse are experienced together, this behaviour seems to be produced more frequently [102].

Much of the literature on child abuse and neglect has related physical abuse with delinquency and aggressive behaviour in adolescence. A close relationship has also been found between physical abuse and conduct disorder which, in turn, has been associated with delinquency and aggressive behaviour [84].

4.2. Psychopathological consequences of child neglect

Having suffered child neglect in childhood has been associated with poor psychological function in childhood, adolescence and adulthood.

The results of studies such as the *Minnesota Mother-Child Project* [103] verify that children who were victims of physical neglect displayed serious social-emotional problems, and most of these problems had an internalising nature. In the same way, in other studies, it has been found that physical neglect and a lack of supervision in childhood is associated with an increase in the risk of producing self-harming behaviour and suicidal tendencies [72,101], suffering from personality disorders with high symptoms of anxiety, depression [104] and dissociative disorders in adolescence and adulthood [105].

4.3. Psychopathological consequences of sexual abuse

Research on sexual abuse suggests that children and adolescents who develop in an abusive environment run the risk of suffering psychological difficulties that are characterised by emotional dysregulation. In particular, it has be found that children who are the victims of sexual abuse show internalising and externalising difficulties, posttraumatic stress disorder symptoms, personality disorders and problems in interpersonal relations with peers [61,106-110].

One of the most worrying aspects for the physical and mental health of the abused adolescent in their childhood is the strong association that exists between sexual abuse and suicidal conduct in this evolutionary stage [99]. The percentage of attempted suicides in the adolescent population of victims of sexual abuse ranges between 7.3 and 11.2% in girls and 3.2 and 4.5% in boys [99,112].

By way of example, in one of the most relevant research projects carried out recently in this field by Martin et al. [112], in which 2,485 adolescents participated, of which 7.4% had been the victim of sexual abuse, they discovered that 27.1% of the sample admitted having suicidal ideation (21.8% of boys and 33.6% of girls); 13.7% had planned to commit suicide (11.3% of boys and 16.4% of girls) and 4.5% of boys and 7.3% of girls had attempted suicide.

4.4. Psychopathological consequences of emotional maltreatment

At present, sufficient evidence is available to confirm that emotional maltreatment in childhood is associated with mental health problems and adaptation problems in adolescence and adulthood [95,113-116].

Emotional maltreatment has been identified as a strong predictor of most psychological problems including personality disorders, anxiety, depression, dissociative symptoms, posttraumatic stress, physical symptoms, suicidal behaviour, sexual dysfunction, eating disorders and low self-esteem [32,74-75,95,114-123].

Author details

Alexander Muela, Elena López de Arana,
Alexander Barandiaran, Iñaki Larrea and José Ramón Vitoria
University of Mondragon Unibertsitatea, Department of Child Well Being, Eskoriatza, Spain

5. References

[1] Aber J., Zigler E. Developmental considerations in the definition of child maltreatment. In: Fitzgerald H. E., Lester B. M., Yogman M. (Eds.), Developmental perspectives on child maltreatment. San Francisco: Jossey-Bass; 1981. p. 1-29.
[2] Besharov DJ. Toward better research on child abuse and neglect: Making definitional. Child Abuse & Neglect 1981; 5(4) 383-390.
[3] Cicchetti D., Barnett D. Toward the development of a scientific nosology of child maltreatment. In Grove WM., Cicchetti D. (Eds.), Thinking clearly about psychology: Essays in honor of Paul E. Meehl. Vol. 2. Personality and Psychopathology. Minneapolis: University of Minnessota Press; 1991. p. 346-377.

[4] Giovannoni, J. Definitional issues in child maltreatment. In Cicchetti D., Carlson V. (Eds.), Child Maltreatment: Theory and research on the causes and consequences of child abuse and neglect. New York: Cambridge University Press; 1989. p. 3-37.

[5] Giovannoni J, Becerra RM. Defining child abuse. Nueva York: Free Press; 1979.

[6] Jiménez J, Moreno M, Oliva A, Palacios J, Saldaña D. El maltrato infantil en Andalucía. Sevilla: Consejería de Trabajo y Asuntos Sociales; 1995.

[7] Palacios J, Moreno C., Jiménez J. El maltrato infantil: concepto, tipos, etiología. Infancia y aprendizaje 1995; 71, 7-21.

[8] Muela A. Hacia un sistema de clasificación nosológico de maltrato infantil. Anales de Psicología 2008; 24(1), 77-87.

[9] Zuravin S. Research and definitions of child physical abuse and neglect: Current problems. In Starr RH, Wolfe D (Eds.), The Effects of Child Abuse and Neglect. New York: The Guildford Press; 1991. p. 100-128.

[10] Herrenkohl RC. The definition of child maltreatment: From case study to construct. Child Abuse & Neglect 2005; 29, 413-424.

[11] National Research Council. Understanding child abuse and neglect. Washington, D.C.: National Academy Press; 1993.

[12] Cicchetti D, Toth SL. Child maltreatment. Annual Review of Clinical Psychology 2005; 1(1), 409-438.

[13] Cicchetti D, Lynch M. Failures in the expectable environment and their impact on individual development: The case of child maltreatment. In Cicchetti D, Cohen DJ (Eds.), Developmental Psychopathology, Volume 2. Risk, Disorder, and Adaptation. New York: A Wiley-Interscience Publication; 1995. p. 32-72.

[14] Jiménez J, Oliva A, Saldaña D. El maltrato y protección a la infancia en España. Madrid: Ministerio de Asuntos Sociales; 1996.

[15] Gracia E., Musitu G. El maltrato infantil. Un análisis ecológico de los factores de riesgo. Madrid: Ministerio de Asuntos Sociales; 1993.

[16] Briere J, Runtz M. Differential adult symptomatology associated with three types of child abuse histories. Child Abuse & Neglect, 1990; 14(3), 357-364.

[17] Rosenberg DA. Unusual forms of child abuse. In Helfer, ME, Kempe RS, Krugman R (Eds.), The battered child. Chicago: The University of Chicago Press; 1997. 5 ed., p. 431-449

[18] Zigler E., Hall NW. Physical child abuse in America: past, present, and future. In Cicchetti D, Carlson V (Eds.), Child Maltreatment. Theory and research and consequenses of child abuse and neglect. New York: Cambridge University Press; 1989. p. 38-75.

[19] Sameroff A., Chandler M. Reproductive risk and the continuum of caretaking casualty. In Horowitz F(Ed.), Review of child development research (Vol. 4). Chicago: University of Chicago Press: 1975, pp. 187-244.

[20] Kempe CH, Silverman FN, Steele B, Droegemueller W, Silver HK. The battered-child syndrome. Journal of American Medical Association, 1962; 181(1), 17-24.

[21] Gil DG. Violence against children: Physical child abuse in the United States. Cambridge: Harvard University Press; 1970.

[22] Widom CS. Sampling biases and implications for child abuse research. American Journal of Orthopsychiatry, 1988; 58(2), 260-270.
[23] Wolfe DA. Child abuse: Implications for child development and psychopathology (2ª ed.). London: Sage Publications; 1999.
[24] De Paúl J. Diferentes situaciones de desprotección infantil. In De Paúl J, Arruabarrena MI (Eds.), Manual de Protección Infantil. Barcelona: Masson; 2001. p. 3-24.
[25] Cicchetti D, Rizley R. Developmental perspectives on the etiology, intergeneracional transmisión, and sequelae of child maltreatment. New directions for Child Developmental, 1981;11, 31-55.
[26] Korbin JE. A cross cultural perspective on the role of the community in child abuse and neglect. Child Abuse & Neglect, 1979;3, 9-18.
[27] Parke RD, Collmer, CW. Child abuse: An interdisciplinary analysis. In Hetherington EM. (Ed.), Review of child development research (5ª ed., Vol. 5). Chicago: University of Chicago Press; 1975. p. 509-590.
[28] Eisenberg L. Cross-cultural and historical perspectives on child abuse and neglect. Child Abuse & Neglect, 1981;5, 451-473.
[29] Kavanagh C. Emotional abuse and mental injury: A critique of the concepts and a. Journal of the American Academy of Child Psychiatry, 1982;21, 2.
[30] Gelles RJ. Child abuse as psychopathology: A sociological critique and reformulation. American Journal of Orthopsychiatry, 1973;43 (4), 611-621.
[31] Barnett D, Manly JT, Cicchetti D. Defining child maltreatment: The interface between policy and research. In Cicchetti D, Toth S.L (Eds.), Child abuse, child development, and social policy. Norwood, NJ: Ablex; 1993. p. 7-74.
[32] McGee RA, Wolfe DA, Wilson SK. Multiple maltreatment experiences and adolescent behavior problems: adolescents' perspectives. Development and Psychopathology, 1997; 9(1), 131-149.
[33] Belsky J. Child maltreatment: An ecological integration. American Psychologist, 1980;35(4), 320-335.
[34] Bronfenbrenner U. Toward an experimental ecology of human development. American Psychologist., 32, 513-531;1977.
[35] Garbarino J. A preliminary study of some ecological correlates of child abuse: The impact of socioeconomic estress on mothers. Child Development, 1976;47(1), 178-185.
[36] O'Toole, Turbett P, Nalepka C. Theories, professionals knowledge and diagnosis of child abuse. In Finkelhor D, Gelles R J, Totaling GT, Straus MA. (Eds.), The dark side of families. Beverley Hills, CA: Sage; 1983.
[37] Mayhall PD, Norgard KE. Child abuse and neglect: Sharing responsibility. New York: Wiley; 1983.
[38] Muela A. Haurrei emandako tratu txarrak: jatooria, atzematea eta ondorioak. Bilbo: UEU; 2007.
[39] Bennie E, Sclare A. The battered child syndrome. American Journal of Psychiatry, 1969;125, 975-979.
[40] Spinetta JJ, Rigler D. The child-abusing parent: A psychological review. Psychological Bulletin, 1972;77(4), 296-304.

[41] Steele B, Pollock CB. A psychiatric study of parents who abuse infants and small children. In Helfer R, Kempe C (Eds.), The Battered Child. Chicago: University of Chicago Press; 1968. pp. 103-147.
[42] Green A. Self destruction in physically abused schizophrenic children: Report of cases. Achieves of General Psychiatry, 1968;19, 171-197.
[43] Helfer R. The etiology of child abuse. Pediatrics, 1973;51, 777-779.
[44] Sandgrund A, Gaines RW, Green AH. Child abuse and mental retardation: A problem of cause and effect. American Journal of Mental Deficiency, 1974;79(3), 327-330.
[45] Sherrod KB, O'Connor S, Vietze PM, Altemeier WA. Child health and maltreatment. Child Development, 1984;55(4), 1174-1183.
[46] WHO.Violence and Injury Prevention and Disability (VIP); 2011. http://www.who.int/violence_injury_prevention/violence/child/en/ Accessed 07.02.12.
[47] Green AH, Liang V, Gaines R, Sultan S. Psychological assessment of child-abusing, neglecting, and normal mothers. The Journal of Nervous and Mental Disease, 1980;168, 356-360.
[48] Kaplan SJ, Pelkovitz D, Salzinger S, Ganeles D. Psychopathology of parents of abused and neglected children and adolescents. Journal of the American Academy of Child and Adolescent Psychiatry, 1983;22(23), 238-244.
[49] Ammerman RT. Etiological models of child maltreatment: A behavioral perspective. Behavior Modification, 1990;14(3), 230-254.
[50] Wash C, MacMillan H, Jamieson E. The relationship between parental psychiatric and child physical and sexual abuse: findings from the Ontario Health Supplement. Child Abuse & Neglect, 2002;26, 11-22.
[51] Famularo R, Kinscherff R, Fenton T. Psychiatric diagnoses of maltreated children: Preliminary findings. Journal of the American Academy of Child and Adolescent Psychiatry, 1992;31, 863-867.
[52] Narang DS., Contreras JM. Dissotiation as a mediator between child abuse history and adult abuse potential. Child Abuse and Neglect, 2000;24(5), 653-665.
[53] Friedrich WN, Boriskin JA. The role of the child in abuse: A review of the literature. American Journal of Orthopsychiatry, 1976;46(4), 580-590.
[54] Frodi AM, Lamb ME. Infants at risk for child abuse. Infant Mental Health Journal, 1980; 1(4), 240-247.
[55] Anderson SC, Lauderdale, ML. Characteristics of abusive parents: A look at self-esteem. Child Abuse & Neglect, 1982;6(3), 285-293.
[56] Pelton LH. Child abuse and neglect: The myth of classlessness. American Journal of Orthopsychiatry, 1978;48(4), 608-617.
[57] Kaufman J, Zigler E. The Intergenerational Transmission of Child Abuse. En D. Cicchetti & V. Carlson (Eds.), Child Maltreatment: Theory and Research on the causes and consequences of child abuse and neglect (). Cambridge: Cambridge University Press; 1989. pp. 129-150.
[58] Aries P. Centuries of childhood: A social history of family life. New York: Random House; 1962.
[59] Breiner SJ. Slaughter of the innocents: Child abuse through the ages and today. New York: Plenum Press; 1990.

[60] Radbill SX. A history of child abuse and infanticide. In Helfer RE, Kempe CH (Eds.) The battered child (pp. 3-20). Chicago: University of Chicago Press; 1968.

[61] Leon SC, Ragsdale B, Miller SA, Spacarelli S. Trauma resilience among youth in substitute care demonstrating sexual behavior problems. Child Abuse & Neglect, 2008;32, 67-81.

[62] Timmer SG, Urquiza AJ, Zebell NM, McGrath, JM. Parent-child interaction therapy: Application to maltreating parent-child dyads. Child Abuse & Neglect, 2005;29, 825-842.

[63] Veltman MWM, Browne KD. Three decades of child maltreatment research: Implications for the school years. Trauma Violence and Abuse, 2001;2(3), 215-239.

[64] Bolger KE, Patterson CJ. Developmental pathways from child maltreatment to peer rejection. Child Development, 2001;72(2), 549-568.

[65] Carlson EA. A prospective longitudinal study of attachment disorganization/disorientation. Child Development, 1998;69, 1107-1128.

[66] Cicchetti D, Valentino K. An ecological-transactional perspective on child maltreatment: Failure of the average expectable environment and its influence on child development. In Ciccherti D, Cohen D (Eds.), Developmental psychopathology, Risk, disorder, and adaptation (2 ed., Vol. 3). New York: Wiley; 2006.

[67] Hildyard KL, Wolfe DA. Child neglect: Developmental issues and outcomes. Child Abuse and Neglect, 2002;26(6-7), 679-695.

[68] Kim J, Cicchetti D. Longitudinal pathways linking child maltreatment, emotion regulation, peer relations, and psychopathology. Child Psychology and Psychiatry, 2010;51(6), 706-716.

[69] Shaffer A, Huston L, Egeland B. Identification for child maltreatment using prospective and self-report methodologies: A comparison of maltreatment incidence and relation to later psychopathology. Child Abuse and Neglect, 2008;32, 682-692.

[70] Shipman KL, Rossman BR, West, JC. Co-occurrence of spousal violence and child abuse: Conceptual implications. Child Maltreatment, 1999;4(2), 93-102.

[71] Turner HA, Finkelhor D, Ormrod R. The effect of lifetime victimization on the mental health of children and adolescents. Social Science and Medicine, 2006;62, 13-27.

[72] Arata CM, Langhinrichsen-Rohling J, Bowers D, O'Brien N. Differential correlates of multi-type maltreatment among urban youth. Child Abuse & Neglect, 2007;31, 393-415.

[73] Boxer P, Terranova AM. Effects of multiple maltreatment experiences among psychiatrically hospitalized youth. Child Abuse & Neglect, 2008;32, 637-647.

[74] Johnson JG, Cohen P, Smailes EM., Skodol A, Brown AE, Oldham, JM. Childhood verbal abuse and risk for personality disorders during adolescence and early childhood. Comprehensive Psychiatry, 2001;42(1), 16-23.

[75] Thornberry TP, Ireland TO, Smith CA. The importance of timing: the varying impact of childhood and adolescent maltreatment on multiple problem outcomes. Development and Psychopathology, 2001;13, 957-979.

[76] Gibb BE, Alloy LB, Abramson LY, Rose DT, Whitehouse WG, Donovan P, Hogan ME, Cronholm J, Tierney S. History of childhood maltreatment, negative cognitive styles, and episodes of depression in adulthood. Cognitive Therapy and Research, 2001;25(4), 425-446.

[77] Kaplow JB, Widom CS. Age of onset of child maltreatment predicts long-term mental outcomes. Journal of Abnormal Psychology, 2007;116(1), 176-187.
[78] Rikhye K, Tyrka AR, Kelly MM, Gagne GG, Mello, AF, Mello MF, Price LH, Carpenter LL. Interplay between childhood maltreatment, parental bonding, and gender effects: Impact on quality of life. Child Abuse & Neglect, 2008;32, 19-34.
[79] Egeland BR, Sroufe LA. Developmental sequelae of maltreatment in infancy. New Directions for Child Development, 1981;11, 72-92.
[80] Manly JT, Kim JE, Rogosch FA, Cicchetti D Dimensions of child maltreatment and children's adjustment: Contributions of developmental timing and subtype. Development and Psychopathology, 2001;13(4), 759-782.
[81] Brown GR, Anderson B. Psychiatric morbidity in adult inpatients with childhood histories of sexual and physical abuse. American Journal of Psychiatry, 1991;148, 55-61.
[82] Holowka DW, Kinga S, Sahebb D, Pukalla M, Bruneta A. Childhood abuse and dissociative symptoms in adult schizophrenia. Schizophrenia Research, 2003;60(1), 87-90
[83] Hyun M, Friedman SD, Dunner DL. Relationship of childhood physical and sexual abuse to adult bipolar bipolar disorder. Bipolar Disorders, 2000;2(2), 131-135.
[84] Kaplan SJ, Pelcovitz D, Salzinger S, Weiner M, Mandel FS, Lesser ML, Labruna. Adolescent physical abuse: Risk for adolescent psychiatric disorders. American Journal of Psychiatry, 1998;155(7), 954-959.
[85] Kaplan SJ, Labruna V, Pelcovitz D, Salzinger S, Mandel F, Weiner M. Physically abused adolescents: Behavior problems, functional impairment, and comparison of informants' reports. Pediatrics, 1999;104, 43-49.
[86] Read J, Argyle N. Hallucinations, delusions, and thought disorder among adult psychiatric inpatients with a history of child abuse. Psychiatric Services, 1999;50(11), 1467-1472.
[87] Salzman JP, Salzman C, Wolfson AN, Albanese M, Looper J, Ostacher, Schwartz J, Chinman G, Land W, Miyawaki E. Association between borderline personality structure and history of childhood abuse in adult volunteers. Comprehensive Psychiatry, 1993;34(4), 254-257.
[88] Springer KW, Sheridan J, Kuo D, Carnes M. Long-term physical and mental health consequences of childhood physical abuse: Results from a large population-based sample of men and women. Child Abuse and Neglect, 2007;31, 517-530.
[89] Lansford JE, Dodge KA, Pettit GS, Bates JE, Crozier J, Kaplow J. A 12-year prospective study of the long-term effects of early child physical maltreatment on psychological, behavioral, and academic problems in adolescence. Archives of Pediatrics & Adolescent Medicine, 2002;156, 824-830.
[90] Malinosky-Rummell R., Hansen DJ. Long-term consequences of childhood physical abuse. Psychological Bulletin, 1993;114(1), 68-79.
[91] Wolfe DA, Mosk MD. Behavioral comparisons of children from abusive and distressed families. Journal of Consulting and Clinical Psychology, 1983;51(5), 702-708.
[92] Bryer JB, Nelson BA, Miller JB, Krol PA. Childhood sexual and physical abuse as factors in adult psychiatric illness. American Journal of Psychiatry, 1987;144(11), 1426-1430.

[93] Naar-King S, Silvern V, Ryan V, Sebring D. Type and severity of abuse as predictors of psychiatric symptoms in adolescence. Journal of Family Violence, 2002;17(2), 133-149.

[94] Silverman AB, Reinherz HZ, Giaconia RM. The long-term sequelae of child and adolescent abuse: A longitudinal community study. Child Abuse and Neglect, 1996;20(8), 709-723.

[95] Briere J, Runtz M. Multivariate correlates of childhood psychological and physical maltreatment among university women. Child Abuse & Neglect, 1988;12(3), 331-341.

[96] Cavaiola AA, Schiff M. Behavioral sequelae of physical and/or sexual abuse in adolescents. Child Abuse and Neglect, 1988;12(2), 181-188.

[97] Deykin EY, Alpert JJ, McNamara JJ. A pilot study of the effect of exposure to child abuse or neglect on adolescent suicidal behavior. American Journal of Psychiatry, 1985;142(11), 1299-1303.

[98] Dube SR, Anda RF, Felitti VJ, Chapman DP. Childhood abuse, household dysfunction, and the risk of attempted suicide throughout the life span:findings from the adverse childhood experiences study. JAMA: Journal of the American Medical Association, 2001;286, 3089-3096.

[99] Evans E, Hawton K, Rodham K. Suicidal phenomena and abuse in adolescents: A review of epidemiological studies. Child Abuse & Neglect, 2005;29(1), 45-58.

[100] Fergusson DM, Lynskey MT. Physical punishment/maltreatment during childhood and adjustment in young adulthood. Child Abuse & Neglect., 1997;21(7), 617-630.

[101] Paivio SC, McCulloch CR. Alexithymia as a mediator between childhood trauma and self-injurious. Child Abuse and Neglect, 2004;28(3), 339-354.

[102] Carmen EH, Rieker PP, Mills T. Victims of violence and psychiatric illness. American Journal of Psychiatry, 1984;141, 378-383.

[103] Pianta R, Egeland BR, Erickson MF. The antecedents of maltreatment: Results of the Mother-Child Interaction. In Cicchetti D, Carlson V (Eds.), Child maltreatment: Theory and research on the causes and consequences of child abuse and neglect. New York: Cambridge University Press; 1989. pp. 203-253

[104] Johnson JG, Smailes EM, Cohen P, Brown J, Bernstein DP. Associations between four types of childhood neglect and personality disorder symptoms during adolescence and early adulthood: Findings of a community based longitudinal study. Journal of Personality Disorders, 2000;14, 171–187.

[105] Ogawa, JR, Sroufe LA, Weinfield NS, Carlson EA, Egeland BR. Development and the fragmented self: longitudinal study of dissociative symptomatology in a nonclinical sample. Development and Psychopathology, 1997;9, 855-879.

[106] Beitchman JH, Zucker K J, Hood JE, DaCosta GA, Akman D, Cassavia E. A review of the long-term effects of child sexual abuse. Child Abuse & Neglect, 1992;16(1), 101-118.

[107] Berliner L, Elliott DM. Sexual abuse of children. In Briere J, Berliner L, Bulkley JA, Jenny C, Reid T (Eds.), The APSAC handbook on child maltreatment. Thousand Oak, CA: Sage;1996. p. 51-71.

[108] Cantón D, Justicia F. Afrontamiento del abuso sexual infantil y ajuste psicológico a largo plazo. Psicothema, 2008;20, 509-515.

[109] Noll JG, Trickett PK, Susman EJ, Putnam FW. Sleep disturbances and childhood sexual abuse. Journal of Pediatric Psychology, 2006;31(5), 649-480.

[110] Rogosch FA, Cicchetti D. Child maltreatment, attention networks, and potential precursors to borderline personality disorder. Developmental Psychopathology, 2005;17(4), 1071-1089.

[111] Oates RK. Sexual abuse and suicidal behavior. Child Abuse and Neglect, 2004;28(5), 487-489.

[112] Martin G, Bergen HA, Richardson AS, Roeger L, Allison S. Sexual abuse and suicidality: Gender differences in a large community sample of adolescents. Child Abuse and Neglect, 2004;28(5), 491-503.

[113] Gross AB, Keller HR. Long-term consequences on childhood physical and psychological maltreatment. Aggressive Behavior, 1992;18(3), 171-185.

[114] Maciejewski PK, Mazure CM. Fear criticism and rejection mediates an association between childhood emotional abuse and adult onset of major depression. Cognitive Therapy and Research, 2006;30(1), 105-122.

[115] Shaffer A, Yates TM, Egeland BR. The relational of emotional maltreatment to early adolescent competence: Developmental processes in a prospective study. Child Abuse & Neglect, 2009;33, 36-44

[116] Spertus IL, Yehuda R, Wong CM, Halligan S, Seremetis SV. Childhood emotional abuse and neglect as predictors of psychological and physical simptoms in women presenting to a primary care practice. Child Abuse and Neglect, 2003;27(11), 1247-1258.

[117] Burns EE, Fischer S, Jackson JJ, Harding H. Deficits in emotional regulation mediate the relationship between childhood abuse and later eating disorder symptoms. Child Abuse & Neglect, 2012;36, 32-39.

[118] Hund AR, Espelage DL. Childhood emotional abuse and disordered eating among undergraduate females: Mediating influence of alexithymia and distress. Child Abuse and Neglect, 2006;30, 393-407.

[119] Kim J, Cicchetti D. Longitudinal trajectories of self-system processes and depressive symptoms among maltreated and nonmaltreated children. Child Development, 2006;77(3), 624-639.

[120] O'Dougherty-Wright M, Crawford EC, Del Castillo D. Childhood emotional maltreatment and later psychological distress among college students: the mediating role of maladaptive schemas. Child Abuse & Neglect, 2009;33(1), 59-68.

[121] Rich DJ, Gingerich KJ, Rosen LA. Childhood emotional abuse and associated psychopathology in college students. Journal of College Student Psychotherapy, 1997;11(3), 13-28.

[122] Sackett LA, Saunders DG. The impact of different forms of psichological abuse on battered women. Violence and Victims, 1999;14, 105-117.

[123] Wekerle C., Leung E, Wall A, MacMillan H, Boyle M, Trocme N, Waechter R. The contribution of childhood emotional abuse to teen dating violence among child protective services-involved youth. Child Abuse & Neglect, 2009;33 (1), 45-58.

Chapter 2

The Cultural Reinforcers of Child Abuse

Essam Al-Shail, Ahmed Hassan, Abdullah Aldowaish and Hoda Kattan

Additional information is available at the end of the chapter

http://dx.doi.org/10.5772/50693

1. Introduction

Mistreating children at the hands of parents or caretakers has a long history. Sari and Buyukunal (1991), in a study on the history of child abuse, report that from ancient times up to present many societies have exercised what it is recognized today as child abuse for various reasons. On reviewing child abuse literature in the Tobkabi Museum in Istanbul, they report that in ancient Greece fathers were permitted to practice infanticide whereby many infants who had any serious malformations were killed in order to preserve the race characteristics. Greek physicians during the second century were in the habit of advising midwives to examine each newborn and to get rid of those who were considered not fit to be raised. The study also presented the picture of Zal, the first known albino in the literature, exposed at the bottom of a mountain by his father because he was born with white hair. Stories of children being slaughtered in addition to other severe practices of child abuse were also illustrated. Such practices were said to be part of the lifestyle until approximately two centuries ago. Sexual abuse was reported to be common among Eskimos (Sari and Buyukunal, 1991). Their daughters were presented to their guests as an act of hospitality, and the death of those children during their first sexual experience was not a rare event. In India, the girls used to get married very early because it was considered disgraceful for a girl to remain unmarried until the time of menstruation.

Historically, parents used their children for profit. Among the poor families, children were put to work at early ages doing activities such as working on the family's own farm or elsewhere. Generally, boys were more likely to work earlier than girls who usually stay home to help their mothers. In large families, some children were sent to school to receive elementary education or were taught by their parents at home to acquire the necessary knowledge they would need to work and support their families. Only in wealthy families that boys, and to a lesser extent girls, would receive higher standards of education. Not until mid-nineteenth century that compulsory schooling was introduced and education became a common experience for all children.

Although the history of child abuse remains obscure in many parts of the world, it is argued that as from the late seventeenth century onwards children can be seen playing, sketching, and amusing themselves in portraits, which shows that there was a growing concept of childhood. Nevertheless, the number of abused children in modern times generally is still alarming, since the natural state of affairs is a zero-tolerance to child maltreatment, especially the forms of abuse that lead either to death or permanent physical or emotional impairment. In the USA, more than 4 million children were reported to child protection services as alleged victims of child maltreatment in 1999 alone, of which an estimated 1401 child abuse and neglect related fatalities were confirmed by the child protection services' agencies (Nation Committee for the Prevention of Child Abuse [NCPCA] 2000 Annual Fifty State Survey), while the confirmed child abuse deaths in 2002 were about 1400 children (National Data of the U. S. Department of Health and Human Services, April 2004).

The practice of child abuse was based on kinds of philosophies, cultural beliefs and understandings that gave way to a system of laws that, in turn, gave children few, if any, rights. Under the English Common Law, for example, children were considered as property owned by the parents, particularly fathers, who had great latitude over the treatment and discipline of their children. Such legal view was eventually incorporated into early laws in the United States as well. Common law tradition held that the male was head of the household and possessed the authority to act as both disciplinarian and protector of those dependent on him, including his wife and children as well as extended kin, servants, apprentices, and slaves. While common law obligated the male to feed, clothe, and shelter his dependents, it also allowed him considerable discretion in controlling their behavior. Domestic violence, however, was dealt with on the basis of local community standards, which were the most important yardsticks. Puritan parents in New England, for example, felt a strong sense of duty to discipline their children, whom they believed to be born naturally depraved, in order to save them from eternal damnation. Although Puritan society tolerated a high degree of physicality in parental discipline, the community did draw a line at which it regarded parental behavior as abusive, and those who crossed the line would be brought before the courts.

The complexity of the sociocultural underpinnings of child abuse is evident from the historical fact that the legal protections from cruelty was granted to animals long before they were granted to children. One of the first cases in the United States (the case of 8-year-old Mary Ellen Wilson) that arose national attention to child abuse in the early 1870s, got through the legal arguments only after an attorney for the then well-established American Society for the Prevention of Cruelty to Animals (ASPCA) took her case to court and successfully argued for children as being, just like all humans, members of the animal kingdom, hence entitled for the right to be treated with the same legal protection from cruelty as are animals (Shelman and Lazoritz, 2005; Watkins, 1990).

2. Child abuse in Saudi Arabia

Saudi Arabia is a country occupying most of the Arabian Peninsula with a population of about 27 million who are entirely Muslims. The country is governed according to the Islamic

Sharia law whereby the Islamic orthodoxy and conservatism generally dominate the social and cultural characteristics and mechanisms of the Saudi society. Traditional tribal principles and customs, however, have significant influence over a wide range of cultural, behavioral, and attitudinal manifestations in the society. Children are usually well taken care of in terms of basic needs, and are expected to show almost total subordination and obedience to their parents. Corporal punishment by parents is a common practice, especially in less modernized portions of the society. The country generally has one of the lowest rates of serious crimes compared to other countries, despite the fact that nearly 8 million expatriate workers dwell in the country. This fact has been largely due to strict laws that organize all spheres of life, reinforced by the regular police force and members of an official body monitoring the public's compliance with the prevailing religious norms and rules. For the last twenty years or so, most families adopted the tradition of having expatriate housemaids to take care of household menial works including looking after the children in the home.

The first program for detecting, reporting, and working towards preventing child abuse in Saudi Arabia was initiated by one of the leading hospitals in the country in 1994 as a Child Advocacy Committee, with an internal policy and procedure for dealing with all cases of child abuse that reached the hospital. The policy involved the hospital's security department and a mechanism to report cases of suspected or proven child abuse encountered in or admitted to the hospital to legal authorities in the city.

Subsequently, the National Family Safety Program (NFSP) was established in 2005 by a Royal Decree with a vision to establish a foundation that promotes a safe community and help victims of domestic violence Including child abuse victims. The strategic objectives of the NFSP include promoting awareness among individuals and institutions on the damage to individuals and the society caused by domestic violence and child abuse, and training staff members to deal appropriately and effectively with cases of domestic violence and child abuse. Since the implementation of the NFSP in 2007, the numbers of child protection centers that provide NFSP services have increased From 4 to 41 centers.

The National Family Safety Registry (NFSR) was established in 2009 as a web-based data registry system to provide a centralized database for child abuse cases from all over the country. It is aimed to provide a ground for collecting and analyzing data on child abuse cases in order to define the magnitude of the problem and to identify the risk factors leading to child abuse in the country, which is likely to help in formulating prevention strategies and policies.

A total of 616 child abuse cases have been registered in a period of 16 months between October 2010 and February 2012. Of these, 315 (51.1%) are males and 301 (48.9%) are females. The Saudi nationals among the abused children comprise 92.0% of the cases; however, non-Saudi children are mostly treated in private health sectors which are not yet represented by CPC. **Figure 1** shows the age distribution of the abused children included in the registry, , whereby the ages in a small proportion of the cases (2.8%) are missing. The figure shows that 15.9% of the total number of cases involves children younger than one year of age, as shown in **Table 1** below.

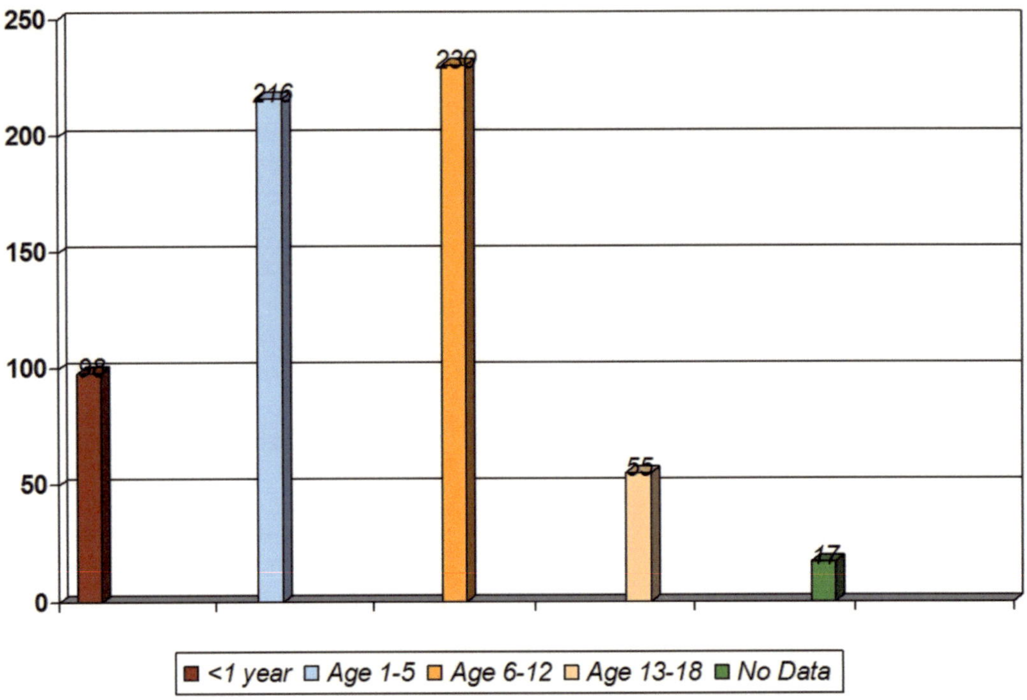

Figure 1. Age Distribution of Abused Children

Age (months)	Male	Female	Total	%
0	3	5	8	8.2
1	3	3	6	6.1
2	4	5	9	9.2
3	4	5	9	9.2
4	1	5	6	6.1
5	7	4	11	11.2
6	8	6	14	14.3
7	5	1	6	6.1
8	7	4	11	11.2
9	4	2	6	6.1
10	2	2	4	4.1
11	4	4	8	8.2
Total	**52**	**45**	**98**	**100**

Table 1. Age and Gender of Abused Infants (<12 months)

3. Defining child abuse

Definitions of child abuse or maltreatment have two main components: harm, which may be a harmful action or a harmful consequence, and a person or persons responsible for the harm (Gough, 1996). As has been pointed out by Gough (1996), childhood itself is a social construct in which ages defining childhood have varied throughout history and across various sociocultural groups of the human societies. However, the word *child*, in its broad literal meaning, refers to "a person between birth and full growth; a boy or girl". The Convention on the Right of the Child (CRC), however, defines a child as "every human being below the age of 18 years unless under the law applicable under the child majority is attained earlier" (*Ref: http://www.unicef.org/crc/crc.htm*). Age of majority pertains solely to the acquisition of control over one's person, decisions and actions, and the correlative termination of the legal authority and responsibility of the parents (or guardian, in lieu of parents) over the child's persons and affairs generally. On the other hand, literally speaking, the word *abuse* is defined as "to use wrongly or improperly; to misuse, or to treat in a harmful, injurious, or offensive way; to speak insultingly, harshly, and unjustly to or about" (Collins English Dictionary, 2009).

A review of the literature on child abuse reveals several definitions to the term that are quite similar in content. For example, a definition of child abuse, as stated in a report on the consultation on Child Abuse Prevention Geneva (World Health Organization, 1999), refers to "any act, or failure to act, that violates the rights of the child that endangers his or her optimum health, survival and development". It adds that "child abuse, or maltreatment, constitutes all forms of physical and/or emotional ill-treatment, sexual abuse, neglect or negligent treatment or commercial or other exploitation, resulting in actual or potential harm to the child's health, survival, development or dignity in the context of a relationship of responsibility, trust or power". A similar definition of the term is stated in the Child Abuse Prevention and Treatment Act (CAPTA), of the federal government of the USA, which states "…at a minimum, any recent act or failure to act on the part of a parent or caretaker, which results in death, serious physical or emotional harm, sexual abuse or exploitation, or an act or failure to act which presents an imminent risk of serious harm." (The Child Abuse Prevention and Treatment Act, the Federal Government of the United States, 2011).

The various definitions of child abuse seem to imply a consensus on several implicit criteria. First, it implies that an act against a child is considered abusive if that act has the potential or likelihood of causing harm to the child, even if no harm has actually resulted from it. Second, it also implies that the forms of acts coming under the definition of child abuse do not always require to have been committed more than once in order to be considered abusive; that is, a single commission of an abusive act may warrant the application of the definition and, where applicable, the activation of subsequent relevant implications and interventions. Third, while most definitions of child abuse assert the non-accidental nature of such acts, they also do not assume the existence of an *intention to harm* in the part of the perpetrator who commits the abusive act. For example, an angry parent may, for example, throw a heavy object at the child that injures him or her, without a pre-existing intention to injure or harm the child; the parent's behavior in this respect, nevertheless, is considered by many as an abusive one.

It is generally agreed that most perpetrators of child abuse are parents or close relatives. For example, the 2002 national data on child abuse in the USA released by the U. S. Department of Health and Human Services (April, 2004) revealed that parents were the abusers in 77 percent of the confirmed cases, other relatives in 11 percent. In addition, Sexual abuse was more likely to be committed by males, whereas females were responsible for the majority of neglect cases.

On the other hand, **Table 2** shows data on the relationship of the abused child to the perpetrators extracted from the NFSR, Saudi Arabia. It illustrates that slightly more than one-third of the total cases of child abuse (37.9%) were reported by either of the parents or relatives, while approximately two-third of the cases were reported by others (which include: teachers, friends, house maids, neighbours, and healthcare professionals). Obviously, this data is not claimed to be representative of the status of child abuse in the whole country since both the registry and the program are at their early stage of life. In addition, these child abuse reports failed to specifically identify the exact perpetrators of the child abuse incidents involved in the reports. Similarly, the section on Saudi Arabia, in the article by Al-Mahroos (2007) that reviewed child abuse and neglect in the Arab Peninsula, did not mention the perpetrators of child abuse cases that the article has outlined with the exception of two reported cases of child abuse committed by two housemaids and were documented by secretly hidden cameras. This shortcoming in data collection is probably related in some way to a lack for a system of obligatory official legal and social interventions in child abuse cases in Saudi Arabia.

Relationship to the Child	**Cases**			
	Male	Female	Total	%
Parents	63	65	128	32.1
Relatives	10	13	23	05.8
Others	133	115	248	62.1
Total	**206**	**193**	**399**	**100**

Table 2. Relation to the Abused Child of Persons Reporting the Abuse

4. Controversies surrounding child abuse

In reality, the terms *child abuse* and *child neglect* are socially defined phenomena. Viewed on technical and legal basis, beating up a child severely, or breaking his or her bones by a total stranger, is likely to be considered by most, without hesitance, as a crime punishable by the law. However, the same act of violence on the child, when committed by the child's parent, may, in many societies, raise some second thoughts that, despite the probable unequivocal condemnation, may delay or prevent the initiation of necessary and appropriate forms of intervention. In other words, child-abuse laws globally raise difficult legal, cultural and political issues, putting the right of children to be free from harm on one hand, against the right of families to privacy and the rights of parents to raise and discipline their children without external interference, on the other. Accordingly, a number of complex issues are at hand when trying to define a specific form of maltreatment. That is because definitions of child abuse or maltreatment reflect cultural values and beliefs. Behaviors that are considered abusive in one culture may be considered acceptable (e.g., corporal punishment) in another culture. Likewise, parental behaviors that are appropriate at one stage in a child's development may be inappropriate at another stage of development. For example, the level of supervision needed for toddlers may differ from that for adolescents. On the other hand, another issue of dispute is the categorical definitions of child abuse or maltreatment. In other words, while some consider a child as either abused or not abused, still others hold the notion that the categorical definition approach fails to acknowledge that abusive and neglectful behaviors can differ markedly in terms of severity, the frequency and duration of occurrence, and the likelihood that they will cause physical or emotional harm. Another disputable dimension of defining child abuse is whether child maltreatment is defined on the basis of the abusive or neglectful adult behaviors committed against a child (e.g., hitting or shaking), or rather on the basis of the harm caused to the child as a result of such behaviors (e.g., displayed physical symptoms such as bruising or swelling). Further, as mentioned above, there is the justified question of whether the intent to maltreat a child is a necessary indicator of child maltreatment. In reality, there can be instances where abuse or neglect can occur even though the perpetrator did not intend to commit it (for example, neglectful parents may have had no intention of neglecting their children).

5. Causes of child abuse

Child abuse occurs across socioeconomic, religious, cultural, racial, and ethic groups. The causes of child abuse or maltreatment are numerous, multiple, and complex. There is no single profile that describes all families within which child abuse occurs. On the other hand, supportive, emotionally gratifying relationships with a healthy network of relatives or friends may help minimize the risk of parents abusing their children, especially during stressful life events. Based on this understanding, research has recognized a number of risk factors commonly associated with child maltreatment. However, the presence of these factors does not necessarily always result in child abuse and neglect. In other words, the factors that may contribute to child maltreatment in one family, such as poverty, may not result in child abuse in another family.

Risk factors associated with child maltreatment have been grouped in four domains: parent or caregiver factors, family factors, child factors, and environmental factors. The interaction of multiple factors across these four domains is recognized to be underlying child maltreatment incidents.

Parent or caregiver factors are related to personality characteristics and psychological well-being, history of maltreatment, substance abuse, attitudes and knowledge, and age. Family factors that may increase the likelihood of child abuse include marital conflict, domestic violence, single parenthood, unemployment, financial stress, and social isolation. Child factors do not imply that children are responsible for being victims of maltreatment. Rather, certain factors can make some children more vulnerable to abusing behavior. The age of the child, his or her physical, mental, emotional, and social development, may increase the child's vulnerability to maltreatment, depending on the interactions of these characteristics with the parental factors outlined above. Environmental factors are often present in combination with parent, family, and child factors. They include poverty and unemployment, social isolation, and community characteristics such as violent neighborhoods, societal attitudes, and promotion of violence in cultural norms and the media.

6. Types of child abuse

Child abuse constitutes all forms of physical and/or emotional ill-treatment, sexual abuse, neglect or negligent treatment, exploitation (commercial or other types of exploitation), resulting in actual or potential harm to the child's health, survival, development or dignity. The abuse takes place in the context of a relationship of responsibility, trust or power. Some types of child abuse are naturally more common, such as cases of child neglect, than other types, such as sexual abuse. Further, certain types of abuse are often difficult to document or characterize, compared to other types that are readily evident in a number of ways.

6.1. Physical abuse

Child physical abuse refers, generally, to the non-accidental use of physical force against a child that results in harm to the child. Physically abusive behaviors include shoving, hitting, slapping, shaking, throwing, pushing, kicking, biting, burning, strangling and poisoning. A parent does not have *to intend* to physically harm his or her child to have physically abused him or her. For example, physical punishment that results in bruising would generally be considered physical abuse. Depending on the age and the nature of the behavior, physical force that is likely to cause physical harm to the child may also be considered abusive; that is, a situation in which a baby is shaken but not injured would still be considered physically abusive. The fabrication or induction of an illness by a parent or carer (previously known as Munchausen syndrome by proxy) is also considered physically abusive behavior (Bromfield, 2005; World Health Organization, 2006).

6.2. Emotional abuse

Emotional abuse (also called *emotional maltreatment, psychological maltreatment* or *psychological abuse*) refers to a parent or caregiver's inappropriate verbal or symbolic acts toward a child and/or a pattern of failure over time to provide a child with adequate non-physical nurture and emotional availability. Such acts of commission or omission have a high probability of damaging a child's self-esteem or social competence (Garbarino, Guttmann, and Seeley, 1986; World Health Organization, 2006). According to Garbarino, et al. (1986), emotional maltreatment takes five main behavioral forms. *Rejecting* is whereby the adult refuses to acknowledge the child's worth and the legitimacy of the child's needs. *Isolating,* involves the adult cutting the child off from normal social experiences, preventing the child from forming friendships, and making the child believe that he or she is alone in the world. *Terrorizing* is that the adult verbally assaults the child, creating a climate of fear, bullying and frightening the child, and making the child believes that the world is capricious and hostile. *Ignoring* involves the adult deprives the child of essential stimulation and responsiveness, stifling emotional growth and intellectual development. Finally, *corrupting* involves the adult 'mis-socializing' the child, stimulating the child to engage in destructive antisocial behavior, reinforcing that deviance, and making the child unfit for normal social experience. However, some scholars classify emotionally neglectful behaviors, such as rejecting and ignoring, as a form of neglect. Obviously there is common conceptual ground between some types of emotional maltreatment and some types of neglect, which serves to illustrate that the different maltreatment or abuse subtypes are not always neatly demarcated.

6.3. Neglect

Neglect refers to the failure by the parent or caregiver to provide a child, where they are in a position to do so, with the conditions that are culturally acceptable as being essential for their physical and emotional development and wellbeing (Broadbent and Bentley, 1997; World Health Organization, 2006). Neglectful behaviors can be divided into different sub-categories. Physical neglect is characterized by the parent's or caregiver's failure to provide basic physical necessities, such as safe, clean and adequate clothing, housing, food and health care. Emotional or psychological neglect is characterized by a lack of parents' or caregivers' warmth, nurturance, encouragement and support; it is noted here that emotional neglect is sometimes considered a form of emotional abuse or maltreatment. Educational neglect is characterized by a parent's or caregiver's failure to provide supportive educational opportunities for the child. Finally, environmental neglect is characterized by the parent's or caregiver's failure to ensure environmental safety, opportunities and resources (Dubowitz, Pitts, and Black, 2004).

6.4. Sexual abuse

Sexual abuse is complicated to define. Some behaviors are considered sexually abusive by almost everyone; for example the rape of an 11 years old child by a parent. Other behaviors are much more equivocal, at least among certain sociocultural groups, such as consensual sex between 19 years old and 15 years old individuals. To judge whether behaviors such as the latter example constitute abuse or not requires a sensitive understanding of a number of definitional issues specific to child sexual abuse. A general definition of child sexual abuse proposes that child sexual abuse involves "the use of a child for sexual gratification by an adult or significantly older child/adolescent" (Tomison, 1995). Similarly, Broadbent and Bentley (1997) define child sexual abuse as "any act which exposes a child to, or involves a child in, sexual processes beyond his or her understanding or contrary to accepted community standards". Sexually abusive behaviors can include the fondling of genitals, masturbation, oral sex, vaginal or anal penetration by a penis, finger or any other object, fondling of breasts, voyeurism, and exhibitionism and exposing the child to or involving the child in pornography (Bromfield, 2005; US National Research Council, 1993). Unlike the other abuse types, the definition of child sexual abuse varies depending on the relationship between the victim and the perpetrator. For example, any sexual behavior between a child and a member of his or her family, such as parent or uncle, would always be considered abusive, while sexual behavior between two adolescents may or may not be considered abusive, depending on whether the behavior was consensual, whether any coercion was present, or whether the relationship between the two young people was equal (Ryan, 1997). A cross-cultural review of child abuse concepts, however, brings into consideration issues of religion and societal norms wherein all sexual behaviors outside the boundaries of marriage are outlawed or criminalized. In societies such as in many Muslim countries, the question is not whether sexual acts are consensual or not; rather, it is about whether or not the sexual acts are occurring between married individuals. In other societies, Australia for instance, consensual sexual activity between 20 years old and 15 years old is considered abusive, while the same activity between unmarried 20 years old and 17 years old is not considered abusive. In some traditional societies, a marriage between an adult male and a below 18 years old girl can be legalized, and there does not seem to be a cutoff age for females at which the marriage is permissible. In fact, in some instances, some females may be made to agree to be married while they are as young as 16 years old or below. The child abuse perspectives related to such instances are very controversial even within such societies themselves.

6.5. Other forms of child abuse

There are additional forms of child maltreatment or abuse that have been identified by some researchers (e.g., Corby, 2006; Miller-Perrin and Perrin, 2007). They include fetal abuse, which involves behaviors by parent mothers that could endanger a fetus, such as the excessive use of tobacco, alcohol, or elicit drugs. Other suggested forms of child abuse include bullying or peer abuse, sibling abuse. One may argue that all these latter forms can indeed be re-classified under the major subtypes of child abuse outlined above. The same argument applies to the so-called institutional abuse (which involves the abuse that occurs in institutions such as foster homes, group homes, voluntary or charity organizations and child care centers) and organizational exploitation (e.g., child sex rings, child pornography, child prostitution), and state-sanctioned abuse. One of the examples given for state-sanctioned abuse is the so-called female genital mutilation in parts of the world, which refers to the circumcision practice. This latter example is particularly controversial on cross-cultural grounds.

It is occasionally argued that to distinguish between the different subtypes of child abuse may be useful for better understanding and to identify them more thoroughly. However, others argue that such a distinction may be slightly misleading because the reality tells us that often there are no strong lines of demarcation between the different abuse subtypes, and that abuse subtypes seldom occur in isolation. The existing evidence shows that the majority of individuals with history of maltreatment report exposure to two or more subtypes (Arata, Langhinrichsen-Rohling, Bowers, and O'Farrill-Swails, 2005; Higgins and McCabe, 2000; Ney, Fung, and Wickett, 1994). In addition, some acts of violence against children involve multiple maltreatment subtypes. For example, an adult who sexually abuses a child may simultaneously hit them (i.e., physical abuse) and isolate or terrorize them (i.e., emotional abuse). Similarly, when parents subject their children to sexual or physical abuse, the emotional harm and betrayal of trust implicit in these acts can indeed be thought of as a form of emotional maltreatment.

The Saudi Arabian National Family Safety Registry (NFSR) has documented not only various types of child abuse but also multiple abusive events occasionally against the same victim. **Figure 2**, therefore, shows the registered events of abuse across subtypes of abuse. The physical abuse events represented 64.4% (N=397) of all events of abuse, followed by neglect (N=286; 46.4%), sexual abuse (N=136; 22%), and finally emotional abuse (N=76; 12.3%) which is traditionally a more difficult to document than other types of child abuse. The registered physical abuse incidents are further classified into sub-categories as shown in **Figure 3**. Further, incidents of neglect are also classified into medical (25.9%), educational (7.7%), nutritional (10.5%), abandonment (9.8%), and general (35.3%) subcategories of neglect. The sexual abuse events are classified into two subcategories: assault (50.9%) and exploitation (49.1%).

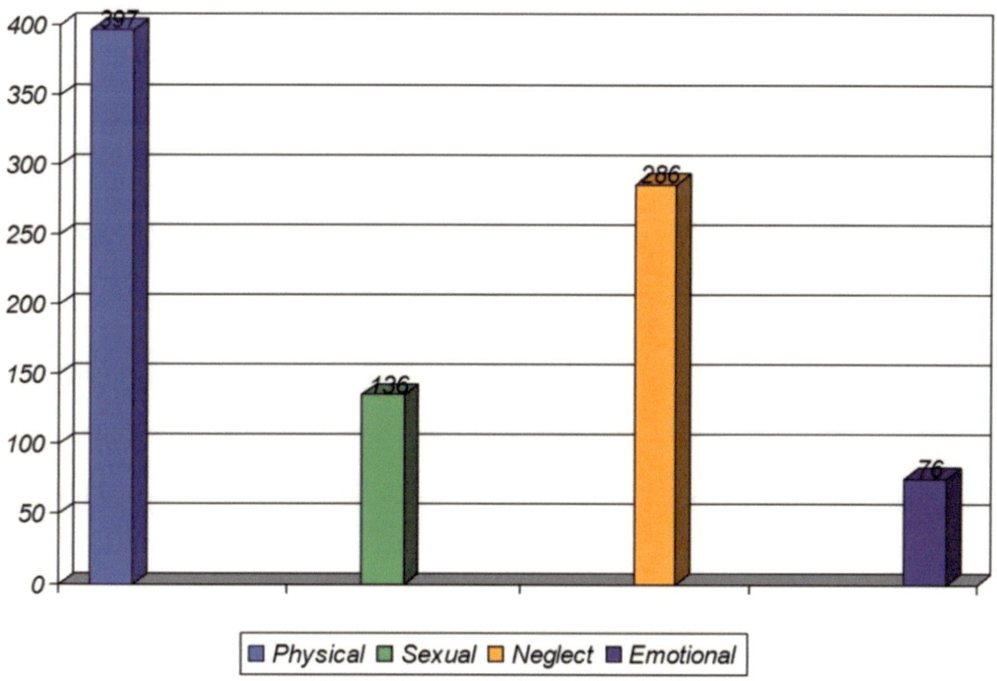

Figure 2. Registered Events of Child Abuse across Types of Abuse

Of the total cases of child abuse (N=616), some cases involved multiple events of abuse hence raising the total events of child abuse registered in the registry to 630 abusive events. Of these events, 303 did not require admission to the hospital, while 327 were serious enough that they required admission to various medical services as shown in **Figure 4** below.

7. Psychological sequelae of child abuse

Some stringent systems that organize actions related to child abuse cases are in place in several countries. As a result, some parents who were proven to be abusive to their children were separated from their children temporarily until remedial steps were taken to ensure that harm was contained or removed and measures were in place to prevent recurrence. In some instances, such separation was permanent. The central issue in this respect is whether the abusive behaviors against a child by his or her biological parent are serious enough to warrant the potential of severing the fatherhood and/or motherhood relationship with the victim child despite the eternal biological connection linking both.

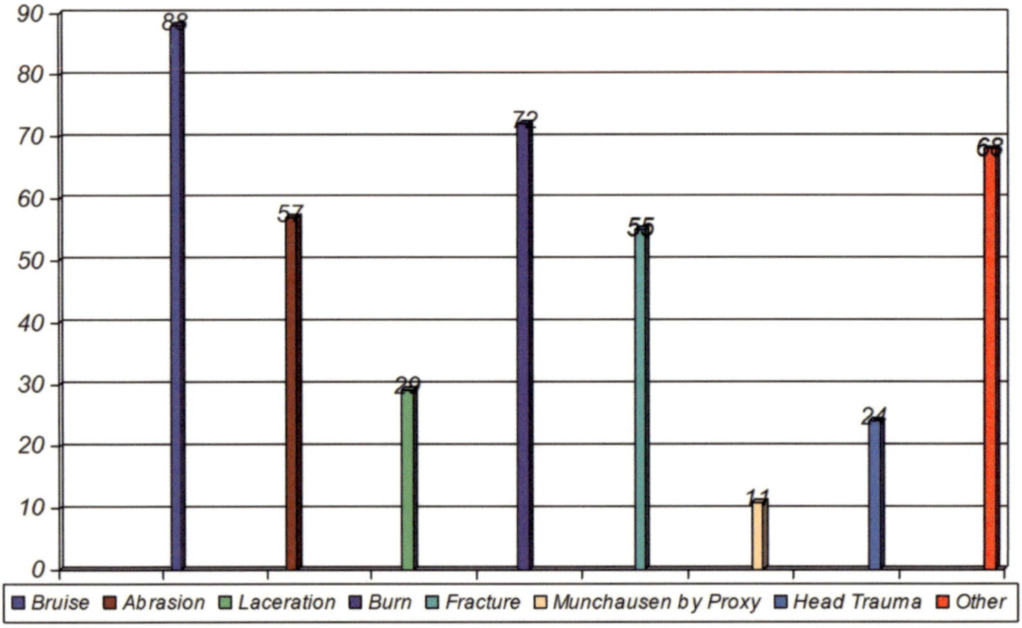

Figure 3. The Subcategories of Physical Abuse Events

In some countries, Saudi Arabia included, despite the establishment of somewhat elaborate governmental bodies and regulations for addressing the problem of child abuse, the courts remain reluctant to allow such bodies and regulations to intrude too far into the private relations between parents and children. The result of such reluctance is that children are not allowed to enjoy an affirmative right to be protected by the official bodies from violence and other forms of maltreatment committed by their custodian parents in the privacy of the home.

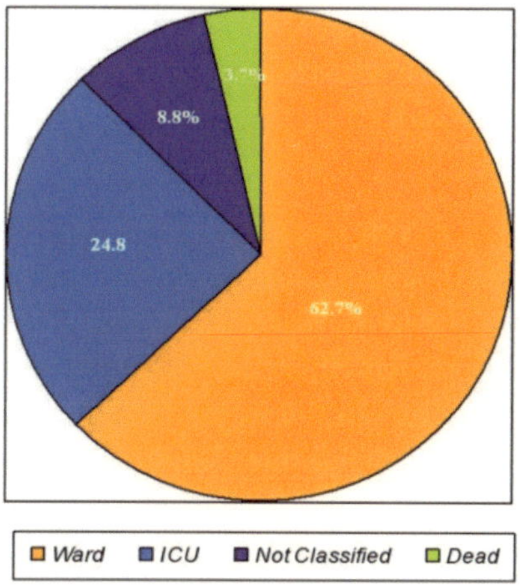

Figure 4. Distribution of Admitted Cases of Child Abuse

With regard to the experience of the NFSP in Saudi Arabia, even after admission, there seems to be some socio-medico-legal challenges that still face the NFSP and will require further legislative and legal workup. To illustrate this point, some abused children who were admitted to the hospital for medical intervention, were soon discharged by their guardians against medical advice (see **Figure 5** below), as there yet to be a legal system and binding regulations that protect the abused child under treatment from being discharged against medical advice by his or her guardian and, in some instances, to return to the same environment in which the abuse took place.

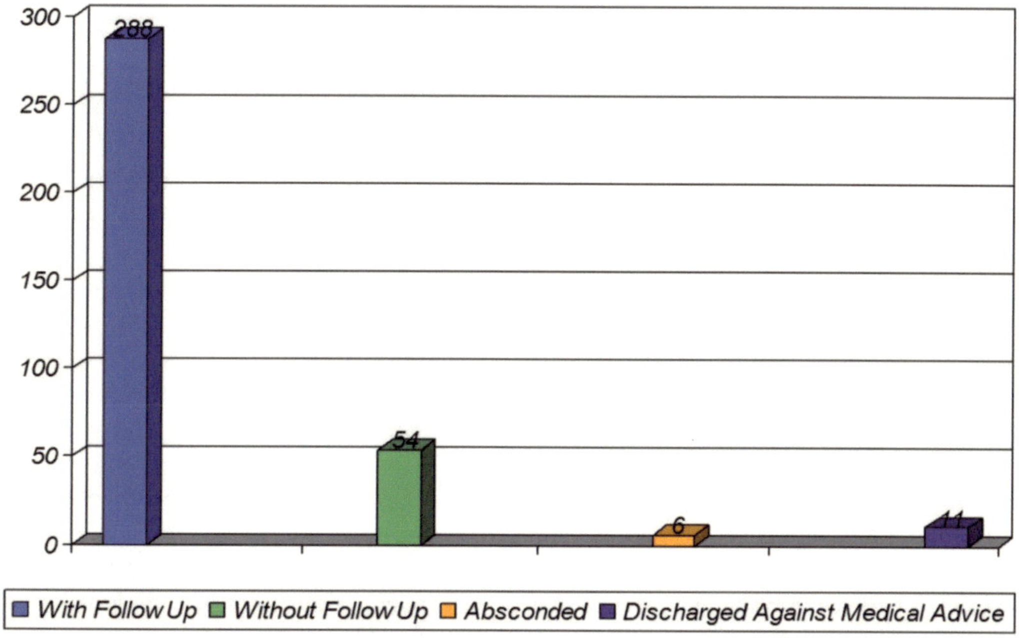

Figure 5. Distribution by Discharge Status

To promote an adequate understanding of the gravity of the psychological impact that child abuse behaviors might inflict on their victims and the society as a whole, it is important first to outline the normal basic needs of a child that are necessary for him or her to develop and grow normally.

Child development is a result of a complex and dynamic process of interplays and shifting influences on physical, emotional, sexual, social and cognitive development. However, the development of the individual child is primarily a social process and the family is the central social context within which this development occurs. In other words, the psychosocial variables and encounters in the immediate surrounds of a child since birth are both intrinsic components of his development and determinants of the outcome of the developmental process. A family is a unique social system, whereby its membership is based on a combination of biological, legal, affectional, geographic and historical ties (e.g., Carr, 2003); entry into the family system usually is through birth (or, less frequently, adoption), and members can leave only by death. Severing all family connections is never possible, a reality that often explains the deep and lasting psychological impacts of some subjectively significant events experienced within the family boundaries by some individuals. In modern times, with new forms of family structures such as single parenthood, the traditional definition of the family may not be very useful (Walsh, 1993). Hence, a child's family may be conceived as a network of people in the child's immediate psychological field, which may include members of the child's household and others who, while not members of the household, play a significant role in the child's life; for example, a separated parent living away with whom the child has regular contact; a grandmother who provides informal day care, and so forth. In clinical terms, the primary concern is the extent to which this network meets the child's developmental needs.

It is important that child abuse and neglect are placed in the context of what is more typical for children to experience as they grow up. Studies that examined family life, in general population samples reveal very great differences within the range of 'normal' family life and childrearing patterns, with social class being one of the strongest influences (Creighton and Russell, 1995).

The development of parenting roles entails what Carr (2003) refers to as 'routines' for meeting children's needs that include safety, care, control, and intellectual stimulation. Developing routines for meeting children's needs for safety include protecting children from accidents by, for example, not leaving young children unsupervised, and developing skills for managing the frustration and anger that the demands of parenting young children often elicit. Failure to develop such routines may lead to accidental injuries or child abuse. Routines for providing children with food and shelter, attachment, empathy, understanding and emotional support need to be developed to meet children's needs for care in these various areas. Failure to do so may lead to various emotional difficulties. Developmental needs for control involve routines for setting clear rules and limits; for providing supervision to ensure that children conform to these expectations; and for offering appropriate rewards and sanctions for rule-following and rule-violations that meet children's need for control. Conduct problems may occur if such routines are not developed. Parent-child play and communication routines for meeting children's needs for age-appropriate intellectual stimulation need to be developed as well, otherwise developmental delays in emotional, language and intellectual development may result.

The impact of child mental health on child development and on the society as a whole is well documented but under recognized. There is limited public awareness of how mental health affects child development and societal wellbeing in general, and of how important mental health needs can and should be met. The importance of mental health for normal child development can hardly be over-estimated. Provision and supporting children's optimal social and emotional development results in positive outcomes for individuals and society, including healthier behavior, greater school successes, improved relationships, and economic savings. Parents, families and other significant caregivers, who are readily available, responsive, and stable, are crucial for children's optimal mental health, and these relationships influence brain development from birth (Carr, 2003). Parents, teachers, and other child-caregivers who care for and work with children need to be better informed about milestones of normal, healthy child development to both reassure caregivers when development proceeds within typical limits and to identify early warning signs that indicate when assistance is necessary. Children and their families can be prepared, in situations of unavoidable life challenges, for stress points and transitions, hence learning the skills to be resilient in periods of stress and challenge, thus protecting and promoting mental health.

There are strong association between exposure to child abuse in all its forms and higher rates of many chronic conditions. There is strong evidence from the Adverse Childhood Experiences series of studies (Middlebrooks and Audage, 2008) that show correlations between exposure to abuse or neglect and higher rates in adulthood of chronic conditions, high-risk health behaviors and shortened lifespan. Child abuse is a major life stressor that has consequences involving the mental health of an adult. For example, it has been identified that childhood sexual abuse is a risk factor for the development of substance-related problems during adolescence and adulthood (Dolezal, McCollum, and Callahan, 2009). The early experiences of child abuse can trigger the development of an internalizing disorder, such as anxiety and depression. For example, adults with a history of some form of child abuse, whether sexual abuse, physical abuse, or neglect, have more chances of developing depression than an adult who has never been abused.

The psychological effects of child abuse are well documented. Children with history of neglect or physical abuse are at risk of developing psychiatric problems (Gauthier, Stollak, Messe, and Aronoff, 1996; Malinosky-Rummell, and Hansen, 1993), or a disorganized attachment style (Lyons-Ruth and Jacobvitz, 1999; Solomon and George, 1999; Main and Hesse, 1990) that is associated with a number of developmental problems, including dissociative symptoms, as well as anxiety, depressive and acting out symptoms. Further, a study by Cicchetti (1990) found that 80% of abused and maltreated infants exhibited symptoms of disorganized attachment, and when some of these children become parents, especially if they suffer from posttraumatic stress disorder, dissociative symptoms and other sequelae of child abuse, they may encounter difficulty when faced with their infant and young children's needs and normative stress, which may in turn lead to adverse consequences for their child's social-emotional development.

8. Conclusion

Human beings, and probably some animals, can go to great lengths and efforts in order to care for and protect their children. Nevertheless, one must be aware that occasionally two contradictory states may exist side by side: caring for children yet abusing them. Child abuse is a complex phenomenon with multiple causes. The work towards eliminating this phenomenon, therefore, is expected to be a task that is as complex as the phenomenon.

To address the problem of child abuse, one must first understand the causes in their real depths. Such understanding requires those concerned with child abuse to approach the issue on the basis of rational deliberations, rather than be driven by the passion and the sympathy with the victims alone. Prerequisites for preventing child abuse are believed to include understanding, in the first place, of why the abusive behaviors against children do occur. In other words, it is important to understand to what extent a particular child-rearing behavior is acceptable or deviant within a particular society or sociocultural group, and whether such a behavior is common or different between groups. The underpinnings of such thinking process include the acknowledgement of the ways in which children are viewed in a given culture. One of the main questions here is that whether children are considered to be the property of the parents. Subsequent issues include the age until which, according to cultural norms, the children require the protection and nurturance of their parents, and the extent until which physical abuse is considered educational and, thus, acceptable. For example, among certain cultural groups it is considered normal, or even desirable, that girls get married during their adolescent life. This desirability involves the girls themselves. Awareness of cultural factors, therefore, must remain high since they influence all aspects of child abuse, from the occurrence and definition through its treatment and successful prevention. Any intervention, to be successful whether for data collection, prevention or even increasing awareness, must take into consideration the cultural environment in which it is to occur. On the other hand, background or baseline conditions beyond the control of families or caretakers, such as poverty, inaccessible healthcare, inadequate nutrition, unavailability of education, can be contributing factors to child abuse. Social upheaval and instability, conflict and war, may also contribute to increases in child abuse and neglect. It is believed that the prevalence of the compromised conditions, such as poverty and political or social conflict, varies to considerable extents across the countries of today's world. Therefore, the means and mechanisms necessary for the fight against child abuse will obviously vary across countries or societies with varying social, cultural, religious, and resource factors. It seems, accordingly, that it is expected from those who are involved, at local or international levels, with the issue of child abuse to be equipped with a thorough cross-cultural understanding of the child abuse phenomenon.

Adequate data on child abuse in Saudi Arabia, and the whole Arabian Gulf region for that purpose, is scarce and scattered (Al-Mahroos, 2007). This is probably due to multiple social, cultural, and bureaucratic factors leading to seemingly a broad consensus at community level on unbroken silence regarding child abuse phenomenon. The few cases that made news in national media were involving tragic deaths or severe harm against children that were perpetrated by expatriate housemaids. Further, the vast majority of the proven or suspected child abuse cases were medically reported (e.g., Al-Mugeiren and Ganelin, 1990; Al-Eissa, 1991; Kattan, 1994). Very little is known about the less severe child abuse cases that might have occurred in the community and were perpetrated by parents or relatives, since lack of data does not necessarily imply low or no incidence of child abuse.

The religion of the country does not permit maltreatment of children. In the contrary, Islam prohibits all kinds of maltreatment against human beings and animals by means of clear verses in the Quran. Even the seemingly permissible corporal punishment has been narrowly restricted by Islam in such a way that it effectively resembles a gesture of disapproval rather than a means for bodily harm. To put it in the correct perspective, the patterns of the reported child abuse in Saudi Arabia are similar to what are seen in other parts of the world, proving that child abuse is an unfortunate tragedy shared by all communities of mankind and is resistive to the teachings of all religions known by humans.

An additional dimension of child abuse in Saudi Arabia that requires further study is the impact of the growth of wealth in the country during the last fifty years or so, which involves tremendous changes in the society including a shift from extended to nuclear family structures, changes from the traditional rearing up methods where grandfathers and grandmothers played significant roles to a modern shape of families where a housemaid plays a significant role in caring after the young ones in the family while both parents are at work. Such housemaids are by and large unskilled workers who have left their own families, and probably their own children, behind them for work in a culturally different country. Intentional and unintentional indiscretions involving children can occur in such a human context. However, this understanding can not attribute any significant portion of child abuse in Saudi Arabia to expatriate housemaid even if the potential does exist.

The Saudi Arabian experience in the realm of child abuse, as outlined above, seems to be in its conception stage. The workers in this realm, by and large, are driven by their own interest in and concern about child maltreatment and their involvement is never a full-time endeavor. The current state of affairs is reactive in nature, such that most of the NFSR child abuse cases were captured during routine hospital visits following the occurrence of injuries or other forms of child abuse that required medical consultation. One can not imagine the number of child abuse incidents that have not been accounted for. The data presented from the NFSR provides glimpses of the problem in rather a superficially descriptive fashion. The individual characteristics of the abused children and their psychological and social profiles would have provided an insight about why these particular children became victims of abuse. In addition, the social and psychological profiles of their parents and their abusers are likewise informative and necessary basis for future planning and legislating.

A full-fledging work against child abuse in Saudi Arabia is expected to include sound and obligatory training of individuals who are likely to work with children and families, such as physicians, psychologists, social workers, teachers, on all dimensions of child abuse issues in order to enhance their abilities to recognize, predict, and intervene. Public awareness of child abuse and its implications on the lives of children, families, and the society as a whole is probably a strategic objective for combating child abuse, and for which various official and non-official bodies in the society can be recruited, such as schools, religious authorities, security forces, etc.

As mentioned earlier, several abused children who were admitted to hospital for treating their physical and emotional injuries, were soon discharged by their guardians against medical advice. There were no guarantees that the same cycle of abuse did not continue against these children after their forced discharge from the hospital pre-maturely. The treating physicians or clinicians had no jurisdiction to prevent such discharge. This legal vacuum requires legislative efforts that are designed to allow children their right to be treated and to be protected from abuse.

Finally, there is active work at various governmental levels to establish a legal and official system to regulate child protection policies in the direction beneficial to the child. Until then, children are largely on their own.

Author details

Essam Al-Shail
Head Section, Paediatric Neurosurgery, Department of Neurosciences, King Faisal Specialist Hospital & Research Center, Riyadh, Saudi Arabia

Ahmed M. Hassan
Department of Mental Health, King Faisal Specialist Hospital & Research Center, Riyadh, Saudi Arabia

Abdullah Aldowaish
Department of Paediatrics, King Faisal Specialist Hospital & Research Center, Riyadh, Saudi Arabia

Hoda Kattan
Department of Paediatrics, King Faisal Specialist Hospital & Research Center, Riyadh, Saudi Arabia

9. References

Al-Eissa, Y. A. (1991). The Battered child syndrome: does it exist in Saudi Arabia? Saudi Medical Journal. Volume 12, pp. 129 – 133.

Al-Mahroos, F. T. (2007). Child abuse and neglect in the Arab Peninsula. Saudi Medical Journal; Volume 28 (2), pp. 241-248.

Al-Mugeiren, M. and Ganelin, R. S. (1990). A suspected case of Munchausen's syndrome by proxy in a Saudi child. Annals Saudi Medicine. Volume 10, pp. 662 – 665.

Arata, C. M., Langhinrichsen-Rohling, J., Bowers, D., and O'Farrill-Swails, L. (2005). Single versus multi-type maltreatment: An examination of the long-term effects of child abuse. Journal of Aggression, Maltreatment & Trauma, 11(4), pp. 29-52.

Broadbent, A. and Bentley, R. (1997). Child abuse and neglect Australia 1995-96 (Child Welfare Series No. 17). Canberra: Australian Institute of Health and Welfare.

Bromfield, L. M. (2005). Chronic child maltreatment in an Australian Statutory child protection sample (Unpublished doctoral dissertation). Deakin University, Geelong.

Carr, A. (2003). The Handbook of Child and Adolescent Clinical Psychology: A Contextual Approach. Hove and New York: Brunner-Routledge.

Cicchetti, D. (1990). Pathways to Resilient Functioning in Maltreated Children: From Single-Level to Multilevel Investigations. In: D. Cicchetti and G. I. Roisman (eds.), Minnesota Symposia on Child Psychology: The Origins and Organization of Adaptation and Maladaptation. Hoboken, New Jersey: John Wiley & Sons, Inc.

Collins, W. (2009). Collins English Dictionary: Complete & Unabridged 10th Edition. William Collins Sons & Co. Ltd.

Corby, B. (2006). Child abuse: Towards a knowledge base (3rd Ed.). Berkshire, England: Open University Press.

Creighton, S. and Russell, N. (1995). Voices from Childhood: A Survey of Childhood Experiences and Attitudes to Childrearing Among Adults in the United Kingdom. London: NSPCC Research Policy and Practice Series.

Dolezal, T., McCollum, D. and Callahan, M. (2009). Hidden Costs in Health Care: The Economic Impact of Violence and Abuse. Eden Prairie (MN): Academy on Violence and Abuse (AVA).

Dubowitz, H., Pitts, S. C. and Black, M. M. (2004). Measurement of three major subtypes of child neglect. Child Maltreatment, 9(4), pp. 344-356

Garbarino, J., Guttmann, E., and Seeley, J. W. (1986). The psychologically battered child: Strategies for identification, assessment, and intervention. San Francisco, California: Jossey-Bass Inc.

Gauthier, L., Stollak, G., Messe, L. and Aronoff, J. (1996). Recall of childhood neglect and physical abuse as differential predictors of current psychological functioning. Child Abuse and Neglect, 20(7), pp. 549-559.

Gough, D. (1996). Defining the problem. Child Abuse and Neglect, 20(11), pp. 993-1102.

Higgins, D. J. and McCabe, M. P. (2000). Relationships between different types of maltreatment during childhood and adjustment in adulthood. Child Maltreatment, 5, pp. 261-272.

Kattan, H. (1994). Child abuse in Saudi Arabia: report of ten cases. Annals of Saudi Medicine. Volume 14, pp. 129-133.

Main, M. and Hesse, E. (1990). Parents' unresolved traumatic experiences are related to infant disorganized attachment status: Is frightened and/or frightening parental behavior the linking mechanism? In: M. T. Greenberg, D. Cicchetti, and E. M. Cummings (Eds.), Attachment in the preschool years: Theory, research, and intervention (pp. 161 – 182). Chicago: University of Chicago Press.

Middlebrooks, J. S. and Audage, N. C. (2008). The Effects of Childhood Stress on Health Across the Lifespan. Atlanta (GA): Centers for Disease Control and Prevention, National Center for Injury Prevention and Control.

Miller-Perrin, C. L. and Perrin, R. D. (2007). Child Maltreatment: An introduction. Thousand Oaks, CA: Sage Publications.

Ney, P. G., Fung, T. and Wickett, A. R. (1994). The worst combinations of child abuse and neglect. Child Abuse & Neglect, 18(9), pp. 705-714.

Price-Robertson, R. and Bromfield, L. (2009). What Is Child Abuse and Neglect? Second edition. Melbourne, Australia: Commonwealth of Australia.

Ryan, G. (1997). Sexually abusive youth: Defining the population. In: G. Ryan and S. Lane (Eds.), Juvenile Sexual Offending: Causes, consequences, and correction. San Francesco: Jossey-Bass.

Sari, N. and Buyukunal, S. N. (1991). A study of the history of child abuse. Pediatrics Surgery International, Vol. 6, pp. 401-406.

Shelman, E. A. and Lazoritz, S. (2005). The Mary Ellen Wilson Child Abuse Case and the Beginning of Children's Rights in 19th Century America. Eric A. Shelman and Steven Lazoritz.

Solomon, J. and George, C. (1999). Attachment Disorganization. New York: Guilford ress.

Tomison, A. M. (2000). Exploring family violence: Links between child maltreatment and domestic violence (Issues Paper No. 13). Melbourne: National Child Protection Clearinghouse.

Walsh, F. (1993). Normal Family Processes (second edition). New York: Guilford.

Watkins, S.A. (1990). The Mary Ellen myth: Correcting child welfare history. Social Work, 35(6), pp. 500-503.

World Health Organization. (2006). Preventing Child Maltreatment: A guide to taking action and generating evidence. Geneva: WHO.

http://www.childwelfare.gov/systemwide/laws_policies/statutes/define.pdf).

Chapter 3

Recognizing the Co-Occurrence of Child and Domestic Abuse in Pregnancy and the First Postnatal Year

Anne Lazenbatt

Additional information is available at the end of the chapter

http://dx.doi.org/10.5772/49963

1. Introduction

Over recent years there has been an upsurge in research that has increased our knowledge and understanding of how pregnancy and the first postnatal year can lay significant foundations for positive child development. This new knowledge has created a consensus of opinion about the need to develop early interventions to help young children get the best start in life. Child abuse and maltreatment can have an impact early in an infant's life, even as early as pregnancy and the postpartum period and can affect infants' physical and emotional health, their learning and their capacity to form positive relationships throughout their lives. Child abuse is a major and complex public health and social welfare problem, caused by a myriad of factors that involve the individual, the family and the community. We know that child abuse or neglect and general trauma, including the witnessing of domestic abuse, are major threats to child health and wellbeing; they alter normal child development and, without intervention, may have lifelong consequences [1].

Infant maltreatment is one of the most serious events undermining healthy psychological wellbeing and development, and no other social risk factor has a stronger association with developmental psychopathology [2]. Parents are almost always the perpetrators and in the United Kingdom (UK) infants are eight times more likely to be killed than older children [3]. However, this may be only the 'tip of the iceberg' as some researchers suggest that well over 50% of fatalities due to maltreatment may be incorrectly coded as deaths due to accidents, natural causes, or other factors on the death record [4]. Evidence highlights that no single factor causes children to be maltreated, rather a 'toxic trio' of factors such as parental mental illness, domestic abuse and drug and alcohol misuse, can increase the risk of neglect or abuse. A recent NSPCC report shows that around 198,000 babies under one year of age in the UK have parents who are affected by domestic violence, substance misuse or mental health problems [5]. An analysis of UK Serious Case Reviews (SCRs) shows that at least one of these three issues is present in many cases, and there is often a high degree of overlap of these factors in cases of child death and serious injury [6]. There is as yet no definitive explanation for this high incidence, though frailty and total dependence are important features. However, it also seems likely that the very real demands and stresses placed on a family by a newborn baby are almost certainly a factor.

2. Domestic abuse

Globally domestic abuse is also a major public and social problem, the prevalence and universality of which is well-documented [7-14]. It is a serious infringement of women's and children's Human Rights with a range of often serious health implications for women and their children [15-19]. Its prevalence in society is shocking and unacceptable with on average throughout the world one in four women experiencing domestic abuse at some point in their lives [18]. The term 'domestic abuse' is used to describe violence perpetrated by an adult against another with whom they have or have had a sexual relationship. This abuse can take many forms including the physical (hitting, kicking, restraining), the sexual (including assault, coercion, female genital mutilation), the psychological (verbal bullying, undermining, social isolation) and the financial (withholding money, unrealistic expectations with the household budget). The UK Department of Health's (2002) [19] definition is: "Any incident of threatening behaviour, violence or abuse (psychological, physical, sexual, financial or emotional) between adults who are or have been intimate partners or family members, regardless of gender or sexuality."

Domestic abuse not only can be physically, emotionally, psychologically and socially devastating to women, it can have similarly devastating effects on children [20-22]. Recent research affirms the notion that few infants and children living with domestic abuse remain unaffected by the experience [23-25, 22, 26], with one in 20 children witnessing frequent physical violence between parents [26]. In addition, the stress of domestic abuse can severely impair women's parenting abilities, making them less able to care for their children and more depressed than other women [27], factors that certainly would affect their infant's wellbeing [28]. The prevalence data suggests that there are very high numbers of children living with domestic abuse and that it is difficult to protect children from exposure to the effects of this violence. It is estimated that in the UK alone 750,000 children [29] are exposed every year. More recent research suggests that one in seven (14.2 per cent) of children and young people under the age of 18 will have lived with domestic abuse at some point in their childhood [30]. For instance, the reports from two different studies which interviewed adult participants reported 86% and 85% respectively that children were present either in the same or adjoining rooms during an incident of domestic abuse [31, 32]. It is not only the exposure to living with domestic abuse that creates vulnerability in children and young people. Children living with domestic abuse are also more likely to be directly physically or sexually abused. Numerous studies report on this problematic co-occurrence. The meta-analysis by Edleson [33] of 31 high quality research studies showed that between 30% and

66% of children who suffer physical abuse are also living in a context of domestic abuse. The variation is largely dependent upon research site and methodology, but either figure is disturbing. The severity of violence is also relevant. Ross, for example, found that in a US study of 3,363 parents there was an almost 100% correlation between the most severe abuse of women and the men's physical abuse of children [34].

The purpose of this chapter is to highlight how pregnancy and the first postnatal year should be described as a 'high-risk' period for violence, prompting the initial episode of domestic abuse, or an escalation of a pre-existing abusive relationship, and the effects of the co-occurrence of child abuse during this time [35, 36]. The chapter is divided into sections that cover issues such as: domestic abuse in pregnancy and early infancy and the understanding of the impact that both domestic and child abuse have on both mother and child; the impact of foetal abuse; domestic abuse as a child protection issue; the co-occurrence of domestic and child abuse in pregnancy; and the role of health professionals especially midwives in recognising and reporting the co-occurrence of domestic and child abuse. The chapter will also report on the findings of a larger study, which was conducted between December 2008 and August 2009, and identified midwives' knowledge, attitudes and experience of domestic and child abuse. Although the evidence base is rapidly expanding on midwives' identification and management of domestic abuse, to the best of our knowledge, no empirical work has been undertaken that focuses on how midwives, working in either hospital or community settings, are assessing the co-occurrence of domestic and child abuse in their client populations.

3. Domestic abuse in pregnancy and early infancy

A family problem such as domestic abuse is therefore clearly a child safeguarding issue. Domestic abuse during pregnancy has emerged as a national and global health issue that has the potential to harm a woman and her unborn child both physically and psychologically. We know that pregnancy and the first year are critical stages in child development, providing the essential foundations for all future learning, behaviour and health. Adverse prenatal and postnatal experiences can have a profound effect on the course of health and development over a lifetime. However, what is clear from the literature is that child abuse is likely to escalate in frequency and intensity over time and may increase at specific critical points, especially during pregnancy and the postpartum period [37] which creates a complex problem because of its dual risks to both a mother and her unborn child [38, 39]. The Confidential Enquiry into Maternal and Child Health estimates that 30% of domestic abuse commences during pregnancy [40, 41] which is why it is acknowledged as a high-risk period for domestic abuse. This period may prompt the initial episode or an escalation of a pre-existing abusive relationship [42, 43, 37].

The findings of a review by Jasinki highlight several factors associated with pregnancy-related abuse such as: poverty, low socioeconomic status; low levels of social support; first-time parenting; unexpected or unwanted pregnancy; ethnicity; drug and alcohol abuse [44]. Prevalence rates for domestic abuse during pregnancy range from 1% to 20% depending on the definition of violence in the study, although most studies report prevalence rates between 3% and 14% [45, 46]. Concurring with the article by Gazmararian et al. [44], World Health Organization reported on 48 worldwide studies that show the incidence of physically abused pregnant women was greater than 5% in 11 of the 15 countries studied [47]. Additionally, between 13% (Ethiopia) and almost 50% (urban Brazil and Serbia and Montenegro) of women in these studies reported that they were abused for the first time during pregnancy [47]. Such findings suggest that domestic abuse during pregnancy is more common than preeclampsia or gestational diabetes [46]. Domestic abuse also produces a range of psychosocial effects upon the mother such as alcohol and drug dependence, unemployment, homelessness, suicide attempts, depression, anxiety, and post-traumatic stress disorder, and heightened maternal and foetal stress [48, 49]. In addition, pregnant women experiencing violence are at a higher risk of becoming victims of homicide than are pregnant women not experiencing violence [50, 51] and domestic abuse has been cited as a prime cause of maternal deaths during childbirth [50]. Evidence shows that within the six weeks following birth, eleven new mothers were known to have been murdered by their male partners during 2000-02, and 14% of all the women who died during or immediately after pregnancy (43 women) had reported domestic abuse to a health professional during the pregnancy [52] Furthermore 12% of the 378 women whose death was reported to the Confidential Enquiry on Maternal Deaths had voluntarily reported domestic abuse to a healthcare professional during their pregnancy [50]. None had routinely been asked about domestic abuse so this is almost certainly an under-estimate.

Although a causal relationship between exposure to violence during pregnancy and adverse perinatal outcomes has not been clearly demonstrated, pregnant women who experience abuse are more likely than are non-abused women to have conditions that place their unborn child at serious risk [53]. Studies have shown that women attending accident and emergency departments with physical injuries owing to violence are more likely to be pregnant than women attending with accidental injuries [54]. Physical violence and trauma during pregnancy increases the risk of foetal abuse, and the risk of adverse pregnancy outcomes such as antepartum haemorrhage, urinary tract infections, premature birth, low birth weight, placental damage, a prime cause of miscarriage or stillbirth, chorioamnionitis, foetal injury and foetal death [38, 55, 56]. The risk for the unborn foetus is also considerable as violence may increase rates of miscarriage, premature birth, low birth weight, chorioamnionitis, foetal injury and neonatal death [57, 58, 38]. Infants under-one year are at the highest risk of injury, or death [59], and it is estimated that around 39,000 babies under-one in the UK have a parent who has experienced domestic abuse in the last year. However, this underestimates the extent of domestic abuse, as it captures only physical violence and not the full breadth of abuse that can operate within an intimate relationship such as sexual, emotional, psychological and financial abuse. Infants as young as one year old can experience trauma symptoms from witnessing domestic abuse. The situation where a woman and her children are both abused by the same male perpetrator is common [60]. The more severely a woman is harmed, the more severely her child is likely to be harmed [59].

3.1. Effects of maltreatment on an infant's early cognitive and psychosocial development

Exposure to abuse affects every dimension of an infant's cognitive and psychosocial development [61]. Development is taken in its broadest sense to include social, emotional, physical, cognitive, language, temperament and fine and gross motor skills development [62]. and abused children may be vulnerable across some or all of these areas. In particular, the attachment relationship between an infant and their primary caregiver has a profound impact on child functioning and future development [61]. Feeling secure, loved and having a safe base to explore from and return to, are ongoing needs met by the parent-caregiver relationship. Numerous studies, including some of the most comprehensive and well controlled, have demonstrated that a secure attachment style is most associated with parental behaviours that are consistently responsive to the child's needs and provide comfort during times of distress [63]. A disorganized attachment style has on the other hand been consistently linked to caregivers who are often abusive and/or neglectful [64]. As a result very young abused or neglected infants may be overwhelmed with intense negative emotions, manifesting in incessant crying, inability to be soothed, feeding problems, sleep disturbances, hyper-arousal and hyper-vigilance, and intense distress during transitions. Toddlers may experience intense separation anxiety, wariness of strangers, social avoidance and withdrawal, and constricted and repetitive play [65, 66]. Hesse and Main have suggested that these behaviours characterize infants with a disorganized attachment style and may be the result of fear in approaching a possibly maltreating caregiver who must also be called upon to provide comfort [65]. Emotional neglect and early childhood deprivation are potentially the most severe risk factors for impaired emotional or intellectual development and are also found as cofactors in most cases of other types of child maltreatment. Neglected infants have been found to have more severe cognitive and academic deficits, social withdrawal and limited peer interactions than those who have been physically abused [68]. The infant suffers either from quantitatively inadequate emotional support, or else from only weak support, delivered by constantly changing individuals. Emotional neglect leads to educational underachievement and difficulties in peer relationships as well as to oppositional behaviour [66, 67].

Maltreatment may also inhibit the appropriate development of certain regions of the brain [65, 69]. Two recent and wide-ranging reviews of research conclude that 'there is considerable evidence for changes in brain function in association with child abuse and neglect' [65]. And, 'It is clear that early deleterious experiences can have significant negative effects on the developing brain that may be long-term' [70]. A neglected infant may not be exposed to stimuli that normally activate important regions of the brain and strengthen cognitive pathways. The connections among neurons in these inactivated regions can literally wither away, hampering the child's functioning later in life [71]. As a result, the brain may become 'wired' to experience the world as hostile and uncaring. This negative perspective may influence the infant's later interactions, prompting them to become anxious and overly aggressive or emotionally withdrawn. Neglect and other forms of abuse may also be associated with neuro-motor handicaps, such as central nervous system damage.

Foetal abuse can also have effects on the developing infant's brain, leading to childhood anxiety and hyperactivity [72]. For instance substance abuse during pregnancy is common and, unfortunately, may have many adverse effects, particularly on the infant, and subsequent parenting and child development. These include an increased risk of foetal alcohol syndrome (FAS), foetal growth restriction, abruptia placenta and premature delivery. Infants may become dependent on drugs that they are exposed to in utero and after birth suffer withdrawal symptoms [neonatal abstinence syndrome, (NAS)]. FAS mostly occurs from teratogenic effects early in the pregnancy when facial features and internal organs are at a crucial stage in their development. Brain damage from alcohol exposure can occur at any time during pregnancy. Prenatal exposure to alcohol is the leading cause of brain damage and development delay amongst children in industrial countries [73]. Although invisible, this alcohol-harm eventually shows up in learning disabilities and behavioural problems, and infants with NAS may require prolonged treatment and spend weeks or even months in hospital as a consequence [74]. Long-term neuro-developmental and behavioural abnormalities are more common in infants exposed to substance abuse in pregnancy, and these include lower intelligence quotient scores, delays in motor skills, speech, perceptual and cognitive disturbances, and behavioural problems.

Recent neurological research suggests that the link between maltreatment and many of these adverse health consequences is through stress and anxiety, which can influence the nervous and immune systems, and can be 'toxic' for the developing brain [75]. Early exposure to 'toxic stress' can cause physical effects on an infant's neurodevelopment which may lead to changes in their long-term response to stress and vulnerability to later psychiatric disorders [76,77]. Recent studies have found an association between childhood abuse and hormonal disruption, manifesting in a dysregulation of the HPA (hypothalamic pituitary adrenal) axis [78]. The HPA axis is not fully developed at birth and is thus subject to environmental experiences that shape its activity, such as the buffering protection of a supportive attachment from an adult. Most infants experience a decline in HPA activity during pre-school years as they learn to cope with identify most threats as mild, and receive appropriate and supportive feedback from parents. Infants faced with stressors such as neglect, severe maternal depression, parental substance abuse or domestic violence, however, may be at risk for poor regulation of the HPA axis [79], as these infants often do not have access to parental support to regulate and manage their stress. This places them at risk of experiencing severe and chronic states of stress that can have negative consequences on functioning [80], and can also impact upon the parenting abilities of those infants when they themselves become adults.

Exposure to stress during developmentally critical periods results in persisting hyper-reactivity of the physiological response to stress, increasing the risk of stress-related disease in genetically susceptible individuals [76, 81]. New technologies such as functional MRI (magnetic resonance imaging) and PET (positron emission tomography) have enabled scientists to identify the chemical and structural differences between the central nervous systems of abused and non-abused young people [82, 83]. Many health problems, including panic or post-traumatic stress disorder (PTSD), chronic fatigue syndrome, fibromyalgia, depression, some auto-immune disorders, suicidal tendencies, abnormal fear responses, pre-term labour, chronic pain syndromes, and ovarian dysfunction can be understood, in some cases, as manifestations of infant maltreatment [84, 85, 77].

3.2. Effects of maltreatment on infant's emotional wellbeing and mental health

The earliest years of life are a critical period when infants are making socio-emotional attachments and forming the crucial first relationships which lay the foundations for future mental health [86, 87]. All types of maltreatment can affect an infant's emotional, psychological and mental wellbeing, and these consequences may appear immediately or years later. The immediate and longer-term impact of abuse can include anxiety, irritability, eating disorders [88]. Longitudinal and retrospective studies cited by Balbernie [86] link disorganised emotional attachment in infancy, as a consequence of abuse and neglect, to a number of severe mental health problems in adulthood, such as depression severe anxiety, addictions, drug and alcohol abuse, post-traumatic stress disorder, self-harming and suicidality; and being bullied. Infants who experience rejection or neglect are more likely to develop antisocial traits as they grow up and are more associated with borderline personality disorders and violent behaviour [89,90]. Most common negative effects of sexual abuse in childhood manifest in emotional and behavioural problems, post-traumatic stress symptoms, depression, suicidal ideation and self-harm behaviours, anxiety, substance abuse, aggression, self-esteem issues, academic problems, and sexualized behaviours [91]. Emotional abuse can have a severe impact on a developing child's mental health, behaviour and self-esteem, particularly when it occurs in infancy. Underlying emotional abuse may be as important, if not more so, than other, more visible forms of abuse, in terms of its impact on the child [65].

4. Impact of foetal abuse

Domestic abuse is clearly a child safety issue, and the unborn child is at significant risk from harm. Violence against pregnant women has been referred to as 'child abuse in the womb' [92]. There has been concern for some time, particularly in the US about the issue of 'foetal abuse', where a foetus may be damaged in-utero by acts of omission or commission [57, 56]. Men can physically harm a foetus by physically assaulting a mother and evidence suggests that controlling men may be particularly violent to women when they are pregnant [93]. Also abdominal trauma resulting in placental damage, uterine contractions, or premature rupture of membranes can directly lead to low infant birth weight [94]. Women who experience abuse are more likely than non-abused women to have conditions that place their foetuses at risk [95]. As stated previously, domestic abuse in particular causes heightened maternal stress [48, 49], which is of critical importance during pregnancy because the consequences extend to her foetus and, later, her newborn. Chronic maternal stress increases cortisol levels [96], and during pregnancy, elevated cortisol levels lead to decreased uterine perfusion and a decreased transfer of essential nutrients for foetal growth, a contributory factor to intrauterine growth retardation. Cortisol also increases uterine irritability, contributing to the increased number of preterm births [97]. However, a causal link between domestic abuse during pregnancy and adverse perinatal outcomes has not been clearly demonstrated. These risks can be considerable as violence may increase rates of miscarriage, antepartum haemorrhage, premature birth, low birth weight, chorioamnionitis, placental damage, sexually transmitted infections, and effects on the developing infant's brain, foetal injury and even foetal death [57, 38, 39].

The Domestic Violence, Crime and Victims Act (2004) [98] which was introduced to increase the protection, support and rights of victims and witnesses, has produced the biggest overhaul of domestic violence legislation for 30 years. The Act aims to ensure better protection for victims and bring more perpetrators to justice through civil and criminal law. Legally, according to this Act if a miscarriage is caused by abuse, the assailant can be charged under S.58 of the Offences against the Person Act, "using an instrument with intent to cause a miscarriage", and if a baby is born prematurely as a result of an assault, and then dies, the assailant may be charged with manslaughter [98]..One of the most consistent empirical findings, however, is the delay of antenatal care among victims of violence [99] which often results in inadequate care during pregnancy. Research indicates that many abused women only begin antenatal care in the third trimester [100], and this may be a serious risk factor for the foetus with the risk of pregnancy complications such as low birth weight and premature birth [101].

5. Domestic violence as a child protection issue

Domestic abuse during pregnancy has the potential to harm both a woman and her unborn child both physically and psychologically. This violence during pregnancy should be seen as a complex problem because of its dual risks to both a mother and her unborn child [102, 103, 104]. However, assessing domestic abuse as a child protection issue has been relatively slow in gaining health professional acceptance, even though the international evidence suggests that there is a clear and irrefutable link between domestic abuse and the co-occurrence of child abuse [105, 106, 107]. If a woman is being abused by a current or former partner, and she has other children living with her, the likelihood is that they are being abused too. Indeed, the situation where a woman and her children are both abused by the same male perpetrator is common [60]. The more severely a woman is harmed, the more severely her child is likely to be harmed [59].

Although pregnant women may experience domestic abuse in the same ways as women who are not pregnant, it has only been recently that attention has been paid to the intricacies of the relationship between pregnancy and child protection [44]. Evidence suggests that domestic abuse during pregnancy, and the first six months of child rearing, is significantly related to all three types of child maltreatment: child physical abuse, neglect, and emotional abuse, up to the child's fifth year, with children under one year being at the highest risk of injury, or death [108, 59]. In addition, where it is believed that a child is being abused; those involved with the child and the family should be alerted to the possibility of domestic abuse. An association of between 45-70% has been found between a father's violence to the mother and his violence to the children [59].

6. Co-occurrence of child and domestic abuse

Children in violent homes face three risks: the risk of observing traumatic events, the risk of being abused themselves, and the risk of being neglected [109]. There is strong evidence to indicate that child abuse and exposure to domestic abuse often co-occur [110, 111], and that a high proportion of infants and children living with domestic abuse are themselves being abused, either physically or sexually, by the same perpetrator [110, 5]. According to published studies, there is a 30 percent to 60 percent overlap between violence against children and violence against women in the same families and many child deaths occur in situations where domestic abuse is also occurring [11]. Although the studies on which these ranges are based employ different methodologies (e.g., definitions of child and domestic abuse, case record reviews, case studies, and national surveys), use different sample sizes, and examine different populations, they consistently report a significant level of co-occurrence [104] and point to the importance of protecting the abused parent to ensure the safety of the child.

Prolonged and/or regular exposure to domestic abuse can, despite the best efforts of the parents to protect the child, seriously affects an infant's development, health and emotional wellbeing in a number of ways. Although, system responses are primarily targeted towards adult victims of abuse, recently, increasing attention has been focused on children who witness domestic abuse, as studies estimate that between 10 and 20 percent of children are at risk for exposure to domestic abuse [111, 112]. A growing body of research suggests that children who live in a household where mothers are being abused by a partner are significantly affected, and experience considerable emotional and psychological distress [20, 113]. Living with or witnessing domestic abuse is identified as a source of "significant harm" for children by the Adoption and Children Act (2004). In the US child abuse and maltreatment have been reported to be a risk marker of domestic violence with each year seeing an estimated 3.3 million children exposed to family violence and abuse [114]. There is also evidence to suggest that in 75-90% of cases, children are in the same or next room when their mother is being abused [115]. Indeed, Mullender et al [113,116] goes as far as saying that in 90 per cent of incidents, infants and children are witnesses to the violence. Infants may be greatly distressed by witnessing the physical and emotional suffering of a parent [19, 104, 116], which can in itself, be psychologically and emotionally harming. This can result in infants becoming more fearful, anxious, and depressed, having temper tantrums, sleep disturbances, and consistently crying, and having extreme difficulties in nurseries and play school [19].

7. The role of healthcare professionals

For some time health care and primary care professionals such as midwives, health visitors, obstetricians, general practitioners and paediatricians have been acknowledged as having a key role in child protection and family violence [117, 118]. They may be the first to detect that a child is at risk, and the consequences of them failing in this recognition can be dire. However, until recently the UK National Health Service (NHS) has largely ignored the problem of identifying women who access health services for injuries caused by domestic abuse, while historically primary care health professionals have experienced difficulties when attempting to identify an abused child [119, 57]. There are now many clear messages from Government, professional organizations and research to indicate that health professionals, such as midwives, should be actively involved in tackling these significant public health and primary care issues [120, 121]. Historically, midwives have experienced certain difficulties when attempting to identify either or both domestic and child abuse [122]. These difficulties have led to low detection rates that are attributed to: midwives' attitudes towards victims of abuse [119, 123]; their general lack of knowledge, education and training; and a lack of understanding of their perceived professional role in addressing both forms of abuse [124, 125]. Furthermore, in a review of fatal child abuse cases by the Department of Health by Sinclair and Bullock [126] it was found that health professionals were more likely than any other group to have knowledge of the child, and over a quarter of children who died at the hands of their parents were unknown to social services. Also a NSPCC publication, "What Really Happened?" [127] highlights how many infant deaths and serious injuries could be prevented if all professionals within primary care were better informed and equipped to identify family abuse. Although research in this area is increasing, it is often difficult to determine the exact nature of the pregnancy-related violence and this is posing difficulties for both practitioners and researchers, who need a clear understanding of the relationship between domestic and child abuse and pregnancy in order to develop risk assessment and screening tools and effective prevention and intervention programmes. Worryingly, although abuse may begin or accelerate during pregnancy few women report the problem to their primary care providers [125].

8. Midwives response to domestic and child abuse in pregnancy

The provision of care to families where issues of possible, or actual child maltreatment have been raised is now seen as one of the most difficult and challenging areas of contemporary maternity practice [128, 129]. Community midwives have always had a role in primary care; however, there is now an explicit need for the profession to direct its attention to issues such as domestic abuse. Even though evidence suggests that 35% of women already suffering domestic abuse experience an increase during pregnancy, and the postpartum, they are rarely identified by midwives [123,125). Midwives have experienced certain difficulties when attempting to identify, either, or both, domestic and child abuse [125], and this finding may represent a reluctance by midwives to discuss the topic of violence with their clients, arising in many cases, from fears and anxieties about causing offence; revealing something which may escalate out of control; of not knowing what to do if abuse is disclosed; of embarrassment; or at a personal level identification with abuse either as a victim or perpetrator [38]. However, this reluctance may also correspond in general to: midwives' attitudes towards victims of abuse [123]; their general lack of knowledge, education and training and available information about questioning and screening protocols [130, 125); and a lack of understanding of their perceived professional role in addressing both forms of abuse [124, 125]. Importantly, at a more basic level the opportunity to 'ask the question' may not always be available i.e. a partner or other family member may be present [130].

To assess and intervene appropriately to situations where domestic or child abuse are known or suspected, midwives, managers and supervisors must have a willingness to identify and report the abuse. They need to have had opportunities to undertake up-to-date education and training and skills necessary to ask questions, and to offer the appropriate multi-professional help and inter-agency support required [131] well as an understanding of domestic violence risk assessment and safety planning in child protection [132]. In addition, regular continual professional development updates should be available for all. The Department of Health 2006 publication Domestic violence: a resource manual for health care professionals [133] supports the need for education and training of health professionals, as the majority of women will use the health care system at some stage in their lives.

The most important factor in identifying domestic and child abuse is the awareness that it often commences or escalates during pregnancy. There are a number of physiological, psychological, emotional and behavioural indicators which can alert a midwife and other health professionals to the possibility of potential or actual abuse. Where abuse is suspected, the midwife has a duty of care to routinely ask the woman about problems with relationships, but only when it is safe to do so, i.e. not when a partner or other person is present. The midwife must not put the woman or her/himself at any further risk. The questioning must be undertaken very sensitively and very carefully. The midwife's role and responsibility is then to provide the appropriate response, believing the woman, showing her that someone cares, not judging her, respecting her reasons and decisions to stay or leave the relationship, offering her support, providing her with helpful information, referring her to appropriate agencies, or any other action that may be required [130]. All midwives should be aware of the services and resources [statutory, community and voluntary] available both locally and nationally to a woman and children suffering domestic abuse. Maternity services should be active in developing a multi-agency, interdisciplinary approach in local procedures and services, to ensure a seamless and effective response to a woman seeking help [128].

It must also be remembered that victims of domestic abuse may also be reluctant to disclose abuse for a variety of reasons which include: reprisals from their partner; an outsider becoming involved; embarrassment; and importantly fear of losing their children if social services become involved. Research, however, has shown that often these women hope that someone will realise that something is wrong and ask them about it [38,130]. Many women may not spontaneously disclose the issues of child or domestic abuse in their lives, but often respond honestly to a sensitively asked question [38]. For midwives routinely to ask women about domestic abuse and to offer support and information is therefore an extremely important issue in both community and primary care settings. However, although midwives approve in theory of routine questioning about domestic violence, and also broadly agree that it is their responsibility; in practice, only about two-thirds are happy to do it [134]. It appears that routine enquiry about domestic violence during antenatal booking is infrequent despite such enquiry being included in clinical practice recommendations and is made less frequently than any other aspect of social history taking [135]. Practical and personal difficulties, including lack of time, staff shortages, and difficulty in obtaining sufficient privacy are frequently cited.

9. Midwifery settings – Differences in community and hospital-based

Findings from research show that significantly fewer midwives in hospital settings are addressing the issue of domestic abuse with their clients, as they appear to be driven by more medically dominant organizational structures and targets, which result in them using a more standardized form of care that stresses measures of efficiency, effectiveness and risk management [125]. According to this study hospital midwives work in a setting that has an ideology which places less emphasis on the psychosocial needs of the individual woman and her child and more on providing care for women experiencing complications, and thus public health issues are seen as low priorities. These findings are consistent with work by Hunter [136] whose results suggest that the occupational ideology of the hospital midwife is 'with the institution' rather than with a more 'woman-centred' approach. On the other hand, more midwives from community-based settings appear to follow more women-centred and child-focused care.

Firstly, community midwives are able to create a healthy living environment for women experiencing domestic violence, by asking about 'abuse' with their clients [137]. Secondly, they integrate health promotion and health empowerment into the primary care setting by working in partnership with the woman in their own homes, frequently talking to them about issues such as domestic and child abuse, and are more aware of providing private facilities in which woman can discuss violent relationships. Thirdly, they develop links with other settings and with the wider community [138]. Community, midwives are more empowered to use a joined-up approach that includes an understanding of evidence-based research in the area, a clear knowledge of local and national multi-professional support agencies, and inter-agency networks and refuges that allows them to give on-going and appropriate information that in itself can empower women to make their own informed choices about how to deal with abuse [125]. The Code of Professional Conduct exhorts midwives to work collaboratively, to enable them to strengthen areas of practice by liaising with other professionals and learning from them [139].

However, the biggest hindrance recorded for both hospital and community midwives is the reluctance of a partner to leave the consultation. Recent changes in midwifery practice designed to 'empower women' and demedicalize childbirth may in reality be reducing the possibility of effective intervention i.e. the traditional concept of women-only space is rapidly disappearing as more and more men are now accompanying their partners to their antenatal and postnatal visits. Women now hold their own notes, eliminating confidential documentation of suspicions of/or identified cases of domestic violence. This can lead women themselves to feel emotionally unable to, or physically prevented from, accessing support, either from their family and friends, or from statutory and voluntary agencies. International research evidence illustrates that maternity services are no longer woman-only spaces because women are now accompanied by their partners when attending antenatal clinics, and partners are often present in primary care appointments [128, 130].

10. Multi-agency pre-birth child protection procedures

Research and experience indicate that very young babies are extremely vulnerable to abuse and that work carried out in the antenatal period to assess risk and plan intervention will help to minimise harm. Any concerns about the welfare of an unborn baby, or about the future care of the baby when born should be shared with the appropriate agency at the earliest opportunity, as plans for safeguarding may need to be put in place before the baby is born. Antenatal risk assessment is a valuable opportunity to develop a pro-active multi-agency approach to families where there is an identified risk of harm. The aim is to provide support for families, to identify and protect vulnerable children and to plan effective care programmes; recognising the long-term benefits of early intervention for the welfare of the child. The UK Local Safeguarding Children Board (LSCB) have produced a set of procedures that explain the action any person should take when they think a child needs protecting because they may have been abused, or are at risk of abuse or significant harm [132]. They also take into account any risk to the unborn child. They clarify the responsibility of the various agencies involved, for reporting and investigating allegations of abuse. However, the process of assessment is consistently criticized in inquiries particularly in relations to professionals' understanding of risk factors (Brandon et al. 1999). In assessing risk there is sometimes a tendency to overlook the mother's male partner.

11. Conclusion

Globally health services including maternity services play an important role in safeguarding children. Within the UK health care professionals ensure that children and families receive the care, support and treatment they need in order to promote children's health and development. Staff such as midwives, health visitors, obstetricians, general practitioners (GPs), and other staff who work as members of the primary care, or hospital maternity team have a safeguarding role to play in the identification of babies and children who have been abused, those who are at risk of abuse, and in subsequent intervention and protection services. In the UK we expect that every pregnant woman will have access to, and engage with, high quality maternity services. It is also increasingly acknowledged that for the majority of women, pregnancy and childbirth are normal life events and that care of these women and their babies may be undertaken exclusively through midwifery-led services. The universal nature of health provision means that maternity professionals such as midwives and obstetricians are often the first to be aware that families are experiencing difficulties. All health care organisations have a duty under the Children Act 2004 to make arrangements to safeguard and promote the welfare of children and young people. Every Child Matters marked a shift of focus from child protection to improving and promoting the health and wellbeing of all children and incorporates several important themes.

However the evidence suggests that domestic abuse is a damaging social problem affecting the health of many women and children within pregnancy and the first postpartum year. It cannot be solved by one profession alone; however, the professional's role in identification and referral plays a critical part in primary care co-ordinated response. In order for such a response to be effective, all professionals need greater exposure to and familiarity with recommended good practice; and must be able to identify and support women and children who are experiencing abuse with a joined-up approach that has adequate resources and support of health service managers. Close inter-agency liaison is required with professionals who are accountable and not afraid to challenge historical working practices, and who are willing to work across traditional boundaries.

Importantly evidence shows it is possible to prevent abuse and neglect and that the pregnancy and infancy offer a unique window of opportunity to work effectively with families at risk. Although we know that sustained maltreatment can have major long-term effects on all aspects of children's health and mental wellbeing, and impair their functioning as adults [81], many health professionals still remain unaware of these long-term health and wellbeing impacts on infants and younger children [119]. We know that the earliest years of life are a critical period when infants are making socio-emotional attachments and forming the crucial first relationships which lay the foundations for future health and wellbeing [84]. All types of maltreatment can affect an infant's emotional, psychological and mental wellbeing, and these consequences may appear immediately or years later. Enhancing the prospects for healthy development in the lives of maltreated infants therefore requires attention to enhancing opportunities for positive, non-violent family and peer interactions. The evidence tells us that pregnancy and the first year of life is a window of opportunity for preventive interventions and a crucial time to reduce later emotional, psychological and developmental difficulties, and develop stronger infant-parent relationships. The importance of preventing child maltreatment and thereby its short and long-term developmental, health and mental health consequences cannot be underestimated. Whilst efficiency savings are clearly key drivers behind much of the recent 'Early Years' policy developments in the UK, it is also clear that there are great opportunities to rethink and redesign how we support parents of very young children. How midwifery, obstetrics, paediatrics, social care, education and criminal justice professionals develop mechanisms for sharing resources and working together creatively to meet the needs of families will be central to the success of this preventative agenda.

Given new evidence that trauma in pregnancy and infancy alters the physiology of the brain, it is time for all health and social care practitioners, teachers and counsellors to be educated about the full health impact of violence and abuse, and to be trained to explore these issues either as the true aetiology of the infant's ill-health, or as an underlying potentiating factor that has contributed to it. Nurses, midwives and health visitors as well as specially trained safeguarding nurse practitioners need to develop an early trusting relationship with parents and other family members to promote sensitive, empathic care of their infant. Nursery school nurses also have a key role in the identification of infants who may have been abused or are at risk of abuse. More and better training is needed to assist health and social care professionals in making appropriate use of core assessments and the common assessment framework (CAF) to support abused and neglected infants, and to ensure appropriate decisions are made about when to intervene. The availability of appropriate treatments to meet the needs of these infants, however, still remains a challenge [140]. Developing effective interventions and services is vital in order to support parents in meeting their children's health and wellbeing needs. A radical rethink of early intervention services is underway, blueprints for integrated working are being developed, bringing with them the opportunity to deliver meaningful and long term changes to the lives of young children across the country. Primary prevention efforts could thus be marketed universally, to further reduce the stigma associated with 'parent training': every parent can benefit from parent skills training, not just the 'bad' ones.

Concerns over inadequate record keeping, poor information sharing, and communication have also been raised by the Commission for Health Improvement [141] between NHS organizations and other agencies with respect to violence and abuse [142]. Developing a system that allows the sharing of information and statistics on abuse would immensely benefit professionals and the families with which they work, as it could provide interpretation of the multiple contributing factors associated with domestic and child abuse. This information would provide baselines to establish education, prevention and treatment programmes [112], to formulate benchmarks for performance evaluation, as well as allow professionals to collaborate and provide assistance and protection to victimized children in a more efficient and effective way. As Lord Laming states in his report:

"Improvements to the way information is exchanged within and between agencies are imperative if children are to be adequately safeguarded. Effective action designed to safeguard the well being of children and families depends upon the sharing of information on a multi-professional, inter-agency basis [143]."

Finally the co-occurrence of risk factors for violence in pregnancy, where the health and safety of two potential victims are placed in jeopardy [53, 54, 55] stresses the importance for all health professionals and the primary care team to be able to recognize and report domestic and/or child abuse at this time Identifying domestic abuse, however, may be a useful risk factor for recognizing child abuse, which is clearly within the appropriate domain of professionals working in maternity or primary care services. Although tensions between the 'best interests of the mother' and the 'best interests of the child' are not always easily responded to, Fleck-Henderso n [144] suggests that best practices for families, where both children and women are at risk of violence, requires professionals to 'see double;' drawing from the knowledge and values of both perspectives to best meet the needs of these families. 'Seeing double' should therefore apply to all professionals in every child abuse case involving domestic violence.

Author details

Anne Lazenbatt

NSPCC Reader in Childhood Studies, School of Sociology, Social Policy and Social Work, Queen's University of Belfast, Northern Ireland, UK

12. References

[1] Flaherty, E.G., Sege R.D, Hurley T.P. (2009) Effect of early childhood adversity on health, *Archives of Paediatrics and Adolescent Medicine*, 160: 1232-1238.

[2] Osofsky JD, Lieberman AF. (2011) *American Psychologist* Feb-Mar; 66(2): 120-28

[3] Smith, Kevin (ed.) et al (2011) *Homicides, firearms offences and intimate violence 2009/2010: supplementary volume 2 to crime in England and Wales 2009/2010.* London: Home Office.

[4] Putnam-Hornstein, EP; Webster, D; Needell, B; Magruder, J. (2011) A Public Health Approach to Child Maltreatment Surveillance: Evidence from a Data Linkage Project in the United States, *Child Abuse Review*,20: 4, p.231-306.

[5] Manning, V. (2011) *National Psychiatric Morbidity Survey*, NSPCC: London.

[6] *Ofsted (2011) Ages of concern: learning lessons from serious case reviews: a thematic report of Ofsted's evaluation of serious case reviews from 1 April 2007 to 31 March 2011.* Ofsted: London.

[7] World Health Organization (2002) *World Report on Violence and Health,* World Health Organisation, Geneva.

[8] Krug, E. G. Mercy, JA. Dahlberg, LL. Zwi, AB. (2002) The world report on violence and health. *Lancet, 5,* 1083-1088.

[9] Coker AL, Davis KE, Arias I. (2002) Physical and mental health effects of intimate partner violence, for men and women, *American Journal of Preventive Medicine;* 23:260–8.

[10] Department of Health (2010) *Responding to Violence Against Women and Children – the role of the NHS,* The report of the Taskforce on the Health Aspects of Violence Against Women and Children: London: Department of Health.

[11] Pico-Alfonso M.A. Garcia-Linares M.I. CelDV-Navarro N. (2005) The impact of physical, psychological, and sexual intimate male partner violence on women's mental health: depressive symptoms, posttraumatic stress disorder, state anxiety, and suicide. *Journal of Women's Health* 15, 599–611.

[12] Walby and Allen, 2004 Walby S. & Allen J. (2004) *Domestic Violence, Sexual Assault and Stalking: Findings from the British Crime Survey,* Home Office Research Study 276, London: Home Office.

[13] Garcia Moreno, Claudia (2003) "Responding to Violence Against Women: WHO's Multi-Country Study on Women's Health and Domestic Violence." *Health and Human Rights* 6(2): 112-127.

[14] Coleman, K, Jansson, K, Kaiza, P. and Reed, E. (2007) *Homicides, Firearm Offences and Intimate violence 2005/6: Supplementary Volume 1 to Crime in England and Wales 2005-6)* (Home Office Statistical Bulletin 02/07, Office for National Statistics)

[15] Smith, K. (ed), Coleman, K, Eder, S and Hall, P (2011) Homicides, firearm offences and intimate violence 2009/10 (Supplementary volume 2 to Crime in England and Wales 2009/10 2nd Edition). Home Office Statistical Bulletin 01/11.

[16] Gielen AC., O'Campo PJ., Faden RR., Kass NE., Xue X. (1994) Interpersonal conflict and physical violence during the childbearing year, *Social Science & Medicine* 39, 781-7.

[17] Coker, A., Sanderson, M., & Dong, B. (2004). Partner violenceduring pregnancy and risk of adverse pregnancy outcomes. *Paediatrics and Perinatal Epidemiology, 18,* 260-269.

[18] Thiara, R.K. and A.K. Gill (eds) (2010) Violence Against Women in South Asian Communities: Issues for Policy and Practice , Jessica Kingsley Publishers.
[19] Abramsky, Tanya, Charlotte H. Watts, Claudia Garcia-Moreno, Karen Devries, Ligia Kiss, Mary Ellsberg, Henrica A. F. M. Jansen, and Lori Heise. (2011). "What Factors Are Associated With Recent Intimate Partner Violence? Findings from the WHO Multi-Country Study On Women's Health and Domestic Violence." *BMC Public Health* 11: 109-125.
[20] Hester *et al.*, 2007 Hester (2007) Asking about domestic violence: implications for practice. In: C. Humphreys, & N. Stanley (eds). *Domestic violence and child protection: directions for good practice*. London: Jessica Kingsley.
[21] McGee C. (2000) Childhood experiences of domestic violence, *Adoption and Fostering*, 20: 8-15.
[22] Osofsky JD. (2003) Prevalence of children's exposure to domestic violence and child maltreatment: implications for practice and intervention, *Clinical Child & Family Psychology Review*, 6(3): 161-170.
[23] Osofsky J.D., Hammer J.H., Freeman N. & Rovaris J.M. (2004) How law enforcement and mental health professionals can partner to help traumatized children. In: J.D. Osofsky (Ed.) *Young Children and Trauma: Intervention and Treatment*, pp. 285–298. Guilford Press, New York.
[24] Mullender, A., Burton, S., Hague, G., Imam, U., Kelly, L., Malos, E., & Regan, L. (2003). "StopHitting Mum!": Children talk about domestic violence. East Molesey, Surrey: Young Voice.
[25] Mullender 2004, Mullender A. (2004) Tackling Domestic Violence: providing support for children who have witnessed domestic violence, Home Office Practice and Development Report 33, London, Home Office. View the report at the Home Office website.
[26] Mullender, A. (2005) '*What children tell us: "He said he was going to kill our mum"* ', in Humphreys, C. and Stanley, N. (eds) (2005) London, Jessica Kingsley.
[27] Humphreys C., Thiara R.K., Skamballis A. & Mullender A. (2006) T*alking about Domestic Abuse: A Photo Activity Workbook to Develop Communication Between Mothers and Young People*, London, Jessica Kingsley
[28] Mian A.I. (2005) Depression in pregnancy and the postpartum period: balancing adverse effects of untreated illness with treatment risks. *Journal of Psychiatric Practice* 11, 389–396.
[29] Radford L., Blacklock N. & Iwi K. (2006) 'Domestic violence risk assessment and safety planning in child protection - Assessing perpetrators' in C Humphreys and N Stanley (eds) *Domestic Violence and Child Protection: Directions for good practice*. London: Jessica Kingsley.
[30] Department of Health (2002) *The Children's Act Report*. HMSO,London.
[31] Radford L, Corral, S. Bredley, C. Fisher, H, Bassett, C. Collishaw, S. (2011) *Child Abuse and Neglect in the UK Today;* NSPCC: London.
[32] Abrahams, C (1994) *Hidden Victims: Children and Domestic Violence,* London: NCH Action for Children.

[33] Brookoff, D, O'Brien, K, Cook, C, Thompson, T and Williams, C (1997) Characteristics of Participants in Domestic Violence. Assessment at the Scene of Domestic Assault, *The Journal of the American Medical Association*, Vol. 277, No. 17, pp1369-1373.

[34] Edelson J. (1999) The overlap between child maltreatment andwoman battering. *Violence Against Women* 5, 134–154.

[35] Ross, S (1996) 'Risk of Physical Abuse to Children of Spouse Abusing Parents', *Child Abuse* and Neglect, Vol. 20, pp589-98.

[36] Stewart DE. & Cecutti A. (1993) Physical abuse in pregnancy. *Canadian Medical Association Journal*, 149: 1257 - 1263.

[37] Silverman MR., Decker E., Reed A. & Raj A. (2006) Intimate partner violence victimization prior to and during pregnancy among women residing in 26 U.S. states: associations with maternal and neonatal health, *American Journal of Obstetrics & Gynecology* 195, pp. 140–148.

[38] Shadigian EM. & Bauer ST. (2004) Screening for partner violence during pregnancy. *International Journal of Gynaecology & Obstetrics*, 84(3): 273-280.

[39] Bacchus L., Mezey G., Bewley S. (2002) Women's perceptions and experiences of routine enquiry for domestic violence in a maternity service. *British Journal of Obstetrics and Gynaecology*, 109: 9-16.

[40] Craig C. (2003) *Domestic Violence and Health Professionals*. Northern Ireland Women's Aid Federation: Belfast.

[41] Confidential enquiry into maternal and child health for England and Wales (2004) *Why Mothers Die 2000-2002 - Report on confidential enquiries into maternal deaths in the United Kingdom* (CEMACH).

[42] Bacchus, L., Mezey, G., & Bewley, S. (2005). Prevalence of domestic violence when midwives routinely enquire in pregnancy. Obstetrical and Gynaecological Survey, 60(1), 11-13.

[43] Jasinski, J. L. (2004). Pregnancy and domestic violence: A review of the literature. Trauma Violence Abuse, 5(1), 47-64.

[44] Gazmararian JA, Lazorick S, Spitz AM. et al (1996) Prevalence of Violence Against Pregnant Women: A Review of the Literature. *Journal of the American Medical Association*, 275: 1915-1920.

[45] Gazmararian JA et al (2000) Violence and reproductive health; current knowledge and future research directions. Maternal and Child Health Journal 4: 79-84. As quoted in: Family Violence Prevention Fund. The facts on reproductive health and violence against women.

[46] World Health Organization (2000) *Violence against women*, Factsheet No 239, World Health Organisation: Copenhagen.

[47] Lemon SC., Verhoek-Oftedahl W.,& Donnelly EF. (2002) Preventive healthcare use, smoking, and alcohol use among Rhode Island women experiencing intimate partner violence. *Journal of Women's Health & Gender-Based Medicine* 11(6), 555-62.

[48] Richardson J., Coid J., Petruckevitch A., Chung WS., Moorey S. & Feder G. (2002) Identifying domestic violence: cross sectional study in primary care. *British Medical Journal* 324, 1-6.

[49] Lewis, Gwynneth, Drife, James. et al (2001) Why Mothers Die: Report from the confidential enquiries into maternal deaths in the UK 1997-9; commissioned by Department of Health from RCOG and NICE (London: RCOG Press).

[50] Campbell, J; García-Moreno, C; Sharps, P. (2003) Abuse During Pregnancy in Industrialized and Developing Countries, *Violence Against Women,* Vol. 10, No. 7, 770-789.

[51] Lewis, Gwynneth, and Drife, James. et al (2005) Why Mothers Die 2000-2002 - Report on confidential enquiries into maternal deaths in the United Kingdom (CEMACH).

[52] Jasinski JL. (2004) Pregnancy and domestic violence: a review of the literature. *Trauma Violence Abuse,* 5(1): 47-64.

[53] McWilliams M, & McKiernan J. (1993) *Bringing it out into the open,* Belfast HMSO.

[54] Mezey, GC., Bacchus L., Haworth A. et al. (2003) Midwives' perceptions and experiences of routine enquiry for domestic violence. *British Journal of Obstetrics & Gynaecology,* Vol 110, 8: 744-752.

[55] Mezey GC., Bacchus L., Bewley S. et al. (2005) Domestic violence, lifetime trauma and psychological health of childbearing women *British Journal of Obstetrics & Gynaecology: An International Journal of Obstetrics & Gynaecology.* 112(2):197-204.

[56] Mezey GC. & Bewley S. (1997) Domestic violence and pregnancy. *British Medical Journal,* 314: 1295.

[57] Shumway J, O'Campo P, Gielen, A. et al (1999) Preterm labour, placental abruption and premature rupture of membranes in relation to maternal violence or verbal abuse. *The Journal of Maternal-Foetal Medicine,* 8(3): 76-80.

[58] Goodall E & Lumley T (2007) *'Not seen and not heard' – child abuse: a guide for donors and funders,* New Philanthropies Capital: London.

[59] Lucas DR., Wezner K., Milner JS., McCanne T., Harris C., Monroe-Posey & Nelson JP. (2002) Victim, perpetrator, family, and incident characteristics of infant and child homicide in the United States Air Force. *Child Abuse & Neglect* 26, pp. 167–186.

[60] Edleson, JL. (2001) Studying the co-occurrence of child maltreatment and woman battering in families. In SA Graham-Bermann and JL Edleson (Eds.), *Domestic violence in the lives of children: The future of research, intervention and social policy.* (pp. 99-110) Washington, DC: American Psychological Association.

[61] Hartley CC. (2002) The co-occurrence of child maltreatment and domestic violence: examining both neglect and child physical abuse, *Child Maltreatment,* 7, 4: 349-358.

[62] Cicchetti D, Rogosch FA, and Toth, SL (2006) Fostering secure attachment in infants in maltreating families through preventative interventions; *Development and Psychopathology,* 18, 623-649.

[63] Glaser D. (2007) The effects of child maltreatment on the brain. *The Link: The Official Newsletter of the International Society for the Prevention of Child Abuse and Neglect;* 16(2):1-4.

[64] Glaser D. (2002) Emotional abuse and neglect (psychological maltreatment): a conceptual framework. *Child Abuse Neglect;* 26: 697–714.

[65] Hesse E, Main M. (2006)*Frightened, threatening, and dissociative parental behavior in low-risk samples: Description, discussion, and interpretations. Development and Psychopathology 2006;18:309-343.*

[66] Jordan B, Sketchley R (2009) *A stitch in time saves nine: Preventing and responding to the abuse and neglect of infants* (NCPC Issues No. 30). Melbourne: National Child Protection Clearinghouse.

[67] Neigh GN, Gillespie CF, Nemeroff CB. (2009) The neurobiological toll of child abuse and neglect. *Trauma Violence Abuse*; 10:389-410.

[68] Radford L, Corral, S. Bredley, C. Fisher, H, Bassett, C. Collishaw, S. (2011) *Child Abuse and Neglect in the UK Today;* NSPCC: London.

[69] Hosking, G and Walsh, I (2005) *The Wave Report 2005. Violence and What to Do about It, Wave Trust: UK.*

[70] Schore, A N. (2003) Early relational trauma, disorganized attachment, and the development of a predisposition to violence. In M. F. Solomon and D. J. Siegel (Eds.), *Healing trauma: Attachment, mind, body, and brain.* New York, NY: Norton.

[71] Shepard, M.F., Elliott, B.A., Falk, D.R., et al., 1999. Publichealth nurses' responses to domestic violence: a report fromthe Enhanced Domestic Abuse Intervention Project. Public Health Nursing 16, 359–366.

[72] Sousa, C., Herenkhol, T. I., Moylan, C. A., Tajima, E. A., Klika, J. B., Herenkohl, R. C., Russo, M. J (2011) Longitudinal study on the effects of child abuse and children's exposure to domestic violence, parent-child attachments, and antisocial behavior in adolescence. *Journal of Interpersonal Violence, 26*(1), 111-136. doi:10.1177/0886260510362883

[73] De Bellis MD. (2001) Developmental traumatology: The psychobiological development of maltreated children and its implications for research, treatment, and policy. *Development and Psychopathology,* 13(3), 539–564.

[74] De Bellis, M., and Thomas, L. (2003) Biologic findings of post-traumatic stress disorder and child maltreatment. *Current Psychiatry Reports,* 5: 108-117.

[75] Cicchetti, D., and Rogosch, F.A. (2001) The impact of child maltreatment and psychopathology upon neuroendocrine functioning. *Development and Psychopathology,* 13: 783-804.

[76] Haegerich TM, Dahlberg LL. (2011) Violence as a Public Health Risk, *American Journal of Lifestyle Medicine;* 5(5): 392-406.

[77] Schore, A N. (2003) Early relational trauma, disorganized attachment, and the development of a predisposition to violence. In M. F. Solomon and D. J. Siegel (Eds.), *Healing trauma: Attachment, mind, body, and brain.* New York, NY: Norton.

[78] De Bellis MD. (2005) The psychobiology of neglect. *Child Maltreatment;* 10 (2):150-72.

[79] Teicher M.H., Dumont N.L., Ito Y., Vaituzis C., Giedd J.N., Andersen S.L. (2004) Childhood neglect is associated with reduced corpus callosum area. *Biological Psychiatry;* 56(2):80-5.

[80] Weniger G, Lange C, Sachsse U, Irle E (2008) Amygdala and hippocampal volumes and cognition in adult survivors of childhood abuse with dissociative disorders. *Acta Psychiatrica Scandinavica,* 118:281–90.

[81] Kendall-Tackett K.A. (2001) Physiological correlates of childhood abuse: chronic hyper-arousal in PTSD, depression, and irritable bowel syndrome. *Child Abuse Neglect;* 24(6):799-810.

[82] Kendall-Tackett K.A. (2003) Treating the lifetime health effects of childhood victimization Kingston, NJ: Civic Research Institute Inc.

[83] Teicher MD (2000) Wounds that time won't heal: The neurobiology of child abuse. *Cerebrum: The Dana Forum on brain science*, 2(4): 50-67.

[84] Bowlby R, King P (2004) *Fifty Years of Attachment Theory: Recollections of Donald Winnicott and John Bowlby*. London: Allen Press.

[85] Belsky, J., Houts, R.M. & Fearon, R.M.P. (2010) Infant Attachment Security and Timing of Puberty: Testing an Evolutionary Hypothesis. *Psychological Science*, 21, 1195-1201.

[86] Balbernie, R. (n.d.). *Early intervention services: An overview of evidence-based practice*. Retrieved August, 2008, from www.waimh.org

[87] Schore, A. N. (2003) Early relational trauma, disorganized attachment, and the development of a predisposition to violence. In M. F. Solomon and D. J. Siegel (Eds.), *Healing trauma: Attachment, mind, body, and brain*. New York, NY: Norton.

[88] Kendall-Tackett KA. (2001) Physiological correlates of childhood abuse: chronic hyper-arousal in PTSD, depression, and irritable bowel syndrome. *Child Abuse Neglect*; 24(6):799-810.

[89] Hunt S. & Martin A. (2001) *Pregnant women, violent men: what midwives need to know*. Books for Midwives Press: Hale.

[90] Hobbs, GF, & Hobbs, CJ. (1999) Abuse of children in foster and residential care. *Child Abuse Neglect*, Dec, 23(12):1239–1252.

[91] Campbell J. & L. Lewandowski, L. (1997) Mental and physical health effects of intimate partner violence on women and children, *The Psychiatric Clinics of North America* 20, pp. 353–374.

[92] Tuten, M; Jones,HE; Tran, G and Svikis, DS. (2004) Partner violence impacts the psychosocial and psychiatric status of pregnant, drug-dependent women, *Addictive Behaviors* 29, pp. 1029–1034.

[93] Sandman CA, Wadhwa PD, Chicz-DeMet A, Dunkel-Schetter C, Porto M. (2007) Maternal stress, HPA activity, and fetal/infant outcome. *Annals of New York Academy Science* 814:266–275.

[94] Dietz, PM., Gazmararian, JA., Goodwin, M., Bruce, FC., Johnson, CH., & Rochat, R. (1997) Delayed entry into prenatal care: the effects of physical violence. *Obstetrics & Gynaecology*, 90 (2), 221-224.

[95] Goodwin, M., Gazmararian, J. A., Johnson, C. H., Gilbert, B. C., Saltzman, L. E., & Group, P.W. (2000). Pregnancy intendedness and physical abuse around the time of pregnancy: Findings from the Pregnancy Risk Assessment Monitoring System, 1996-1997. *Maternal and Child Health Journal*, 4(2), 85-92.

[96] McFarlane, J., Campbell, J. C., Sharps, P., & Watson, K. (2002) Abuse during pregnancy and femicide. *Obstetrics & Gynecology*, *100*, 27-36.

[97] (Domestic Violence, Crime and Victims Act, 2004

[98] Norton, L. B., Peipert, J. F., Zierler, S., Lima, B., & Hume, L. (1995).Battering in pregnancy: An assessment of two screening methods Obstetrics and Gynecology, 85, 321-325.

[99] Coker, AL; Sanderson, M; & Dong, B. (2004) Partner violence during pregnancy and risk of adverse pregnancy outcomes, *Paediatric and Perinatal Epidemiology*, 18, 260–269.

[100] McFarlane, J., Parker, B. and Soeken, K. (1996a) Abuse during pregnancy: Associations with maternal health and infant birth, *Nursing*, pp. 37–42.

[101] McFarlane, J., Parker, B. and Soeken, K. (1996b) Physical abuse, smoking, and substance use during pregnancy: Prevalence, interrelationships, and effects on birth weight, *Journal of Obstetric, Gynecologic, and Neonatal Nursing* 25, pp. 313–320.

[102] Ramsay J., Richardson J., Carter YH., Davidson L. & Feder G. (2002). Should health professionals screen women for domestic violence? Systematic review. *British Medical Journal*, 325:1-13.

[103] Hall, T. and Wright, S. (2003) *Making it count: A practical guide to collecting and managing domestic violence data.* London: NACRO.

[104] Lundy M. & Grossman SF. (2005) The mental health and service needs of young children exposed to domestic violence, *Families and Sociology*, 86(1):17-29.

[105] Butchart A. & Villaveces A. (2003) *Violence against women and the risk of infant and child mortality*, Bulletin of the World Health Organization: Geneva.

[106] Mullender A., Burton S., Hague G., Imam U., Kelly L., Malos E. & Regan L. (2003) *'Stop Hitting Mum!': Children Talk about Domestic Violence*, East Molesey, Surry, Young Voice.

[107] Sousa, C., Herenkhol, T. I., Moylan, C. A., Tajima, E. A., Klika, J. B., Herenkohl, R. C., Russo, M. J (2011) Longitudinal study on the effects of child abuse and children's exposure to domestic violence, parent-child attachments, and antisocial behavior in adolescence. *Journal of Interpersonal Violence, 26*(1), 111-136. doi:10.1177/0886260510362883

[108] Amaro H., Fried L E., Cabral H., Zuckerman B. (1990) Violence during pregnancy and substance use, *American Journal of Public Health*, 80 (5), 575-579.

[109] Appel AE. & Holden GW. (1998) The co-occurrence of spouse and physical child abuse: a review and appraisal. *Journal of Family Psychology*;12:578–99.

[110] Carter J. & Schechter S. (1997). Child abuse and domestic violence: Creating community partnerships for safe families-Suggested components of an effective child welfare response to domestic violence. San Francisco, CA: Family Violence Prevention Fund.

[111] Creighton S. (2004) *Prevalence and incidence of child abuse: international comparisons*, NSPCC Research Department: London.

[112] Mullender A., Burton S., Hague G., Imam U., Kelly L., Malos E. & Regan L. (2003) *'Stop Hitting Mum!': Children Talk about Domestic Violence*, East Molesey, Surry, Young Voice.

[113] Filipas HH. and Ullman, SE (2006) Child sexual abuse, coping responses, self-blame, posttraumatic stress disorder, and adult sexual revictimization, *Journal of Interpersonal Violence* 21, pp. 652–672.

[114] British Medical Association. (1998) *Domestic violence: a health care issue*? BMA: London.

[115] Mullender, A. (2005) *'What children tell us: "He said he was going to kill our mum" '*, in Humphreys, C. and Stanley, N. (eds) (2005) London, Jessica Kingsley.

[116] Department of Health. (2002) *The Children's Act Report.* London: HMSO.

[117] Lupton, N. North, I. & Khan, N. (2001) Working together or pulling apart? The National Health Service and child protection networks, The Policy Press: Bristol.

[118] Lazenbatt A. & Freeman R. (2006) Recognizing and reporting child physical abuse: a cross sectional survey of primary health care professionals, *Journal of Advanced Nursing, 56, 3: 227- 237.*

[119] Department for Education and Skills (2004) National Service Framework for Children, Young People and Maternity Services: Core Standards. London: Department of Health.

[120] Department for Education and Skills (2006) *Working Together to Safeguard Children: A Guide to Inter-Agency Working to Safeguard and Promote the Welfare of Children* London: Department of Health.

[121] Bewley, S. (1997) Pregnancy and violence. In: Bewley, S. Friend, J. & Mezey, G. *Violence against women.* RCOG Press: London.

[122] Lazenbatt A., Cree LF. & McMurray. (2005) The use of exploratory factor analysis in evaluating midwives' attitudes and stereotypical myths related to the identification and management of DV in practice, *Midwifery: an international journal*, 21, 322-334.

[123] Peckover S. (2003) Health visitors' understanding of domestic violence. *Journal of Advanced Nursing*, 44(2), 200-8.

[124] Lazenbatt A., Taylor J. & Cree L. (2008) A Healthy Settings Framework: an evaluation and comparison of midwives' responses to addressing domestic violence in pregnancy, *Midwifery*.

[125] Sinclair R. & Bullock R. (2002) *Learning from past experiences – a review of significant case reviews,* The Stationary Office: London.

[126] Dale P., Green R. & Fellows R. (2002) *What Really Happened? - Child Protection Case Management of Young Children with Serious Injuries and Discrepant Parental Explanations.* London: NSPCC Publications Unit.

[127] Protheroe L., Green J. & Spiby H. (2001) An interview study of the impact of domestic violence training on midwives. *Midwifery,* 20(1): 94-103.

[128] Smith F. (2003) Safe-guarding the young, *Paediatric Nursing & Midwifery,* 15, 10:24-25.

[129] Taket A., Nurse J., Smith K. et al. (2003) Routinely asking women about domestic violence in health settings. *British Medical Journal,* 327: 673-676.

[130] Paluzzi PA. & Houde-Quimbly CH. (1996) Domestic violence Implications for the American College of Nurse-Midwives and Its Members. *Journal of Nurse-Midwifery,* 41(6): 430-435.

[131] Radford L., Blacklock N. & Iwi K. (2006) 'Domestic violence risk assessment and safety planning in child protection - Assessing perpetrators' in C Humphreys and N Stanley (eds) *Domestic Violence and Child Protection: Directions for good practice.* London: Jessica Kingsley.

[132] Department of Health (2006) Tackling the health and mental health effects of domestic and sexual violence and abuse, London: Department of Health.

[133] Price, S. (2004) "Routine questioning about domestic violence in maternity settings" in Midwives, Vol.7, no.4 April.

[134] Buck, L. (2007) Why don't midwives ask about domestic violence? *British Journal of Midwifery*, Vol. 15, 12: 753 – 758.

[135] Hunter B. (2004) Conflicting ideologies as a source of emotion work in midwifery. *Midwifery*, 20: 261-272.

[136] Poland B., Green L. & Rootman I. (2000) *Settings for health promotion: linking theory and practice*. Sage: London.

[137] Whitelaw S, Baxendale A, Bryce C. et al (2001) Settings-based health promotion: a review, *Health Promotion International* 16(4): 339-353.

[138] Nursing & Midwifery Council (2004) *Rules and Standards.* London: Nursing & Midwifery Council.

[139] Brandon,M., Thoburn,J., Lewis,A. & Way,A. (1999) *Safeguarding Children with the Children Act 1989*. The Stationery Office: London.

[140] Commission for Health Improvement (2004) *Protecting children and young people: results of an audit of NHS Organisations in England*. www.chi.nhs.uk/eng/about/pulications/child protection/index.shtml Last accessed May 4th 2008.

[141] Truman, P. (2004) Problems in identifying cases of child neglect, *Nursing Standard,* vol 18, no 29, p3-38.

[142] Department of Health. (2003b) *The Victoria Climbie' Inquiry: Report of the Inquiry by Lord Laming,* The Stationary Office: London.

[143] Fleck- Henderson AF. (2000) Domestic violence in the child protection system: Seeing double, *Children and Youth Services Review* 22, pp. 333–354.

Chapter 4

Attachment Theory in the Assessment and Promotion of Parental Competency in Child Protection Cases

Chantal Cyr, Karine Dubois-Comtois, Geneviève Michel, Caroline Poulin, Katherine Pascuzzo, Valérie Losier, Marilyne Dumais, Diane St-Laurent and Ellen Moss

Additional information is available at the end of the chapter

http://dx.doi.org/10.5772/48771

1. Introduction

Maltreatment is a complex problem affecting the lives of thousands of families and children. In fact, not only is maltreatment a major societal issue carrying substantial socio-economic costs in relation to medical and social allowances, but it also has devastating effects on child development. There is thus a pressing need to better understand the dysfunctional interactions occurring between abusive/neglecting parents and their children in order to improve evaluation and intervention strategies with these families. In the past few years, attachment theory has provided a solid foundation for understanding the risk and resiliency factors involved in the development of maltreated children and guided the development of assessment and intervention protocols for this at-risk population. Attachment theory and related empirical studies thus provide relevant knowledge about the processes through which maltreatment may negatively impact child development, as well as the clinical applications and best-suited practices for this population.

According to the ecological-transactional perspective child attachment is an important protective factor for the development of children with a history of abuse and neglect [1]. More precisely, this perspective [2]sustains that maltreated children's adaptation is affected by several systemic levels, some closer to the child such as the system including family relationships, and others more distal, such as the community and cultural values systems. Though the ecological-transactional model acknowledges the influence of different systemic levels, systems closest to the child are considered has having the greatest impact on child development. Problematic and dysfunctional parent-child interactions, which are characteristic of families subject to maltreatment, have a more direct effect on child development than more distant variables such as poverty or parents' psychological state of mind. Therefore, based on this model, parent-child interactions and child attachment to parent act as relational mediating processes between distal systemic variables and child adaptation, and thus become primary interventional targets for promoting child development.

The objective of this chapter is to present attachment theory as a useful framework for assessing and promoting parental competency in child protection cases. In the first section of this chapter, we present key concepts of attachment theory, which are at the heart of all attachment-based clinical protocols. In the second section, the two main attachment-based intervention models are discussed: 1) the long-term model which addresses parents' representations of attachment relationships, and 2) the short-term model which uses video-feedback to modify inadequate parental behavior. In addition to describing these intervention models, this section provides a review of studies having tested the efficacy of these protocols with parents and children reported for child maltreatment. In the third and final section, we present how a short-term attachment-based intervention protocol may be used in the assessment of parental capacity in child protection cases.

2. Attachment theory: Key concepts

Studies in attachment have consistently shown the undisputed role of attachment in child development. In particular, studies have repeatedly demonstrated that the quality of child attachment to parent is one of the best indicators of the child's mental health and later adaptation [3,4]. All children, with some rare exceptions, develop an attachment relationship with their caregiver and view this figure, even if inadequate, negligent or abusive, as a potential source of comfort in stressful situations. The display of attachment behaviors by the child stems from a biologically driven system in which the child is dependent on the caregiver's responsiveness to their needs to ensure survival. As such, the child's capacity to form a bond with a caregiver does not depend on the type of care received. What varies among children is the quality of the attachment relationship developed towards the caregiver, i.e. the degree of trust the child has towards the caregiver's emotional availability, ability to protect, comfort and soothe in distressing situations. According to attachment theory and empirical studies, individual differences in child attachment behaviors are primarily based on two types of factors. The first, proximal to the child, is quality of caregiving, while the second is made up of more distal variables likely to affect parental care, such as the parent's own state of mind in relation to past attachment experiences.

Quality of caregiving

Parental sensitivity and attachment security

Child attachment pattern to parent is closely linked to the latter's sensitivity, i.e. the parent's capacity to detect, interpret, and respond appropriately and within a reasonable delay to the child's needs and signals [5,6]. Based on interaction experiences with a sensitive parent, children learn, as early as 12 months of age, that their parental figure will help appease their distress in stressful situations [7].Accordingly, by the end of their first year of life, children will be inclined to seek parental proximity in stressful situations to regulate emotions and organize behaviors and, once comforted, to use their parental figure as a secure base from which to explore [6].

Alternatively, an insensitive parent, who misinterprets or fails to respond to child signals, encourages the development of insecure child attachment patterns. More specifically, following repeated experiences with a rejecting or distant parent, the child is more inclined to develop an insecure-avoidant attachment pattern, characterized by the minimization of distress signals and proximity-seeking behaviors in order to suppress the activation of negative emotions, which are difficult for the parent to manage. In response to more inconsistent parental behaviors (sometimes sensitive, sometimes insensitive), the child is likely to develop an insecure-ambivalent attachment pattern. This attachment pattern is characterized by an exaggeration of distress signals and proximity-seeking behaviors by the child towards the attachment figure in order to maximize chances of receiving parental comfort. However, resistant behaviors with respect to physical contact and parental comfort are also characteristic of this attachment pattern, resulting from the child's anger towards the parents' inconsistency. While the distress of avoidant and ambivalent children may not be adequately appeased, these children still manage to develop an attachment strategy that organizes behaviors and emotions towards the attachment figure in situations of stress.

Parental frightening/frightened behavior or extreme insensitivity and disorganized child attachment

While some children with an insecure attachment develop organized strategies to access the attachment figure when distressed, others show a breakdown of attachment strategies or fail to develop coherent approach strategies to gain access to the parent. In the presence of their attachment figure, these children exhibit confused and disoriented behaviors, and may even display frightened facial expressions or body postures. This particular group of children are identified as presenting insecure disorganized attachment behaviors. Recent studies have shown that mothers who demonstrate frightening or frightened behaviors during interactions with their child (e.g. intense withdrawal, hostility, momentary state of dissociation, facial expression of fear, hypervigilance, predatory behavior, sexualized or deferential) are likely to promote the development of insecure disorganized attachment behaviors in their children [8-10]. At the communication level, research has also showed that mothers of disorganized preschooler tend to utter frightening remarks and ridicule their child [11]. As Hesse [12] stated, children showing disorganized attachment behaviors are caught in an unsolvable paradox: their potential source of comfort is also their source of fear [13]. Disorganized children are therefore less likely to adequately explore their environment, for their attachment system is chronically activated by feelings of fear or apprehension caused by the presence of their attachment figure [14].

Disorganized attachment is the type of attachment most strongly linked in childhood to socio-emotional adaptation difficulties, cognitive deficits, psychopathology, low self-esteem, as well as psychopathology in adolescence and adulthood, including anxiety disorders, dissociation, and suicidal thoughts [3,15-20]. Studies have also showed that attachment disorganization is maintained over time and evolves into a controlling strategy at the beginning of school age, where children becomes aggressive and punitive towards their parent, or on the contrary, answer the affective needs of the latter [21,22]. This parent-child role-reversal phenomenon, commonly called "parentification", has often been observed in parent and maltreated-child dyads [23].

Given that abusive and neglecting behaviors of maltreating parents are highly frightening for children, it is not surprising to find that the majority of maltreated children exhibit disorganized attachment behaviors, i.e., up to 86% are classified as insecure disorganized children according to various studies [20,24]. In particular, a model by Main and Hesse [25] propose that parents who have not been able to resolve past traumas from their own childhood (abuse, loss) are likely to show short moments of dissociation, such as sudden lapses with reality [26], altering their behavior when interacting with their child, which may activate the child's fear and attachment systems. In support of this hypothesis, a recent study with a high-risk population has shown the mediating role of frightening parental behaviors in the transmission of unresolved parent attachment representations (unresolved loss or experience of abuse) to the child showing disorganized attachment behaviors[27]. A second model,articulated by Lyons-Ruth et al. [8], suggests that it is the parent's inability to regulate thechild's physiological and emotional states that contributes to the child's development of a disorganized attachment. In other words, the inability to face potentially traumatizing events hinders the parent's capacity to regulate the child's own physiological experience of fear[28].Hence, parents of disorganized children fail to repair situations that elicit fear in their child. Instead of being sensitive following a frightening situation for the child, these parents remain helpless or show hostility[8]. Through these extreme insensitive behaviors, parents do not appease their child's fear and attachment systems, but instead actually exacerbate stress and become themselves an important source of fear for the child.

Parental state of mind with regards to attachment

Parental state of mind with regards to attachment refers to the representations of attachment relationships and cognitive strategiesparents have developed since childhoodto organize and understand present and past attachment experiences. Parental attachment state of mind is an important precursor of child disorganized attachment as it is likely to interfere with parental sensitivity. Notably, studies have demonstrated thatmothers of children with a secure attachment are more likely to discuss attachment experiences coherently and make metacognitive judgements (e.g. reflective functioning) to reassess the significance and the meaning of past childhood experiences. Conversely, mothers of children with insecure disorganized attachment are unable to solve past traumatic experiences (e.g. abuse, loss) [29-30]. Their discourse has shown to be incoherent when describing past traumatic events and related emotionsas well as sometimes disconnected from reality.

Abusive and neglectful parents are definitely at-risk of developing unresolved attachment representations. Indeed, many of them have suffered sexual or physical abuse, or have been abandoned and placed in foster homes in their childhood [1,31]. The personal background of these parents, all too often filled with traumatic events, clearly puts them at risk of developing unresolved attachment representations. When painful experiences remain unresolved, they continue to exert an (unconscious) influence on the parent's psychological processes and behaviors, inhibiting the parent'sability to properly perceive, interpret and adequately respond to the child's needs and signals and thus contributing to the emergence and maintenance of insecure disorganized attachment behaviors in the child.

Several studies have demonstrated the mediating role of maternal sensitivity in the transmission of attachment from parent to child [32]. Another study of high-risk dyads identified the role of frightening parental behaviors in the transmission of disorganization [27]. Although studies having identified precursors to attachment disorganization in maltreated children are scarce, findings stemming from the field of attachment support the need to develop intervention protocols aiming improvements in parental sensitivity in order to promote attachment security and reduce attachment disorganization [33].

3. Attachment-based intervention strategies and protocols designed for maltreated children and their parents

Based on Bowlby's [34] work and empirical studies on the intergenerational transmission of attachment, Berlin et al. [35]suggest that interventions inspired by attachment theory should be guided by three major therapeutic principals. The first two relate to intervention targets and the way change is likely to occur. Attachment-informed interventions are concerned with the promotion of child attachment security because it constitutes an important protective factor in the development and well-being of the child. Therefore, key targets should be empirically associated with child attachment. Whether target of intervention is to change parents' representations of attachment or behaviors with the child, in both cases, emphasis is placed on the parent-child attachment which is used as the main intervention vehicule to promote child attachment security and optimize child development. The third principal refers to the intervention process in which a relationship of trust between parent and practitioner, the latter in the role of a secure base for the parent, is necessary to promote change.

For the past few years, several intervention protocols have been developed based on research in the area of parent-child relationships and attachment. Accordingly, two meta-analytic studies [33,36] have shown that short-term behavioral interventions aimed at changing parental behavior towards the child are more effective in improving parental sensitivity and child attachment security and reducing the incidence of disorganized attachment behaviors, than those aimed at changing parental representations or providing parental social support. However, none of the studies included in these meta-analyses exclusively examined maltreating parents and their children. Recently, three majorattachment-based intervention protocols have emerged as effective for improving child attachment security of maltreated children. These protocols, which are either short-term (approximately 6-10 weeks) or long-term (approximately 20 weeks to 2 years), have been developed for mother-child dyads in infancy and preschool age, and usually involve weekly home visits. Long-term protocols aim mainly the modification of parents' representational models, while short-term protocols focus on the modification of parental behaviors. In both models parent and child are present during intervention sessions, but in long-term protocols, parents may receive social support and participate in separate individual psychotherapy sessions.

Long-term protocols: The modification of representational models

Changing representational models refers to the modification of representations of the self, others, and attachment relationships developed by the parent throughout the years. The therapeutic objective is to bring the parent to understand how their representations of their child and of their relationship can be inadequate, distorted, and linked to insecure representations of past childhood relationships. According to Bowlby [34], the parent's capacity to give new meaning to attachment representations is possible through open dialogue, in which the therapist supports the parent in the reinterpretation of past childhood experiences and the recognition that these experiences may affect the actual quality of caregiving towards the child. According to this model, it is this reflective process that promotes parental responsiveness, sensitivity, and availability, which in turns foster child attachment security and development.

The Infant/Child-Parent Psychotherapy (IPP or CPP)

The intervention model developed by Fraiberg et al. [37] with parents and infants, and later extended by Lieberman and Van Horn[38]to parents and preschoolers, is centered on the modification of representations. CPP has its origin in attachment theory, developmental psychopathology, and trauma theory [38].The principal assumption of the IPP/CPP is that difficulties in the parent-child relationship (parental insensitive behaviors) are not only due to deficits in parenting knowledge and skills, but also, and most importantly, to insecure internal representational models developed by the parent in response to past childhood experiences. In particular, this intervention involves dyadic therapy sessions in which the therapist uses the child's naturally occurring play behaviors with the parent as a way to translate the developmental and emotional meaning of the child's behavior towards her parent and improve mother-child interactive quality [39,40].This approach is mostly supportive, nondirective, and non-didactic, and includes developmental guidance based on the parent's concerns, or other strategies like role modeling, emotional support or insight-oriented techniques to promote, through a trusting therapeutic relationship, the parent's understanding and empathy towards the child [39,41].

Several studies have assessed the efficacy of CPP and IPP for maltreated children and their mothers. For example, the study conducted by Cicchetti et al. [41], noteworthy for its randomized control trial, compared the IPP to a Psychoeducational Parenting Intervention protocol in which mothers were giving didactic training in child development, parenting skills, coping strategies, and assistance in developing social networks in order to promote overall parenting skills. A randomized control trial, which involves random assignment of participants to an experimental group (receiving the intervention) and a control group (without intervention, or receiving an intervention having different targets and objectives from those of the experimental group), constitutes an extremely rigorous method that allows one to conclude that observed effects are due to the intervention and not simply explained by the passage of time, or other confounding variables. In this study, both intervention protocols involved mothers and their child (mean age=13 months), and dyads were met at a frequency of one session per week during one year. These two protocols were compared to two other groups: 1) a community standard control group, which received the usual community services available to maltreating families, and 2) a normative comparison group, which consisted of non-maltreating, high socioeconomic risk families from the community.

Results of this study indicated a substantial increase in secure attachment and a substantial decrease in disorganized attachment for children in the IPP and Psychoeducational group compared to those in the community standard services and normative comparison groups. However, no intervention effect was observed regarding maternal sensitivity. Moreover, a second study with the same sample revealed significant differences in stress (cortisol) regulation trajectories over time as a function of intervention groups [42]. More specifically, children receiving community standard services showed more dysregulated trajectories of stress (cortisol) beginning mid-treatment, in comparison to children in the IPP and Psychoeducational Intervention groups, for whom trajectories remained similar to those of non-maltreated children across time. In another study, this team also examined the effect of CPP on preschool children's (4 years old) representations of self, mother and relationships [43]. Using a randomized control trial, mother-child dyads were assigned to CPP, a Psychoeducational Parenting Intervention, or a community standard services group. Children in the CPP group showed significant decreases in negative representations of self and mother, as well as increases in their positive mother-child relationship expectations. Results by this research team thus support the efficacy of the IPP and CPP as successful long-term interventions in altering the predominantly insecure attachment organizations of infants and preschoolers from maltreating families, which is not the case with typical intervention services. These results point to the importance of providing services early on in the child's development by working jointly with the parent-child dyad in order to promote child attachment security, remediate early developmental difficulties, and prevent the development of later psychopathology.

Other studies by Lieberman et al. [44] assessed the efficacy of the CPP with mothers and their preschooler (3-5 years old). Using a randomized control trial, these researchersprovided dyads witha one-hourintervention session per week, for an average of 50 weeks. CPP, as a preschool version of the IPP, targeted changes in maladaptive behaviors through developmentally supported and appropriate interactions; and guided mother-child dyads in creating a joint narrative of traumatic events while working towardsa resolution. The efficacy of the CPP on variables such as child behavior problems, post-traumatic stress symptoms, and presence of life stressors, was compared with a regular case management group which included individual psychotherapy with mothers. Study results showed a decrease in behavioral problems and post-traumatic stress symptoms for children in the CPP group in comparison to the case management group. Ata 6-month follow-up of this sample, reductions in child behavior problem were maintained, showing that the effects of the CPP were stable across time [45]. According to the authors, CPP assisted parents in finding effective ways to processtheir own traumatic stress, which in turn improved child emotion regulation and aided in the correction of child cognitive distortions. However, while this study presents excellent methodological qualities, it did not measure parental sensitivity or child attachment.

CPP has also proven its' feasibility and effectiveness in a community and clinical setting as part of the Florida's infant and Young Child Mental Health Pilot Program designed for maltreating parents and their children (0-5 years old) [39]. Osofsky et al. [39] found improvements in parental sensitivity and responsiveness, and positive parental discipline. In addition, children showed improvements in positive affect, problem-solving or motor development, and mother-child dyads showed more reciprocal exchanges. This study did not however include a comparison or control group with random assignment.

Short-term protocols: Modification of parental behaviors

Changing parental behaviors refers to the modification of inadequate, insensitive, and frightening parental behavior into more sensitive caregiving behaviors. The therapeutic objective is therefore to bring parents to recognize, interpret, and properly respond to child distress and exploration signals. Video feedback has been considered as avaluable strategy to attain this objective. After filming a parent-child interaction, the therapist views video sequences with the parent in order to reinforce the latter's positive and sensitive behaviors towards the child. Video feedback allows the parent to witness personal positive behaviors, appropriate parenting skills, and most importantly their positive effect on child behaviors. Also, by highlighting the parent's strengths, this approach allows both the parent and the child to experience a new and pleasant relational exchange. According to this model, it is through these positive experiences that parents give new meaning to their relationship and increase their responsiveness, sensitivity, and availability towards their child, which in turn foster child attachment security and development. Although some parents may present limited strengths at the start of the intervention, emphasizing even simple positive behaviors such as saying "good job" to the child, can help the parent reconsider negative self-perceptions and discover hidden strengths, which can then lead to an increase in parental sensitivity. Once this is possible, positive behaviors may be consolidated and applied to other parent-child interactive situations [46].

To date, however, only two research teams have assessed short-term protocols based on attachment theory for maltreated children and their parents: the Moss, Dubois-Comtois, Cyr, Tarabulsy, St-Laurent, and Bernier (2011) research team [47] and the Bernard, Dozier, Bick, Lewis-Morrarty, Lindhiem, and Carlson (2012) research team [48].

The Attachment and Behavioral Catch-up protocol (ABC).

The ABC is a short-term attachment-based intervention consisting of 10-weekly home visits for which both the parent and the child are present. The main objective of the ABC [48] is to enhance sensitive, nurturing care among parents and to decrease frightening behaviors towards the child. While each session has a specific focus, the intervention aims mainly at helping parents become more nurturing towards their child especially when the latter shows signs of distress. Parents are also encouraged to be sensitive to child needs despite the fact that some children may show rejecting behaviors (session 1 and 2). The practitioner's goal is therefore to help parents reinterpret their child's behavior, as well as their own personal issues, which may stem from past childhood attachment experiences and interfere with their present ability to provide sensitive care (session 7 and 8). In situations when the child is not in distress, parents are encouraged to support the child's exploration and feelings of competency. This is accomplished by following the child's lead with delight during moments of play (session 3 and 4). Parents are also asked to monitor their own overwhelming or intrusive behaviors towards their child during play activities (session 5 and 6). The practitioner thus uses structured activities to help parents enact particular skills. The practitioner also comments on parents' behaviors during these activities, as well as through video-feedback sessions in order to reinforce their positive parental behaviors, strengths, and understanding of the session content. The last two sessions are used to consolidate gains acquired during the first 8 weeks of intervention. Finally, weekly homework is assigned so that parents can practice the use of their newly developed skills and record their own behaviors and those of their child throughout the week.

Bernard et al. [48] tested the efficacy of the ABC with parents and children (1-2 years old) reported to child protection services. Using a randomized control trial design, dyads were assigned to the ABC or a control intervention group, i.e., the Developmental Education for families (DEF), which aims the enhancement of cognitive and linguistic development of the child. Although child attachment was not assessed before the intervention, results from the 1-month post-intervention follow-up revealed a higher proportion of securely attached children and a lower proportion of disorganized children in the ABC group than in the DEF intervention group. These results support the efficacy of short-term attachment-based interventions for improving attachment security and decreasing later incidence of psychopathology in high-risk samples.

The Attachment Videofeedback Intervention (AVI)

The Attachment Video feedback Intervention, developed by Moss et al. [47] is a short-term attachment-based intervention for parents and their children consisting of 8-weekly home visits. The fundamental strategy of this approach is to focus on parental positive behavior to help the parent witness personal strengths and promote change. More specifically, during each intervention session of approximately 90 minutes, the practitioner reinforces the parent's sensitive behavior through a video-feedback discussion with the parent following a filmed parent-child interactive sequence. At each session, activities and toys are proposed to the dyad according to child age and parental behaviors to be modified. For this 10 to 15-minute filmed activity, the parent is given only one instruction targeting specific aspects of parental sensitivity to be improved (e.g. follow your child's lead, describe what your child is doing, describe your child's feelings during the activity). For younger children, caregiving activities such as breastfeeding or bath time can be used as filmed interactions. Following this activity, a video-feedback discussion of approximately 20 minutes is conducted by the practitioner who watches the interaction sequence with the parent. At first, the practitioner intentionally stops the film during positive moments in order to reinforce the parent's sensitive behaviors towards the child, reciprocal interactions, and moments when the parent had a positive impact on the child. The practitioner also inquires about the parent's feelings and thoughts during specific moments. The parent is also invited to share observations relating to the self and the child (see Table 1 for a description of a typical session).Intervention sessions also include a discussion with the parent regarding attachment related themes, emotion regulation, and concerns regarding the child (e.g. anger, discipline). While the first video feedback session emphasizes child behaviors (e.g. proximity seeking, exploration, meaning of distress signals), the focus is gradually shifted on to parents' behaviors (e.g. interpretation of signals, adequate and nurturing responses).

Moss et al. [47] tested the efficacy of the AVI with parents and children (0-5 years old) reported to child protection services. Using a randomized control trial, dyads were either assigned to the AVI or to a case management control group receiving regular child protection services. Results revealed that parents exposed to the AVI were more sensitive after the intervention than those who received the usual servicesof the child protection services. Substantial increases in attachment security and decreases in attachment disorganization were also found for children of the AVI group. In addition, a decrease in behavior problems was observed for older children of the intervention group. Results of this study clearly support the value of short-term attachment-based interventions as a cost-effective means for improving child attachment security as well as for promoting sensitive caregiving behaviors in parents identified as neglectful and/or abusive, and at-risk of having their parental rights terminated.

Overall, attachment-based intervention protocols represent promising and valuable intervention strategies for maltreated children and their parents.Given the relatively limited number of studies on intervention strategies for maltreated children and their parents, determining whether one type of protocol is more effective than another is premature. It is also difficult to determine the distinct benefits of short versus long-term programs, or best-suited intervention target (parental representations and/or parental behaviors). We can only deplore the rarity of studies that have evaluated the medium to long-term effects of these interventions. Accordingly, greater research is needed in order to examine whether the beneficial effects of these seemingly promising interventions are maintained over time.

Studies must also consider the potential influence of variables that can moderate the efficacy of intervention protocols (e.g. parental mental health, parental attachment state of mind, domestic violence). For example, some variables may influence the ability of some parents and children to benefit from specific types of intervention. In particular, studies have shown that mothers who have experienced trauma during their own childhood or have unresolved attachment representations in response to loss or past experiences of physical or sexual abuse, do not profit from a behaviourally-driven attachment-based intervention aiming the improvement of parental sensitivity [49,50]. Perhaps, sensitivity is more likely to improve if parents are able to witness their inappropriate, and sometimes frightening, behaviors in relation to their child. This hypothesis is supported by results from the Bernard et al. [48] study in which sessions specifically aiming the identification of parental frightening behaviors were integrated into the intervention protocol, and for which child attachment disorganization decreased and child attachment security improved. However, this study did not examined intervention effects on parental sensitivity. In addition, while the Moss and al. study [47] did not specifically target parental frightening behaviors during video-feedback sessions, they attributed part of their success to the training received by clinicians working with the families. Not only were clinicians trained by attachment researchers (experts) in the recognition of children's distress signals and parental sensitive/insensitive behaviors, but they were also trained in the identification of parental frightening, extremely intrusive, and helpless behaviors. As suggested by Bakermans-Kranenburg et al. [33], to reduce child disorganization and its correlates, interventions should focus on both improving parental sensitivity and reducing parental frightening behaviors.

The clinician as a secure base for the parent

According to Bowlby [34], in order for intervention strategies to be effective, it is essential that the therapist be perceived as a secure attachment figure by the parent. By listening, being available and consistent, the therapist can be viewed as a sensitive personwho can help the parent find new meaning to past and current attachment representations or behaviors towards the child. By accompanying the parent in the re-interpretation of childhood experiences and by having the parent discover personal strengths, the therapist helps the parent experience a significant and gratifyingrelationship with another adult. The parent canthen refer to this new sensitive attachment figure to better interpret and appease their own distress as well as that of their child. The practitioner's empathy and ability to proceed with therapy in a progressive manner, respecting the parent's rhythm, are key elements for the development of a relationship of trust and the promotion of changes in the parent-child relationship. The more the parent learns to rely on this relationship of trust, the more the parent learns to become his or her own security base.

Beyond these qualities, practitioner training and supervision are essential aspects of successful intervention protocols with parents. Research has shown that clinicians who intend to apply intervention strategies based on the principles of attachment theory must acquire in-depth knowledge of the theory and of child developmental processes, and must develop excellent observational skills with respect to parent-child interactions [51]. For example, in the Moss et al. [47] study, the training, which included the presentation of multiple video case-studies, focused on the teaching of attachment theory concepts as well as associated intervention techniques. In addition, the appropriate attitudes to be adopted by clinicians partaking in the intervention protocol were clearly written out in the intervention manual received by clinicians during the training. Moreover, clinicians learned to be flexible and to make appropriate judgments in order to adequately adjust themselves to the particular needs of each family, the age of the child, and the complex problems surrounding families. In order to ensure the integrity of the intervention, regular supervision was also offered to clinicians. Supervision was carried out by a psychologist, whom also was an expert in attachment and the application of the AVI. As indicated by Olds [52] and Goodson, Layzer, St-Pierre, Bernstein, and Lopez [53], the absence of extensive training makes prevention or intervention efforts ineffective, and can even exacerbate the difficulties already present in the parent.

	Phases	Duration	Relational intervention session
1.	Arrival at the home	• 10 min.	Brief review of events which affected the parent and child since the last encounter
2.	Discussion	• 20 min.	• Theme chosen by the parent • Theme related to parent-child relationship, emotional regulation or parent's preoccupations concerning parent-child relationship (e.g. bedtime, discipline, etc.) • Allows practitioner to develop relationship of trust with parent and helps the latter to make links between her present parental preoccupations and how she interacts with her child
3.	Filmed playtime	• 10-15 min.	• Parent-child interaction filmed during playtime activity • Activity and toys supplied by practitioner in accordance to the child's age and dyadic aspects to be worked at (e.g. physical proximity, child's need to explore, interpreting child's distress signals, etc.) • A single instruction is given to the parent (e.g. to act as usual, follow her child's rhythm, imitate her child, etc.) • No intervention is made during interaction; the practitioner is merely an observer
4.	Video feed-back	• 20 min.	• Video feedback done by practitioner who views the interaction sequence with the parent • Practitioner asks parent how she feels and what she notices of herself and her child • Practitioner intentionally pauses at positive moments where he reinforces parental sensitivity, reciprocity and moments when the parent has a positive impact on her child
5.	End of ses-sion	• 10 min.	• Homework: Practitioner encourages the parent to reproduce an activity with her child during the week

Table 1. Progress of an Attachment Video feedback Intervention session according to a protocol by Moss and Colleagues

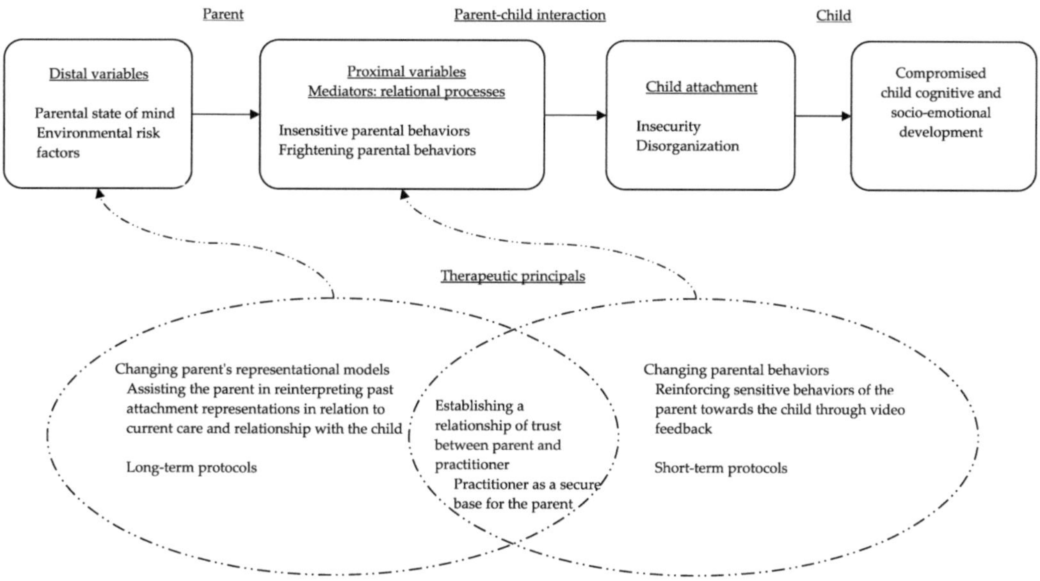

Figure 1. Development of the maltreated child and attachment-based intervention targets to promote child development

Figure 1 presents the intergenerational transmission of child attachment disorganization and the compromised development of maltreated children. It also illustrates how the different therapeutic principals can guide and act as important elements in the process of change and modification of the parent-child relationship.

4. Applying attachment-based intervention in a new context: The assessment of parental capacity in child protection cases

While the contribution of attachment theory in the assessment of parental capacity in child protection cases has been proposed by many researchers [54-57], key concepts of this theory have rarely been integrated intoassessment protocols. This is surprising given that attachment theory is closely linked to the concept of parental capacity, i.e., the parent's capacity to care for their child, to protect from potential threats, and to offer an environment that promotes child emotional, cognitive, and physical development [58].A competent parent, in terms of parenting capacity, is able to adapt to the inherent developmental changes of their child: not only is the parent sufficiently competent in responding to the child's needs while adjusting to the child's changing developmental capacities, but the parent is also able to find solutions to the daily struggles encountered as a parent [54,58]. It is through a high-quality relationship, in which the parent demonstrates interest, respect, and sensitivity towards the child that a parent's competency becomes apparent [59]. The concept of parental competency is therefore closely related to the concept of parental sensitivity, as defined by attachment theory.

The assessment of parental capacity in cases of children reported for abuse or neglect is particularly important, in that it often informs the court of the child's best interest. Specifically, it plays a role in whether the child should be removed or not from his family of origin, and if removed, the type of placement suggested for that particular child. This assessment is subsequently used by clinicians as a way to determine the most appropriate intervention plan for the family. Therefore, the assessment of parental capacity plays a major role in the life of a child. Given the seriousness of the decisions made following theseassessments, it is important that they be carried out by carefully trained professional, for whom personal biases do not interfere with the objectivity of the evaluation process. Many, concerned with the quality of parental capacity assessments, have suggested guidelines for evaluators. For example, the *American Psychological Association* (APA) suggested guidelines regarding the necessary professional competencies required for the evaluation process, as well as the ethical considerations to respect during assessments of parental capacities [60].Other researchers and clinicians have highlighted key elements to consider in such evaluations [54,61-64]. In particular, Budd [61,62] carefully outlined a list of principles that should guide such evaluations.

The first principle proposed by Budd [61,62] is that assessments of parental capacity should center on the parent's limitations and strengths, as well as on the quality of the parent-child relationship. This principal rests on the idea that parental capacity should be understood in response to child needs, that is, how the parent's limitations and capabilities may be potential risk or protection factors for the child, and how they may influence the parent's ability to profit from clinical services. Indeed, as mentioned by the APA [60], the evaluator must not only focus on the parent's actual capacity, but also assess the parent's potential. This is in line with Haynes'[65]view, who describes core features in the assessment of parental competency as parental: 1) capacity to care (ex: parental sensitivity, emotional commitment, empathy); 2) capacity to protect (ex: safe environment, supervision, tolerance to frustration, educational practices and adequate discipline); and 3) capacity to change (ex: intellectual limits and strengths, severity of psychopathological symptoms, insights/reflective functioning, social and family support).

The second principal emphasizes the importance of favoring a functional approach in the evaluation of parental capacity, as to focus on behaviors and skills towards the child in everyday performance and daily routines. As indicated by White [58], in an extensive summary pertaining to research relating to parental capacity, it is the quality of the parent's immediate and daily behaviors towards the child that influences the child's overall well-being and development.

The third principal implies the use of a minimal parenting standard to the assessment of parental capacity. Indeed, many authors [54,61,66]have suggested that parents facing adversity should not be compared to parents presenting optimal abilities. For parents in child protection cases, meeting the minimal requirements needed to ensure child physical and emotional security should be considered sufficient and acceptable. For example, parents who experience symptoms of depression or intellectual deficits may be limited in their ability tooffer their child a safe and secure emotional environment. Nevertheless, the impact of these limitations may be reduced if the parent demonstrates insight, the ability to recognize personal limits, or the capacity to benefit from friends/family social support or a clinical treatment. Although this parent's functioning may be affected by risk factors, he or she should be considered as meeting the minimal standards required for adequate parental capacity if parental behaviors and abilities are sufficiently adequate during parent-child interaction. Accordingly, parent-child interactive quality should be regarded as a central feature in parenting assessment capacity.

Despite these aforementioned guidelines, in practice, assessmentreports of parental capacityoften remain incomplete and follow a minimalist and low-quality protocol. Budd et al. [67]examined 170 parenting capacity assessment reports for child protection cases. Researchersidentified numerous flaws that put into question the validity of these reports. In particular, results showed an over-simplification of conclusions, often based on premature evaluations, and following only one meeting with the parent outside the family home. Moreover, researchers found a lack of crucial information pertaining to the child and the quality of parent-child relationship. More information was provided on parental limitations than on parental strengths. In particular, direct observations of child and parent-child interaction were limited and assessments generally relied on questionnaires and interviews with the parents.

Harnett [68] also raises the important point that parental capacity is generally evaluated under very short time frames. This suggests that parents' capacity to change is not really evaluated according to longitudinal observations of parents' interactive behavior with the child, but instead is generally estimated following short meetings with the parent. In order to assess parents' capacity to change, parents need to be able to demonstrate their ability to question themselves and take responsibility for their actions, but mostly they need to show their capacity to benefit from an intervention and change. Certainly, these abilities represent important indicators of the parent's capacity to change. It has been suggested to assess parental competency from the perspective of the parent's ability to build parenting skills, while clinical workers aim at promoting positive parenting behaviors [68,69].Accordingly, Harnett [68] proposes applying an intervention for improving the parent-child relationship as a way to evaluate parental capacity to change. However, to date, no such protocol, including an intervention centered on parent-child interaction, has been submitted to a scientific evaluation. The challenges associated with the assessment of parental capacity highlight the need to develop standardized intervention strategies that could accurately assess parental capacity to change. Such a procedure would lead to more accurate and useful evaluation reports, allowing for better decision making in the court justice system and more adaptive intervention plans for the child and family.

The parental capacity assessment protocol at the Child Protection Services of Montreal-University-Institute

Recently, the Child Protection Services of Montreal-University Institute (CPS-UI) have launched the *Clinicfor the assessment and intervention of young children and their families,*for children aged 0 to 5 and their parents who have been reported for child maltreatment and for whom a parental capacity evaluation is required. In collaboration with this clinic, we developed a specialized protocol for the assessment of parental capacity [70,71]. The innovative aspect of this protocol is that we integrated into the evaluation procedure a short-term attachment-based intervention[47]as a way to assess parental capacity tochange. This attachment-based protocol is currently under scientific investigation by our research team.

We believe that an attachment-based approach is particularly appropriate for assessing parental capacity in child protection cases. Given that an assessment of parental capacity requires the description of parental deficits and limitationsin the final evaluation report, as well as during court hearings, evaluators must be able to quickly put into evidence with the parent their inappropriate behaviors during the sessions. To identify these inappropriate behaviors within a framework that highlights the positive side of the parent can: 1) increase the parent's feelings of trust towards the evaluator and the ability to commit in the evaluation process, and 2) orient intervention efforts on the reinforcement of the parent's self-recognition and repair of inappropriate behaviors, while making use of the parent's personal strengths. Through video-feedback parents may witness their own frightening-frightened behaviors with their child, and then begin a process of change and reparation in which they increasingly learn to take responsibility for their actions.

The parental capacity assessment protocol

The parental capacity assessment protocol implemented at the clinic of the CPS-UI consists, on average, of 5 meeting of approximately 3 hours each, carried out during a 4 to 8 week period. A typical evaluation meeting includes 4 components.

Component 1: At each meeting, the evaluator observes parent-child interactions during daily activities and routines.

Component 2: A discussion period is scheduled with the parent toassess the different factors potentially explainingthe parent's behaviors and ability to recognize his or her own difficulties. This discussion is based on an adaptation [64] of the parental competence assessment guide fromSteinhauer [63], which allows for the collection of various information regarding the parent's social and familial context, the health and development of the child, the impulse control of the parent, and the parent's history of prior use of clinical services. This guide also allows the evaluator to obtain information regarding parental practices (e.g.educational methods, discipline, care for basic needs) and the parent-child relationship by orienting evaluators observations on child attachment behaviors and parental sensitivity in response to the child needs during daily activities.

Component 3: In addition to gathering information regarding the parent's ability to care and protect the child, an intervention protocol is used as a way to assess parental capacity to change. Here, we have used the attachment-based strategy developed by Moss et al. [47], to which we have added a focus on parental frightening or inappropriate behaviors. Therefore, this adapted version of the AVI protocol not only aims at reinforcing, via video-feedback of parent-child interactions, 1) the parent's sensitive behaviors (e.g identify and interpret child distress signals, answering them in an acceptable delay), but also 2) the recognition by the parent of his own frightening behaviors and the repair of these behaviors through sensitive behaviors.

Component 4: The last component is conducted at the end of the evaluation process. It consist of the presentation of the strengths and limitations to the parent, and the writing of the evaluation report.

Preliminary results: The adapted AVI protocol as an effective tool for improving the quality of parent-child interactions and for assessing parent's capacity to change

In the scope of this research project, we have tried to answer two main objectives. The first objective concerned the efficacy of the intervention as a tool for improving parental sensitivity. The second objective was to verify whether the parental capacity assessment protocol, which included an intervention centered on parent-child interaction, was useful for assessing parents' capacity to change.

Preliminary statistical analyses were conducted with a sub-sample of participants. This sub-sample consisted of 23 families, including 12 that were evaluated according to the AVI protocol as the activation technique for assessing parental capacity to change, and 13 were evaluated according to a second protocol, just as intensive, but relying on the standard activation techniques used by psycho-educators of the CPS-UI (e.g. modeling). The children (55% boys) had an average age of 18.21 months (*S.D.* = 18.96, range = 1 to 60 months). The majority of children were reported for neglect, although half of thesample were also victims of physical abuse. An important number of parents also experienced a troubled past including maltreatment or out-of-home placements.At a socio-demographic level, study participants represented a very high-risk sample with more than half not having a high school diploma and living below the poverty threshold.

Using a randomized clinical control trial design, we examined changes in the quality of parent-child interactions during a snack time procedure [19]. More specifically, we observed parents' capacity to be sensitive tochild needs and signals and to take on appropriate parental role, as well as the ability of each member of the dyad to openly and freely express emotions and intentions. In support of our hypothesis, results showed that dyads involved in the AVI assessment protocol demonstrated significant improvements in interactive quality, with mothers showing higher levels of sensitivity and dyads showing more reciprocal and synchronized interactions [71]. On average, 6 sessions of video-feedback were offered to participants.

Moreover, at the end of each parental capacity assessment, we questioned evaluators from both protocols regarding the changes they observed in the parent-child dyads. We also asked about the usefulness of our protocol for the assessment of parental capacity. Results of statistical analyses revealed that, according to evaluators, parents' level of commitment facilitated parents capacity to learn new strategies, regardless of the complexity of the case (difficulties met during the evaluation process, the severity of abuse suffered by the child, etc). In addition, results revealed that evaluators of the AVI assessment protocol observed significantly more changes within the family, resulting in improved parental sensitivity, greater secure or organized child attachment, and improved overall child development [72]. These results support the efficacy of the AVI as a tool for promoting quality of parent-child interactions of families reported to CPS.

Also, our results point to the usefulness of the AVI intervention as a valuable tool for assessing parental capacity to change. Given that the potential for parents to change is more likely to result from the application of the AVI protocol than as a result of the "psycho-educational' protocol, and that evaluators from the AVI are more likely to observe this improvement, we conclude that the AVI strategy is a valuable tool for accurately assessing parents' capacity to change and show greater sensitivity towards their child.

5. Conclusion

The work stemming from attachment theory offers a critical theoretical framework that helps identify 1) parental behaviors that influence the quality of the parent-child interaction and the development of the child, and 2) effective intervention strategies to promote sensitive behaviors, which are at the root of a secure child attachment pattern. Taken as a whole, the different attachment-based intervention protocols, whether short or long-term, are particularly promising. While the assessment of some of these protocols has not relied on randomized control trials, they all have been subjected to a scientific investigation. As a result, all evaluated protocols with maltreated children and their parents have supported the beneficial outcomes of this type of intervention strategy on the quality of the parent-child relationship and on the various aspects of the child's development : increase in parental sensitivity, child attachment security, and decrease in child disorganized attachment; greater development or adaptation of the child (e.g. increase in motor development, decrease in child's negative representations of the self and of the maternal figure, decrease in behavioral problems and of symptoms of post-traumatic stress). In summary, the various attachment-based protocols show impressive success rates for vulnerable populations and are therefore important practices to adopt with respect to maltreated and at-risk children. It is important to note, however, that the continuous training and supervision of the evaluators, including extensive understanding of child developmental processes and observation techniques for relational patterns are central in maintaining the integrity and successfulness of the intervention.

Following the preliminary scientific evaluation of the adapted AVI protocol for the assessment of parental capacity at the CPS-UI clinic, we conclude that the contribution of attachment theory to the assessment of parental capacity in child protection cases is considerable and significant. Not only did this intervention strategy allowed for the improvement of parental sensitivity and reciprocity during parent-child interactions of a high-risk vulnerable population, but it also enhanced quality of assessments conducted by evaluators of the CPS, particularly with respect to the evaluation of parents' capacity to show potential for change. This clinical improvement is notable, considering the impact of the decisions made following these evaluation. It is clear that a better understanding of the capacity for parents to change during the evaluation process enables family services that are better suited to answer the specific needs of parents and their child. Nevertheless, to date, these preliminary results offer only a partial understanding of the effects of an attachment-based intervention on the quality of a parental capacity assessment. Future analyses will be conducted with a larger number of participants and will examine the role of other variables that could potentially positively or negatively affect outcomes. Finally, more research is needed to corroborate the results stemming from our project.

By helping parents, often perceived as inadequate, identify their strengths, practitioners guide parentsin the recognition of abilities and qualities, despite the fact that these may initially be limited or scarce. Working with a parent in such a context can only facilitate the parent's willingness to acknowledge deficits and inappropriate/frightening behaviors towards the child, and help to promote the development of more sensitive behaviors. Also, attachment-based protocols can facilitate parents' collaboration with child protective services. In summary, the use of an intervention protocol based on attachment-theory with parents and children reported for maltreatment, whether for assessing parental capacity, or for intervention purposes, is clearly a promising avenue.

Author details

Chantal Cyr, Geneviève Michel, Caroline Poulin,
Valérie Losier, Marilyne Dumais and Ellen Moss
University of Quebec at Montreal, Dept. of Psychology, Montreal, Canada

Chantal Cyr
Child Protection Services of Montreal-University Institute, Canada

Diane St-Laurent and Karine Dubois-Comtois
University of Quebec at Trois-Rivières, Canada

Karine Dubois-Comtois
Montreal Sacré-Coeur Hospital, Canada

Katherine Pascuzzo
McGill University, Canada

6. References

[1] Cicchetti D, Valentino K (2006) An Ecological-transactional Perspective on Child Maltreatment: Failure of the Average Expectable Environment and its Influence on Child Development. In: Cicchetti D, Cohen D J, editors. Developmental Psychopathology. New Jersey: Wiley. pp. 129-201.
[2] Cicchetti D, Lynch M (1993) Toward an Ecological/transactional Model of Community Violence and Child Maltreatment: Consequences for Children's Development. Psychiatry. 56: 96-118.
[3] Lyons-Ruth K, Jacobvitz D (2008) Attachment Disorganization: Genetic Factors, Parenting Contexts, and Developmental Transformation from Infancy to Adulthood. In: Cassidy J, Shaver P R, editors. Handbookof attachment second edition: Theory, Research, and Clinical Applications. New York: Guilford Press. pp. 666-697.
[4] Weinfield N S, Sroufe A L, Egeland B, Carlson E A (2008) The Nature of Individual Differences in Infant-Caregiver Attachment. In: Cassidy J, Shaver P R, editors. Handbook of Attachment. New York: Guilford Press. pp. 520-554.
[5] Bowlby J (1982) Attachment and Loss. Am. j. of orthopsychiatry. 52: 664-678.

[6] Ainsworth M D S, Blehar M C, Waters E, Walls S (1978) Patterns of Attachment: A Psychological Study of the Strange Situation. Hillsdale, N.J.: Lawrence Erlbaum Associates.
[7] Sroufe A L (1996) Emotional development: The Organization of Emotional Life in the Early Years. New York: Cambridge University Press.
[8] Lyons-Ruth K, Bronfman E, Parsons E (1999) Maternal Frightened, Frightening, or Atypical Behavior and Disorganized Infant Attachment Patterns. In: Vondra J, Barnett D, editors. Atypical Patterns of Infant Attachment: Theory, Research, and Current Directions. Mono. of the society for research in child dev. (Serial #258, 64): 67-96.
[9] Madigan S, Bakermans-Kranenburg M J, van IJzendoorn M H, Moran G, Pederson D R, Benoit D (2006) Unresolved States of Mind, Anomalous Parental behavior, and Disorganized Attachment: A Review and Meta-analysis of a Transmission Gap. Attach. and human dev. 8: 89-111.
[10] Schuengel C, Bakermans-Kranenburg M J, van IJzendoorn M H (1999) Frightening Maternal Behavior linking Unresolved Loss and Disorganized Infant Attachment. J. of consulting and clinical psychology. 64: 54-63.
[11] Cyr C, Dubois-Comtois K, Moss E (2008) Les Conversations Mère-Enfant et l'Attachement des Enfants à la Période Préscolaire. R. can. des sciences du comp. 40: 140-152.
[12] Hesse E (1999) The Adult Attachment Interview: Historical and Current Perspectives. In: Handbook of Attachment: Theory, Research, and Clinical Applications. Cassidy J, Shaver P R, editors. New York: Guilford Press. pp. 395-433.
[13] Main M, Hesse E (1990)Frightening, Frightened, Dissociated or Disorganized Behavior on the Part of the Parent: A coding System for Parent-Infant Interactions. Unpublished manuscript, University of California at Berkeley.
[14] Solomon J, George C (1999) The Development of Attachment in Separated and Divorced Families. Effects of Overnight Visitation, Parent and Couple Variable. Attach. and human dev. 1: 2-33.
[15] Carlson E A (1998) A Prospective Longitudinal Study of Attachment Disorganization/ Disorientation. Child dev. 69: 1007-1028.
[16] Carlson V, Cicchetti D, Barnett D, Braunwald K (1989) Disorganized/Disoriented Attachment Relationships in Maltreated Infants. Dev. psychology.25: 525-531.
[17] Dubois-Comtois K, Cyr C, Moss E (June 2005) Self-Reported Behavior Problems of Insecure Organized, Disorganized and Controlling children in middle childhood. Poster presented at the Canadian psychological association convention. Montréal, QC.
[18] Lyons-Ruth K, Connell D B, Grunebaum H U, Botein S (1990) Infants at Social Risk: Maternal Depression and Family Support Services as Mediator of Infant Development and Security of Attachment. Child dev. 61: 85-98.
[19] Moss E, Cyr C, Dubois-Comtois K (2004) Attachment at Early School-age and Developmental Risk: Examining Family Contexts and Behavior Problems of Controlling Caregiving, Controlling-Punitive, and Behaviourally Disorganised Children. Dev. psychology. 40: 519-532.

[20] van IJzendoorn M H, Schuengel C, Bakermans-Kranenburg M (1999) Disorganized Attachment in Early Childhood: Meta-Analysis of Precursors, Concomitants, and Sequelae. Dev. and psychopathology.11: 225-249.

[21] Main M, Cassidy J (1988) Categories of Response to Reunion with the Parent at Age 6: Predictable from Infant Attachment Classifications and Stable over a 1-month Period. Dev. psychology. 24: 415–426.

[22] Moss E, Cyr C, Bureau J-F, Tarabulsy G M, Dubois-Comtois K (2005) Stability of Attachment During the Preschool Period. Dev. psychology. 41: 773-783.

[23] Howes P W, Cicchetti D (1993) A Family/Relational Perspective on Maltreating Families: Parallel Processes across Systems and Social Policy Implications. In: Cicchetti D, Toth S L, editors. Child Abuse, Child Development, and Social Policy. Norwood, N.J.: Ablex. pp. 249-300.

[24] Cyr C, Euser E, Bakermans-Kranenburg M J, van IJzendoorn, M H (2010) Attachment Security and Disorganization in Maltreated and High-Risk Families: A Series of Meta-Analyses. Dev. and psychopathology.22: 87-108.

[25] Hesse E, Main M (2006) Frightened, Threatening, and Dissociative Parental Behaviour in Low-Risk Samples: Description, Discussion, and Interpretations. Dev. and psychopathology. 18: 309-343.

[26] Putman F W (2006) Dissociative Disorders. In: Cicchetti D, Cohen D J, editors. Dev. and psychopathology. New Jersey: Wiley. pp. 657-695.

[27] Madigan S, Moran G, Pederson D R (2006) Unresolved States of Mind, Disorganized Attachment Relationships, and Disrupted Mother-Infant Interactions of Adolescent Mothers and Their Infants. Dev. psychology. 42: 293-304.

[28] Schuder M R Lyons-Ruth K (2004) "Hidden Trauma" in Infancy: Attachment, Fearful Arousal, and Early Dysfunction of the Stress Response System. In: Osofsky J D, editor. Young children and trauma: Intervention and treatment. New York: Guilford Press. pp. 69-104.

[29] Main M, Kaplan N, Cassidy J (1985) Security in Infancy, Childhood, andAdulthood: A Move to the Level of Representation. In: Bretherton I, Waters E, editors. Growing Points in Attachment Theory and Research. Mono. of the society forresearch in child dev. 50: 66-106.

[30] Hesse E (1999) The Adult Attachment Interview: Historical and Current Perspectives. In Cassidy J, Shavers P, editors. Handbook of Attachment: Theory, research, and clinical applications.New York: The Guilford Press. pp. 395-433.

[31] Trocmé N, Fallon B, MacLaurin B, Daciuk J, Felstiner C, Black T, & al (2003) Étude Canadienne sur l'Incidence des Signalements de Cas de Violence et de Négligence envers les Enfants: Données Principales. Ottawa, ON: Ministre des Travaux publics et des Services gouvernementaux du Canada.

[32]van IJzendoorn M H (1995) Adult Attachment Representations, Parental Responsiveness, and Infant Attachment: A Meta-analysis on the Predictive Validity of the Adult Attachment Interview. Psychological bulletin. 117: 387-403.

[33] Bakermans-Kranenburg M J, van IJzendoorn M H, Juffer F (2003) Less is More: Meta-Analyses of Sensitivity and Attachment Interventions in Early Childhood. Psychological bulletin. 129: 195-215.

[34] Bowlby J (1988). A secure base: Parent-child Attachment and Healthy Human Development. New York: Basic Books.

[35] Berlin L, Zeanah C H, Lieberman A F (2008) Prevention and Intervention Programs for Supporting Early Attachment Security. In: Cassidy J, Shaver P R, editors. Handbook of Attachment: Theory, Research and Clinical Applications (2nd ed.). New York: London: Guilford Press. pp. 745–61.

[36] Bakermans-Kranenburg M J, van IJzendoorn M H, Juffer F (2005) Disorganized Infant Attachment and Preventive Interventions: A Review and Meta-Analysis. Inf. mental health j.26: 191-216.

[37] Fraiberg S, Adelson E, Shapiro V (1975) Ghosts in the Nursery. A Psychoanalytic Approach to the Problems of Impaired Infant-Mother Relationships. J.of the am. academy of child & adolescent psychiatry.14: 387-421.

[38] Lieberman A F, Van Horn P (2008) Psychotherapy with Infants and Young Children: Repairing the Effects of Stress and Trauma on Early Attachment. New York: Guilford.

[39] Osofsky J D, Kronenberg M, Hammer J H, Lederman C, Katz L, Adams S, & al (2007) The Development and Evaluation of the Intervention Model for the Florida Infant Mental Health Pilot Program. Inf. mental health j. 28: 259-280.

[40] Toth S L, Gravener J A (2012) Bridging Research and Practice: Relational Interventions for Maltreated Children. Child and adolescent mental health.

[41] Cicchetti D, Rogosch F A & Toth S (2006) Fostering Secure Attachment in Infants in Maltreating Families through Prevention Interventions. Dev. and psychopathology. 18: 623-649.

[42] Cicchetti D, Rogosch F A, Toth S L, Sturge-Apple M L (2011) Normalizing the Development of Cortisol Regulation in Maltreated Infants through Preventive Interventions. Dev. and Psychopathology. 23: 789-800.

[43] Toth S L, Maughan A, Manly J T, Spagnola M, Cicchetti D (2002) The Relative Efficacy of two Interventions in Altering Maltreated Preschool Children's Representational Models: Implications for Attachment Theory. Dev. and psychopathology. 14:877-908.

[44] Lieberman A F, Van Horn P, Ippen C G (2005) Towards Evidence-Based Treatment: Child-parent Psychotherapy with Preschoolers exposed to Marital Violence. J. of the am. academy of child and adolescent psychiatry. 44: 1241-1248.

[45] Lieberman A F, Ghosh Ippen C, Van Horn P (2006). Child-parent Psychotherapy: 6-month Follow-up of a Randomized Controlled Trial. J. of the am. academy of child and adolescent psychiatry. 45: 913–918.

[46] St-Laurent D, Larin S, Tarabulsy G, Moss E, Bernier A, Dubois-Comtois K, Cyr C (2008) Intervenir auprès de Familles Vulnérables selon les Principes de l'Attachement. L'infirmière clinicienne. 5 :21-29.

[47] Moss E, Dubois-Comtois K, Cyr C, Tarabulsy G, St-Laurent D, Bernier A (2011). Efficacy of a Home-Visiting Intervention Aimed at Improving Maternal Sensitivity, Child

Attachment, and Behavioral Outcomes for Maltreated Children: A Randomized Control Trial. Dev. and psychopathology. 23: 195-210.

[48] Bernard K Dozier M, Bick J, Lewis-Morrarty E, Lindhiem O, Carlson E (2012) Enhancing Attachment Organization Among Maltreated Children: Results of a Randomized Clinical Trial. Child Dev. 83 : 623-636.

[49] Duchesne D, Dubois-Comtois K, Moss E (2007) La Théorie d'Attachement comme Outils d'Intervention auprès des Parents d'Accueil et des Enfants Placés. R. prisme. 46: 96-113.

[50] Moran G, Pederson D, Krupka A (2005) Maternal Unresolved Attachment Status Impedes the Effectiveness of Interventions with Adolescent Mothers. Inf. mental health j. 26 : 231-249.

[51] Cyr C, Moss E, St-Laurent D, Dubois-Comtois K, Sauvé, M (2012) Promouvoir le Développement d'Enfants Victimes de Maltraitance : L'Importance des Interventions Relationnelles Parent-Enfant. In : Gagné M H, Drapeau S, Saint-Jacques M C, editors. Les Enfants Maltraités : de l'Affliction à l'Espoir. Pistes de Compréhension et d'Action. Les presses de l'Université Laval (pp. 41-70) QC, Canada.

[52] Olds D (2002) Home Visiting by Paraprofessionals and by Nurses. Pediatrics. 110 : 486-496.

[53] Goodson B D, Layzer J I, St Pierre R G, Bernstein L S, Lopez M (2000) Effectiveness of a Comprehensive Five-year Family Support Program for Low-income Children and their Families: Findings from the Comprehensive Child Development Program. Early childhood research quarterly. 15: 5-39.

[54] Azar S T, Lauretti A F, Loding B V (1998) The Evaluation of Parental Fitness in Termination of Parental Right Cases: A Functional-contextual Perspective. Clinical child and fam. psychology r. 1: 77-100.

[55] Budd K S, Holdsworth M J (1996) Issues in Clinical Assessment of Minimal Parenting Competence. J. of clinical child psychology. 25: 2-14.

[56] Schmidt F, Cuttress L J, Lang J, Lewandowski M J, Rawana J S (2007) Assessing the Parent-Child Relationship in Parenting Capacity Evaluations: Clinical Applications of Attachment Research. Fam. court r. 45: 247-259.

[57] Steinhauer P, Leitenberger M, Manglicas E, Pauker J, Smith R, Gonçalves L (1993) Guide d'evaluation de la compétence parentale.Toronto: L'Institut pour la Prévention de l'enfance maltraitée.

[58] White A (2005) Assessment of Parenting Capacity: Literature Review. Ashfield: NSW Department of Community Services: Centre for Parenting & Research.

[59] Masson O (august 2005). Les Compétences Parentales ne sont Déterminées ni par les Liens Biologiques, ni par le Sexe. 4è Congrès Mondial de Psychothérapie. Buenos Aires, Argentine.

[60] American Psychological Association (1998). Committee on Professional Practice and Standard. Available:http://www.apa.org/about/governance/bdcmte/standards.aspx. Accessed 2012 April 29.

[61] Budd K S (2001) Assessing Parenting Competence in Child Protection Cases:A Clinical Practice Model. Clinical child and fam. psychology r. 4: 1-18.

[62] Budd K S (2005) Assessing Parenting Capacity in a Child Welfare Context. Children and youth services r. 27: 429-444.

[63] Steinheuer P D (1993) Assessing Parenting Capacity Manual Guidelines. Institute for the Prevention of Child Abuse.

[64] De Rancourt L, Paquette F, Paquette D, Rainville S (2006) Guide d'Évaluation des Capacités Parentales : Adaptation du Guide de Steinhauer : 0 à 5 ans (3éd.). Centre jeunesse de Montréal – Institut universitaire : Montréal.

[65] Haynes J P (2010) Parenting Assessment in Abuse, Neglect, and Permanent Wardship Cases. In: Benedeck E P, & al, editors. Principles and Practice of Child and Adolescent Forensic Mental Health. Washington, D. C.: American Psychiatric Publishing, Inc. pp. 157-170.

[66] Jacobsen T, Miller L J, Kirkwood K P (1997) Assessing Parental Competency in Individuals with Severe Mental Illness, A Comprehensive Service. The j. of mental health administration. 24: 189–199.

[67] Budd K S, Poindexter L M, Felix E D, Naik-Polan A T (2001) Clinical Assessment of Parents in Child Protection Cases: An Empirical Analysis. Law and human behavior.25:93–108.

[68] Harnett P H (2007) A Procedure for Assessing Parents' Capacity for Change in Child Protection Cases. Children and youth services r. 29: 1179-1188.

[69] Fablet D (1999) Accompagner les changements d'identité professionnelle. In : Blanchard-Laville C, Fablet D, editors. Développer l'analyse des pratiques professionnelles dans le champ des pratiques socio-éducatives. Paris: L'Harmattan. pp. 163-182.

[70] Cyr C, Poulin C, Losier V, Michel G, Paquette D (2012, in revision). L'évaluation des capacités parentales au CJM-IU : Un Protocole d'Évaluation et d'Intervention Fondé sur la Théorie de l'Attachement. R. de psychoéducation.

[71] Cyr C, Lopez L, Moss E, Paquette D (march 2011). Promoting Quality of Interactive Behavior in Maltreated Child-Parent Dyads: The Efficacy of an Attachment-based Intervention. Poster presented at the society for research in child development. Montreal, QC.

[72] Losier V, Cyr C, Dumais M, Lemaire J, Paquette D (march 2012) L'évaluation des Capacités de Changement des Parents : Perception des Intervenants (tes) de la Clinique Externe Spécialisée du Centre Jeunesse de Montréal. Affiche présentée à la société québécoise de recherche pour la psychologie. Montréal, QC.

Chapter 5

Human Trafficking of Young Women and Girls for Sexual Exploitation in South Africa

Thozama Mandisa Lutya

Additional information is available at the end of the chapter

http://dx.doi.org/10.5772/39202

1. Introduction

Young South African women and girls are trafficked internally (within South African borders) and externally (outside the borders of South Africa) for the purposes of sexual exploitation and other purposes, such as domestic labour, for criminal activities, as well as organ transplants.

External trafficking has occurred in this country since colonial times. Molo Songololo (2005), a children's rights organisation, reports that between 1726 and 1834, as many as 36 169 slaves were brought from Indonesia, Java, Ceylon, India, the East Indies, Mauritius, Malaysia and other countries to South Africa to work in mines, and as domestic workers. This was a practice instituted by the colonial authorities to boost the southern African economy by importing cheap labour. Three infamous examples typify the beginning of the trade in human beings internally and externally (Martens, 2003; Martens, Pieczkowski & Van-Vuuren-Smyth, 2003). One known notorious incident was the recruitment, with promises of economic prosperity and educational advancement, of Saartje Baartman, who was transported from the Cape Colony and exploited by European citizens in England and France (Martens et.al, 2003). The promises made to her in her country of origin were not fulfilled – instead, her naked live body was displayed as an object of attraction for everybody to view. She eventually died in France, where her private parts were put on display in a museum. Another, less well-known, example involved European girls who were trafficked into the Cape Colony for the purposes of involuntary prostitution to meet the demand of men for prostitutes (Molo Songololo, 2005). More recently, Mozambican children were trafficked into South Africa to be kept as concubines in the Carletonville mines (Martens, 2003; Martens et.al 2003).

In the last two decades, increasingly, reports of human trafficking for sexual exploitation have surfaced in the print and visual media, fuelled by the South African Police Service

(SAPS) raids on brothels. One incident that made headlines in 1998 was human trafficking for sexual exploitation of Asian women, whose dead bodies were found on a railway track by the SAPS. These Asian women were brought into the country under false pretences – they were told they would be working in high-end restaurants where they could mingle with and marry rich men. When they arrived in South Africa, they became entangled in debt bondage and their passports were taken from them (Reuters, 1998). Since then, academic institutions and civil organisations have increasingly been reporting on the subject of internal and external human trafficking for sexual exploitation. Furthermore, government and non-governmental organisations (NGOs) are raising awareness on the topic, educating South African citizens about this form of crime.

Internal trafficking also has historical origins dating back to the late nineteenth and early twentieth century. At the turn of the century, a criminal leader called Nongoloza Mathebula (1867-1948) and his gang abducted and kidnapped women and boys from neighbouring areas to the mine compounds and kept them as sex slaves in the wake of the discovery of sexually transmitted diseases among prostitutes selling their bodies to mine workers (Van Onselen, 1998).

When the political struggle was at its highest (during the 1980s until 1990) and into the early 1990s, 'jack-rollers' kidnapped and abducted young women and girls who appeared to be superior and were less appealing to men from lower socio-economic backgrounds. The targeted victims led quiet lives and had been seriously pursuing educational goals. They were also physically attractive. The jack-rollers would confine them in secluded residences where the victims were repeatedly raped and physically assaulted (Mokwena, 1991). These practices were not considered human trafficking at the time. However, South Africa has defined these practices as criminal since becoming a signatory to United Nations Human Rights-oriented legislation. Such practices are now classified as trafficking for sexual exploitation in Part 6 Section 71 (1-2) b of the Criminal Law (Sexual Offences and Related Matters Act, Act (32 of 2007), as amended.

Internal trafficking is the most commonly reported form of human trafficking in South Africa. Human trafficking research reports produced in this country have revealed evidence of children being trafficked from poor socio-economic areas such as rural areas and farms in the Eastern Cape and KwaZulu-Natal to developed parts of the country, such as urban areas in the Western Cape and Gauteng (Bermudez, 2008; Molo Songololo, 2005). Another research report has identified case studies of teenagers recruited and transported under false pretences to work as prostitutes in hidden brothels across South Africa (Unicef, 2003; UNODC, 2007). In between these research reports, newspapers, television documentaries, workshops, seminars and conferences have provided evidence of the prevalence of internal trafficking. A criminal investigator aligned with the Organised Crime Unit of the SAPS in Port Elizabeth has also exposed organised Nigerian syndicates trafficking children from city centres to city centres across South Africa (Van der Watt, 2009). Furthermore, children as young as ten are being kidnapped and abducted by organised criminal gangs who first feed them drugs in preparation for work as prostitutes (Chetty, 2009; Molo Songololo, 2005;

UNODC, 2007). Some of the members of these syndicates were filmed by a crew of the local television programme Special Assignment while the syndicates were trafficking children from Durban to Bloemfontein and Johannesburg in 2004. Some of these criminals have since been caught by the SAPS. The conditions within which the trafficked children were held was described by one of the investigators as 'deplorable, not fit for a pig and downright shameful' (UNODC, 2007).

Although human trafficking occurs for other purposes in this country, sexual exploitation is the most frequently reported reason. Human trafficking for sexual exploitation occurs within a context of high levels of contact crimes (interpersonal violent crimes occurring between persons who are known to each other). As illustrated in Figure 1 below, for the period from 2009 to 2010, the SAPS recorded approximately 2.1 million criminal cases: 31.9% of these cases were contact crimes (Sigsworth, 2008).

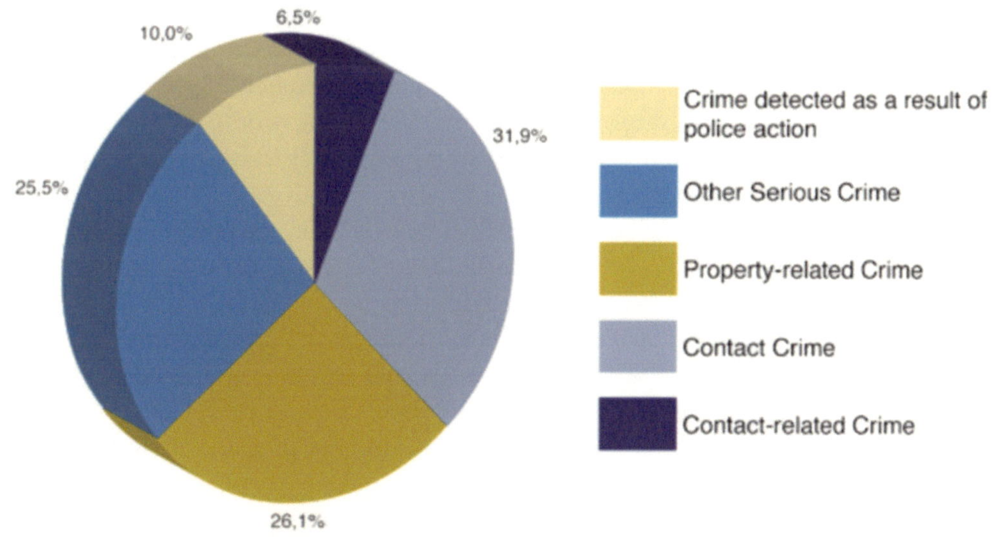

Figure 1. Crime figures for 2009/2010 ([70])

Of these contact crimes, sexual violence comprised of 10.1% (see Figure 2, below). Although the details have not been released for the period 2009/2010, in the period 2008/2009, prostitution and other sexually exploitative acts accounted for 15.3% of the total number of sexual offence cases.

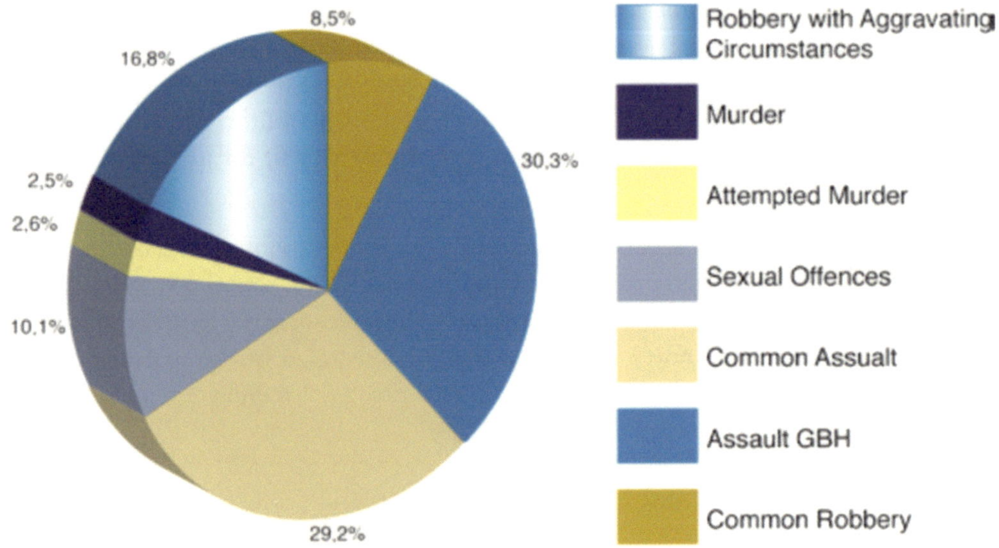

Figure 2. Contact crimes for 2009/2010 (70)

Despite high levels of contact crimes, especially sexual violence against women and children, the South African criminal justice system has been ineffective in its approach to sexually violent crimes affecting women and girls. Only approximately 5% of reported and prosecuted sexual violence cases receive a custodial sentence (Sigsworth, 2008). Regardless of the large amount of research and scholarly work on human trafficking, there is currently still no specific law to prosecute the crime in the country – South Africa literally does not have a crime called human trafficking. Parts of existing legislation are used to prosecute to human trafficking activities (SALRC, 2008; Stuurman, 2009). However, there are some sections from the Criminal Law (Sexual Offences and Related Matters) Amendment Act (32 of 2007) and the Children's Act (Act 38 of 2005) reserved only for the sexual exploitation of trafficked women and children. Part six of the Criminal Law (Sexual Offences and Related Matters) Amendment Act (32 of 2007) is reserved to prosecute trafficking in persons for sexual purposes. Chapter 18 of the Children's Act 38 of 2005 is reserved to prosecute trafficking in children.

South Africa is a hotbed for human trafficking for a variety of other state-related factors. It is a source, transit and destination country for human trafficking (Le Roux, 2009b; SALRC, 2008; Stuurman, 2009; UNICEF, 2003). It is reputed among neighbouring countries to be economically advanced and therefore may be seen as potentially offering golden opportunities to poor immigrants. Since South Africa opened its borders to foreign citizens from neighbouring countries such as Zimbabwe, Lesotho, Mozambique and Namibia in 1994, a large number of documented and undocumented immigrants have entered the country as refugees, asylum seekers and tourists (Irish, 2005). On arrival in South Africa, many of these immigrants experienced xenophobia from the local population, which creates feelings of insecurity and fear. They have been accused of stealing jobs from South African citizens, for example. As a result, some had their possessions stolen or burned by South African citizens. The insecurity felt by refugee women and girls on arrival in South Africa (Chetty, 2009; Minnaar, 2009, Mutongwizo, 2009; Palmary, 2005; Prince, 2009) aggravates the problem. They tend to rely on fellow citizens for economic opportunities instead of assimilating into and seeking help from South African citizens (Malapa, 2008). However, fellow citizens do not always provide legitimate economic opportunities. There is some evidence that some immigrants recruit fellow nationals for prostitution (Martens, 2003; O'Connor, 2009; SALRC, 2004).

1.1. Aim of the book chapter

In this chapter, the problem statement relating to human trafficking is addressed. Concepts such as 'human trafficking', 'sexual exploitation', 'child trafficking' and 'girl' are defined. A distinction is made between voluntary and involuntary prostitution. A theoretical framework to elucidate the vulnerability of young women and girls to human trafficking is also provided, particularly within the socio-economic and socio-cultural context within which human trafficking in South Africa occurs. South African responses to human trafficking are identified, taking into account the fact that the relevant legislation has not yet been passed into law, because certain social and legal politics are preventing the rapid processing of this law. A strategy or policy that could effectively reduce the human trafficking of young women and girls for sexual exploitation in South Africa is proposed.

2. Problem statement

The purpose of writing this chapter is to illustrate the plight of victims of human trafficking for involuntary prostitution. Given this plight, it is important to research and write about human trafficking for sexual exploitation over other forms of human trafficking. Matters of particular concern are the age of victims of human trafficking for sexual exploitation, the increasing numbers of sex trafficking victims, socio-cultural factors contributing to the crime, the context within which human trafficking for involuntary prostitution occurs, the limited South African responses to human trafficking, as well as the politics of legal reform hindering the promulgation of the Prevention and Combating of Trafficking in Persons Bill.

Human traffickers recruit, kidnap and abduct young girls between the ages of 11 and 17 (Dyantyi & Pritz, 2009; Muller & Holley, 2009; UNICEF, 2003; Van der Watt, 2009). When these girls encounter human traffickers who make lucrative offers, or promise them economic prosperity, or when these girls are kidnapped and abducted, they are usually alone, without a capable guardian (Lutya, 2010b). The traffickers target this age bracket because of a client preference for younger girls – such clients believe that younger girls are compliant and docile, and therefore more likely to comply with their sexual demands (Bernat & Zhilina, 2010; Bernant & Winkeler, 2010; UNICEF 2003). In addition, the increasing number of HIV/Aids infections has popularized the socio-cultural myth of the virgin cure: some HIV/Aids infected men believe that sexual intercourse with a virgin will cure them of the disease (Dyantyi & Pritz, 2009; Fitzgibbon, 2003; Gould, 2008). The United Nations estimates that 79% of all trafficked victims are moved for the purposes of sexual exploitation (Tshwane Alliance for Street Children, 2009; Tyakume, 2009). Most of these victims are recruited, abducted or kidnapped from socio-economically deprived areas and are then moved to economically developed parts of the country (Bermudez, 2008; Bernat & Zhilina, 2010; Bernat & Winkeler, 2010; Molo Songololo, 2005).

Currently, South Africa does not have the means to distinguish between voluntary and involuntary prostitution. Public hearings are still being conducted by the South African Law Reform Commission to debate a suitable approach to prostitution. The country will have to decide whether to legalize or regulate, continue to criminalize or abolish prostitution.

If they cannot be rescued by the police or are not reported missing by family members, victims of sex trafficking cannot be identified easily (SALRC, 2008). They are often assumed to be just another group of morally depraved girls searching for 'easy money' (Bernat & Zhilina, 2010; Bernat & Winkeler, 2010). During the transportation process, if they are questioned by the authorities, human traffickers falsely identify victims as relatives (Bernat & Zhilina, 2010; Bernat & Winkeler, 2010). Even though they could be offered help by strangers, victims of sexual exploitation find it difficult to just leave their captors. They are consistently threatened with violence or may have been physically assaulted by human traffickers (Delport, Koen & MacKay, 2007; UNICEF, 2003; Van der Watt, 2009).

Although South Africa has made significant progress with regard to the prevention, protection, prosecution and partnerships to respond to human trafficking, there are still a number of ambiguities and gaps in the knowledge of human trafficking in South Africa. Furthermore, the politics of legal reform are hindering the promulgation of the Prevention and Combating of Trafficking in Persons Bill.

3. Definition of concepts

3.1. Human trafficking

The Prevention and Combating of Trafficking in Persons Bill (2009) defines human trafficking to include the recruitment, sale, supply, procurement, transportation, transfer, harbouring, disposal, or receipt of persons or the adoption of a child facilitated or secured through legal or illegal means within and across the borders of the Republic by means of threat, force, intimidation or other forms of coercion, abduction, kidnapping, fraud, deception, debt bondage, abuse of power, or the giving or receiving of payment in order to achieve the consent of the other or by abusing vulnerability for the purpose of exploitation.

There is, however, still some confusion with regard to the definition of human trafficking. Ambiguity arises from the inclusion of the word 'exploitation', with little explanation or an inadequate explanation of what constitutes 'exploitation' (Gould & Fick, 2008). Consequently, it is easy to include any exploitative situation under the umbrella of human trafficking. The broadness of the definition of exploitation could mean that a common sense interpretation of exploitation is used to describe a human trafficking situation (Gould &

Fick, 2009). For instance, a holiday visit of a child which turns into exploitation could be seen as human trafficking, instead of as a vulnerable situation that could lead to human trafficking if the child was to be removed under false pretences. Human trafficking has not yet occurred. The child has not yet been recruited, transferred, harboured, deceived or intentionally bought for exploitation, even when the child has been abused sexually, physically and emotionally by the relatives. The act of victimising the child becomes a spontaneous act during the period of stay at the relatives' home, but cannot be prosecuted as trafficking.

3.2. Sexual exploitation

According to the Prevention and Combating of Trafficking in Person Bill (2010), sexual exploitation implies the commission of any sexual offences against the victim of human trafficking. Literally, sexual exploitation implies the act of misusing or mistreating another person through sex. The various ways in which a person could be misused through sex are forced marriage, sex work, forced pregnancy for the purpose of selling the child, as well as personal gratification. Forced marriage and personal gratification are acts that occur within private homes, and that are often perpetrated towards young women and girls who have not been recruited, transported, sold, supplied, procured through deceit, fraud or debt bondage – the essential components of the South African definition of human trafficking. It seems that a clear distinction between a human trafficking victim and a child who has been forced into a marriage is lacking, as well as between a human trafficking victim and a young woman or a girl who is sexually exploited by a member of her family.

There needs to be legal and social criteria that can be used by social services and criminal justice authorities to identify victims of human trafficking. Currently, the Prevention and Combating of Trafficking in Persons Bill does not provide clear guidelines pertaining to the victims of human trafficking. Sections 11 and 12 refer to professionals that could assist in the identification, referral and reporting of a victim of trafficking, but these sections fail to describe the characteristics of the victim. A list of factors have been presented by SALRC (2008) describing the circumstances within which a victim could be experiencing when encountered by professionals. It might be best if the Bill requires that all these factors should be present at the time of identification, namely sexual violence, confinement, forcing drugs on the victim, threats by family members, and mental as well as sexual health related problems, to name just a few. However, these factors could be present in a person who has not been trafficked. Legally speaking, to be defined as a victim of human trafficking a person should have experienced crimes vital in the definition of human trafficking, at least social dislocation, and should be unfamiliar with the environment within which she was or is confined.

3.3. Child trafficking

According to section 1 of the Children's Act (Act 38 of 2005) child trafficking for sexual exploitation means the recruitment, transportation, receipt, harbouring, and transfer of children through deceit, fraud, abduction and kidnapping for the purpose of sexual exploitation due to a position of vulnerability. In relation to children, section 1 of the Children's Act (Act 38 of 2005) states that commercial sexual exploitation implies the procurement of a child to perform sexual activities for financial or other rewards including acts of prostitution or pornography, irrespective of the person using or receiving the reward.

3.4. Girl

According to the South African Constitution (108 of 1996), a girl is any female person, daughter, or young woman under the age of 18. This person may still be residing with her parents, in a hostel or heading a household. Girls as young as seven are abducted, kidnapped or misled by traffickers to accept offers that promise to yield financial incentives. A set of gendered factors place girls in more vulnerable situations for abduction and kidnapping by human traffickers for sexual exploitation. Firstly, young girls are perceived as disease-free and therefore possess the potential to attract more customers/clients/users than older women. The International Labour Organization reports that the high incidence of HIV/Aids infections among young women has propelled users of sex workers to select girls' more than young women. This preference has led to many young South African girls' being recruited, abducted and kidnapped for sexual exploitation (Lutya, 2010a). Some girls have been abducted and kidnapped on their way to school, running an errand for their parents or venturing outside with friends (Lutya, 2010a). Secondly, the desire to own the latest labels and technological gadgets pushes some girls into pursuing their materialistic hopes. If they are offered a job, such girls may accept the job with little or no scrutiny in the hope of generating an income in order to reach this materialistic goal (Lutya, 2010a). It is possible that the need to achieve the patriarchally approved gendered notion of femininity, defined by aesthetics – fancy clothes, make-up, groomed hair and nails – as well as the desire to fit in and receive external confirmation (Russell & Tyler, 2002) may drive some girls to accept dubious jobs from traffickers. Gender and consumption could be ways in which some girls define who they are in relation to boys and society: that means they become feminine through consumer culture, a behaviour society expects of young women and girls (Russell & Tyler, 2002). In essence, any person under the age of 18 is vulnerable to human trafficking in three ways: legally (if the person is financially inadequately equipped to reside independently and in pursuit of financial independence), socially (if the person is in need of social affirmation) and individually (if the person hopes to obtain affirmation of her physical aesthetic attributes).

3.5. Difference between voluntary and involuntary prostitution

A prostitute is working on a voluntary basis if her decision to perform sex work has not been influenced, forced on her or coerced by anyone. She is working as a prostitute involuntarily if another person has forced, confined and manipulated her to work as a prostitute. In this paper, the term 'voluntary prostitution' pertains to any work that is performed by a prostitute, either indoors or outdoors, where the prostitute obtains the money from the customer for her own gain. By contrast, involuntary prostitution refers to any sex work that is performed indoors or outdoors where the prostitute works under the supervision and monitoring of another person. The money obtained from selling sex is taken by the monitor or supervisor (pimp). The difference between these two concepts is that a voluntary prostitute exercises agency by deciding on the job, area and type of client to serve, whilst an involuntary prostitute is forced to do the work in a chosen area and to serve clients preferred by the supervisor or monitor.

4. Theoretical framework

There are three theoretical attributes which can be used to explain human trafficking for the sexual exploitation of young women and girls in South Africa: victim vulnerability, victim precipitation, as well as the victim-criminal relationship (Daems, 2005; Nettlebeck, Wilson, Potter & Perry, 2000). These attributes should be present and stabilise in a victim's life for a long time (Nettlebeck et.al 2000). Victim vulnerability pertains to the presence of factors, contextual and situational, in a victim's life that could make the victim more vulnerable to victimisation (Clark, 2005). It could be the victim's lifestyle; personal characteristics or the amount of time the victim spends or interacts with the offender (UNICEF, 2003; UNODC, 2007). Secondly, a victim's words, actions and behaviour may precipitate the offender's actively and passively victimising her (UNODC, 2007). In the context of human trafficking for sexual exploitation victim precipitation thus occurs when the victim accepts recruitment, travels with a chaperone and allows herself to be transported with or without the documentation required by immigration officials. In addition, the lack of a reasonable solution to socio-economic challenges facing her, the potential victim may seek help from traffickers. Eventually, the time spent by the victim in the company of human traffickers may provide traffickers with opportunities for the victimisation of girls.

Victim vulnerability is best explained when a person is surrounded by factors that could result in victimisation. It is attributed to a variety of internal and external factors that are multidimensional, such as their age and lack of maturity, which affects young women and girls more than adults, whilst socio-economic factors create potential victimisation for both children and adults (Clark, 2005). Many young South African women and girls spend a significant amount of free time in entertainment establishments that sell liquor (shebeens, nightclubs and bars), abusing intoxicating substances such as drugs and alcohol, engaging in risky sexual behaviour, as well as participating in criminal activities (Gould, 2005; Gould & Fick, 2008). These lifestyles place them within close proximity to human traffickers. Closeness to human traffickers of potential victims may not result in actual victimisation: some young girls do not accept offers from strangers. The contextual situation within which girls entertain themselves, coupled with their immaturity and the absence of a capable guardian, may make it easier for traffickers to recruit them successfully. Eccentric behaviours by a potential victim do not necessarily create vulnerability to victimisation, but poor control of feelings, inadequate social skills and confrontational responses to problematic situations may increase vulnerability to victimisation (Nettlebeck et al 2000).

Regardless of personal characteristics, a victim's lifestyle and the amount of time some young women and girls spend with human traffickers, the contextual and situational factors surrounding victims make them vulnerable to human trafficking for sexual exploitation. The factors that drive most young women and girls to shebeens and bars, and into crime and promiscuity (such as unfavourable home and family conditions, including a lack of parental supervision and monitoring, inter-parental violence, sibling violence and parental use of intoxicating substances) combined with socio-economic challenges exacerbate the vulnerability of young women and girls to human traffickers (Clark, 2005; Lutya, 2010b; Lutya, 2007). When these factors are stronger in a child's life, careful scrutiny of an offered job may not feature in the young woman or girl's mind.

Although victims of human trafficking are often caught by surprise at the turn of events at the places of destination, the acceptance of a job provided through illegal means of which some young women and girls may be unaware can be regarded as victim precipitation. Victim precipitation refers to a person's willingness to move to another destination with the recruiter or chaperone. At times, victims may initiate the act, or agree to its occurrence, or may be joined by the perpetrator, which makes them accomplices in the perpetration of their victimisation (Muftic, Bouffard & Bouffard, 2007). By asking for help from human traffickers, the victim precipitates the occurrence of the crime. However, the victim may not be aware of the consequences of her actions, because the negative consequences of accepting or asking for help from human traffickers may be hidden, and she may fail to recognise a legal or conventional solution to her contextual and situational problems. In this regard, this chapter does not apportion blame, find fault or assign guilt to human trafficking victims, but attempts to illustrate some of the ways in which the contextual and situational factors surrounding victims could facilitate victimisation (Muftic, Bouffard & Bouffard 2007).

Prior to accepting jobs from human traffickers, victims are often confronted with socio-economic and individual challenges such as unemployment and poverty, domestic violence, a lack of knowledge of the crime, stereotyped perceptions of prostitutes, as well as socio-cultural factors hindering access to opportunities for economic advancement. Faced with such factors, they may accept (non-existent) opportunities that they believe could rescue them from this context. In turn, they are opening up chances for sexual exploitation. Moreover, human traffickers can be people that the victims trust, such as a close associate, family member, an employment agent or a neighbour (Lutya, 2009; O'Connor, 2009 & Prince, 2009). The relationship shared by the victim and the perpetrator, as well as the image presented by the employment agent may not be suspicious enough to encourage the potential victim to scrutinise the person's motives.

There is sometimes a relationship between a human trafficker and the victim, enabling them to interact, communicate and associate on a regular basis (UNODC, 2007). During this process, both parties play roles that define the existence of this relationship (UNODC, 2007). The victim may either actively or passively precipitate, provoke or instigate the formulation of this relationship, but is victimised in return (Molo Songololo, 2005 & Tyakume, 2009). An association between a human trafficker and a victim cannot always be construed as inappropriate, due to the quality of a relationship between the human trafficker and the victim. As stated above, human traffickers can range from close associates to strangers and apparently legitimate employment institutions. Therefore, the victimisation of a young woman or girl in the process should not be blamed on the victim. Blaming the victim implies that the victimised young woman or girl behaved outside social norms by associating with a relative, friend, neighbour or seeking the services of employment agencies (Tyakume, 2009).

Vulnerability, a persistent search for better opportunities and interaction with persons that might turn out to be traffickers feature strongly in the lives of many young South African women and girls. However, given their biological and socio-economic vulnerability (Molo Songololo, 2005 & Tyakume, 2009), there is little victims can do to avoid association with the human traffickers. They may lack the ability or have only limited ability to change the disadvantaged positions that place them closer to human traffickers (Molo Songololo, 2005 & Tyakume, 2009), and they could reside in areas characterised by a disregard for law and order (Clark, 2005), where residents are likely to resort to violent means of resolving conflict and achieving their goals. Constantly battling to define themselves in socially acceptable ways, to rid themselves of socio-economic weakness, vulnerability and susceptibility to victimisation, they could precipitate victimisation and associate with persons that increase their chances of becoming victims. Other young women and girls in similar situations may not feel pressured to seek assistance from human traffickers, but may resort to ill-paid jobs to make ends meet. The personality characteristics of potential victims may therefore determine whether vulnerability will lead to actual victimisation.

5. Why is human trafficking associated with vulnerability?

The position of disadvantaged young South African women and girls places them in locations that are easily accessible to human traffickers. They come across human traffickers, wondering, bewildered and struggling with challenges that define them as passive victims (Bernat & Zhilina, 2010). They are often deprived of basic necessities such as food, shelter and medical care (Bernat & Winkeler, 2010). Because of the lack of these resources they feel less valuable as human beings, to such an extent that any person who either pays any attention to them to reduce their plight or promises to provide for them financially is welcome, regardless of the negative intentions of this person (Bernat & Zhilina, 2010). Ordinarily, being female is often equated with victimhood: societies often perceive young women and girls to be in need of rescue, or protection in order to remain in a pure state of femininity (Hargreaves, Vetten, Scheineder, Malepe & Fullere, 2006). Accepting and seeking assistance from a human trafficker is not an unusual move for a young woman or girl. It is a way of seeking incentives that will make her feel less unworthy, economically deprived, depressed, anxious and stressed – psychological variables that hamper a young woman's or girl's personal development (Hargreaves, 2006). Her goal is to move away from positions of deprivation that make her feel inferior, persistently undermined and unworthy (Hargreaves, 2006). In South Africa, child prostitutes, children heading households, girls who have been dislocated, are addicted to drugs and/or affiliated to gangs, as well as displaced and dislocated women and children consistently seek to meet people who might rescue them from such situations of victimhood and vulnerability to positions associated with conventional social acceptability.

It is estimated that about 30 000 South African children work as prostitutes and that 247 000 are in exploitative labour-related situations (Delport et al 2007). The number of child-headed households is growing, as South African parents die from illnesses related to their HIV/Aids status, and other terminal illnesses. There were 148 000 child-headed households in South Africa in 2007 – that translates to 0.8% of the 18 292 000 children between 0 and 17 years in this country (Children's Institute, 2009). Most of these children live in poor provinces (Children's Institute, 2009), which are commonly targeted by human traffickers for recruitment into sexual exploitation, such as the Eastern Cape, Mpumalanga, KwaZulu-Natal and the Limpopo Province (Bermudez, 2008 & UNICEF, 2003). About one in ten school learners use some form of intoxicating substance. A high number of these learners have been offered drugs in classrooms and playgrounds during schooling hours (Burton, 2008).

South African girls between 13 and 18 are involved in gangs independently of boys and some courier narcotics for male drug dealers (Govender, 2008 & Naidoo, 2008). Male gang members have been known to kidnap young girls, feed them with 'Tik' (methamphetamine), and, once they are addicted, force them to work as sex workers to pay back the drug money (Naidoo, 2008). If they are not couriering drugs for male drug dealers (Naidoo, 2007), some young women and girls are used to recruit other girls into child trafficking rings for work as prostitutes (Parker, 2008). In the absence of parental supervision and monitoring, this behaviour could lead to human trafficking for sexual exploitation.

Displaced and dislocated young women and girls are another group of females that are vulnerable to human trafficking for sexual exploitation. Street children, refugees, children used by adults to commit crimes, as well as children in gangs, can easily be recruited clandestinely into human trafficking for sexual exploitation. Because of their need for sympathy, shelter, food and a sense of belonging, displaced and dislocated children could accept offers presented by human traffickers without verifying the details of the alleged job (Bolowana, 2004; Parker, 2008 & Van der Watt, 2009). In South Africa, due to the growing demand for sex with children, dislocated and displaced children are easily accessible and visible (Bolowana, 2004). The Tshwane Alliance for Street Children (2009) reports that about 10 000 children live on the streets of South Africa. In Tshwane (Pretoria) alone, it is estimated that 3 500 children live on the streets.

Refugee women and girls experience gender-specific victimisation that could result in their accepting offers from human traffickers. Whilst they are trying to re-invent coping mechanisms in the countries of exile (Wambugu, 2003), they risk being forced into marital unions with older men, as well as discrimination from the citizens of their adopted countries (Palmary, 2005). In some instances, families have forced war-raped female relatives to marry their rapists to avoid the shame that they believe war rape would bring to the family

(Palmary, 2005). Rather than to marry their rapists, a number of these women have turned to prostitution to try to counter the trauma of rape and family rejection.

In addition, the xenophobic treatment experienced by legal and illegal immigrants in South Africa make foreign women and children more vulnerable to human trafficking, despite family and community rejection. Often accused of taking away jobs from the locals, intermittently, they have their houses destroyed and property stolen in retaliation for others' economic deprivation. In this context, it might seem like a better choice to accept an offer from a fellow national than from a South African citizen, regardless of the negative repercussions the offer might bring.

Owing to these personal characteristics and situational circumstances of young South African women and girls, and of refugees and immigrants in South Africa, analysing their situations becomes a matter of the utmost importance. Although other types of human trafficking have been identified to occur within South African borders, 90% of the young women assisted between the ages of (12-24) have been trafficked for sexual exploitation (Le Roux, 2009a; Le Roux, 2009b). The employment commitments of South African parents are such that some spend considerable amounts of time travelling to and from work, thus leaving little time to supervise and monitor their daughters closely (Le Roux, 2009b). The increasing number of households headed by children with limited or no financial resources to provide for their younger siblings puts pressure on these children that could see the children who are heading such households accepting offers which turn out to be sexually exploitative.

6. Contextualising human trafficking

Socio-economic factors, a lack of parental supervision and monitoring, exposure to violence, households headed by children and a lack of a legal position on prostitution compound the problem of human trafficking of young South African women and girls for sexual exploitation. The experience of financial deprivation coupled with home and family circumstances, as well as limited knowledge pertaining to child-rearing drive some young women and girls into traffickers' nets. With no consistent legal position on prostitution, getting out of the victimisation process can be difficult.

6.1. Socio-economic factors

Although unemployment decreased from 30% in 2007 to 19% in 2008 (Statistics South Africa, 2009), women and young girls are still the worst hit by unemployment in South Africa. The Children's Institute (2009) reports that 75% of black children, 43% of coloured children and 4.9% of white children live in households generating an income below R350.00 a month: 67% of these children are female and 69% are between the ages of 12 and 17 years. Furthermore, 38% of South African children live in households with an unemployed adult. However, the employment and unemployment of parents may not necessarily translate to the avoidance or non-avoidance of victimisation from human trafficking. A parent should be present in a child's life, monitoring and supervising his or her movements. An average South African parent, especially among the poor, spends approximately eight hours at work and four hours travelling to and from work (Statistics South Africa, 2009).

6.2. Lack of parental supervision and monitoring

In most instances working and travelling parents leave behind unsupervised and unmonitored children. When they are left to their own devices, with no authority figure to control unruly behaviour, some children are likely to visit areas that could bring them closer to human traffickers. On hearing of their children's misbehaviour during their absence, some parents may use corporal punishment to discipline their children (Dawes, Kropiwnicki, Kafaar & Richter, 2005 & Le Roux, 2010b). This may not be a helpful response to children's problematic behaviour, but some parents may select this response because work challenges, financial shortfalls, as well as fatigue from travelling, are likely to bring about stress and frustration which could make some parents impatient with ill-disciplined children (Dawes et al., 2008). However, a lack of parent-child interaction and corporal punishment may drive some children to play truant or to run away from home (Le Roux, 2010b).

6.3. A culture of violence

Violence in South Africa is a widespread and increasingly common phenomenon: the belief in the use of violence to solve problems is pervasive, embedded and entrenched in traditional norms and values (Bruce, Dissel & Menziwa, 2007; CSVR, 2008 & Hargreaves et al, 2006). A recent survey has revealed that children who have witnessed violence at home – family members punching, kicking, beating, slapping and attacking another with a weapon –and community violence, as well as interaction with negative peers and use of substances, have a greater chance of being victims of school violence (Leoschut, 2008). The implication is that multiple victimisations are experienced by children in direct contact with violent neighbourhoods, peers and families.

Although criminologists predict that black males between 16 and 24 are more likely to become victims and perpetrators of violent crime, in South Africa, women and children are the most likely to become victims of violent crime (Mistry, Snyman & Van Zyl, 2001)). There were 197 284 reported cases of domestic violence between 2009 and 2010, the highest numbers coming from the industrialised areas, such as Gauteng and the Western Cape and the poor provinces, namely the Eastern Cape and KwaZulu-Natal (UNODC, 2007). The Teddy Bear Clinic and Childline report that in Gauteng alone, 1 200 children were raped in 2008 (Mashaba, 2009). In 1999, every day, four women died at the hands of their intimate partners in South Africa: 50% were killed by cohabiting partners, boyfriends murdered 30% of these women, and husbands were responsible for 18.4% of all female homicide cases (Mathews et al., 2004). Only 9% of gender-based violence cases – violence towards strangers as well as intimate partners – receive a conviction in South Africa (Sigsworth, 2008). In most instances, victims may drop the case before the end of the trial.

With human trafficking occurring in a clandestine and hidden manner, within similar power-related contexts between the victim and the offender, it becomes difficult to identify victims and report cases of human trafficking. The normalisation of violence, criminal justice approaches to gender-based cases, as well the secretiveness with which human trafficking occurs, makes it possible for human trafficking to thrive.

There is a link between human trafficking for sexual exploitation, poverty, gender violence and inequality in South Africa (Tyakume, 2009). It is common in South African families which experience deprivation, unemployment and poverty for girl children to be the first to be sent away, either to live with relatives, to marry older men or to be sold in exchange for cash (Delport et al., 2007). Some of the cases of human trafficking for sexual exploitation involve parents' directly selling their children to human traffickers (Richter, 2009). In this regard, foreign nationals have been known to recruit female relatives from East and West African countries, and upon their arrival in South Africa, force them into prostitution for economic survival (Richter, 2009). As these practices are widespread, it appears that they could be morally accepted as forms of economic survival (Tyakume, 2009).

6.4. Child-headed households

Although a significant number of South African adolescents attend school (Children's Institute, 2009), parental unemployment, the HIV/Aids-related deaths of parents, early marriages and exposure to inter-parental violence at home result in limited chances for educational and economic advancement for some adolescents. When parents die, some parents leave behind adolescent girls to raise the younger children. Children who are heading households are often left with no resources to care adequately for their siblings. The need for resources might lead some young girls to child prostitution, which places them at risk of being coerced, kidnapped, abducted or deceptively recruited by human traffickers. Furthermore, the opportunities for relocation to economically developed South African provinces and abroad are not easily accessible to young women and adolescents. Very few young women have money for visas, plane tickets and start-up funds, or the skills required to get a job in the country of destination (Delport et al., 2007). If such opportunities are offered to them, they may accept a 'job' with no verification of the information offered to them.

6.5. Lack of a legal position on prostitution

The lack of a definite legal position on the act of prostitution creates confusion with regards to the acceptability of this activity. According to the Sexual Offences Act (Act 23 of 1957), prostitution, running a brothel, forcing a person to work as a prostitute and earning an income from prostitution are criminal activities. Nevertheless, it is possible for SAPS officers not to arrest prostitutes on the streets, but to intimidate them, interrogate them and allow them to carry on with night activities (Fick, 2007). The brothels that are raided might be closed down temporarily and then maybe allowed to carry on with their operations once the police leave the premises (Gould & Fick, 2008). Furthermore, the publication of advertisements for exotic dancers, masseuses and sex work in newspapers creates the impression that prostitution is an acceptable form of employment in this country. Young women and girls brought into prostitution by human traffickers are often caught up in the social perceptions and attitudes towards the industry that appear to be unable to separate voluntary and involuntary prostitution. The male 'need' for sex is often used by society as a reason for turning a blind eye on prostitution (Parker, 2008).

7. Cultural factors contributing to human trafficking

Some entrenched cultural norms and values that could be detrimental to the psychological and personal development of young women and girls survive in South Africa. Notably, child marriages due to HIV/Aids, child placement, as well as materialism and immediate gratification are some of the cultural practices drawing young women and girls to human traffickers in this country.

7.1. Child brides

With the high levels of HIV/Aids infection afflicting one in nine South Africans (HSRC, 2009), older men are currently reviving age-old customs, bordering on human trafficking, by kidnapping and abducting young girls for sexual exploitation to cure themselves of the infection (Prince, 2009). These girls are turned into child brides at a tender age. At times, the parents of these girls know about these marriages, but prefer to overlook the situation and accept *lobola* from the groom. Some of the parents receive approximately R500.00 or a sheep, goat or calf in exchange for their daughters (Oliphant, 2009). The mere fact that the girls are abducted or kidnapped, and kept as sex slaves and against their will could imply human trafficking for sexual exploitation. However, this practice is defined as a traditional custom, legitimately acceptable in some Eastern Cape communities. Historically, traditional leaders had specified orders regulating the practice, which was called *ukuthwala intombi* [taking of a bride by force]. The regulation of the occurrence of this cultural practice has changed. Currently, South Africa has ratified numerous human rights instruments which make it a crime for a man to take an adolescent girl for marriage without consent. This would apply to a situation where the main purpose of abducting girls is purely for sex slavery to cure Aids, or to satisfy the preconceived notion of women as carriers of HIV/Aids and young girls as pure.

7.2. Child placement

It appears that the everyday reality of some people has become a method to victimise young women and girls. It is customary for large South African families that are struggling socio-economically to send some of their children to relatives, usually residing in economically advantaged areas, in order to access economic and educational opportunities (Dyantyi & Pritz, 2009). This practice is currently being used to draw children into human trafficking for sexual exploitation. For example, a wealthy uncle from an economically privileged suburb invited his two nieces from an informal settlement in Port Elizabeth (in the Eastern Cape) to reside with him. He initially promised to provide education and access to other essential resources to his nieces. Instead, he confined them in his house and forced them to work as prostitutes and took away their earnings (Bermudez, 2007).

Even when they are not misled by relatives, some young women and girls may pursue relationships with older men, who in turn provide material objects in return for sex (Leclerc-Madlala, 2003). In some instances, human traffickers use this kind of scenario – they first spoil young girls between the ages of 13 and 17 with an expensive night out (UNODC, 2007). Once the outing is over, they force them to work as prostitutes in order to return the money used for the night out.

Child placement and intergenerational sex are embedded in South African society, and are tolerated as strategies for unemployed young women and girls to earn an income (Dunkle et al.,2007; Dyantyi & Pritz, 2009; Leclerc-Madlala, 2003). This situation makes the identification of victims and communication of the prevention of the crime difficult to accomplish.

7.3. Materialism and immediate gratification

There is a growing culture of materialism and immediate gratification among young women and girls in South Africa. The ownership of cell phones, brand-label clothes, as well as partying at entertainment areas such as nightclubs and parties is a lifestyle desired by most South African adolescents (Lutya, 2010a). During such parties and social events, adolescents consume high volumes of alcohol, with some taking drugs and others involved in risky sexual behaviours (Dunkle, 2007). Survival sex is one mechanism which poverty-stricken teenagers use to access the material goods they desire (Leclerc-Madlala, 2003). They become intimately involved with older men who can purchase the wares the teenagers want in return for sexual favours. The male companion may then persuade the young female to perform sex work in order to generate more money. Eventually, the female companion is moved, harboured and commercially exploited for the benefit of the male companion.

In summary, although not all HIV/Aids-infected South African men kidnap and abduct young women and girls for early marriage, the cultural practice of *ukuthwala intombi* has received major criticism from government, civil society and human rights activists. As a result of these points of view, public hearings on this practice have occurred in order to ascertain the opinions of the citizens. The purpose of the public hearings is not to conflate cultural practices with human trafficking or to refuse some citizens their right to practise their culture. It is to ensure that the practice of *ukuthwala intombi* does not violate the rights of young women and girls or contribute to increasing levels of sexual violence. Furthermore, the practice of child placement is vital for social network support and family linkages. Family support is important for the survival of young women and girls from poverty-stricken backgrounds in the absence of government services and sufficient income-generating resources. Support from relatives prevents young women and girls from entering into relationships with older men for the purposes of generating an income. However, it should be done with the intention to provide for a struggling family, instead of human trafficking for sexual exploitation.

8. South African responses to human trafficking

The government and civil society are currently mobilizing society and the legal system to intensify prevention, protection and prosecution services, as well as partnerships to respond to this crime (Eye on Human Trafficking, 2007). Several partnerships have been created to broaden and give more publicity and information on human trafficking patterns and forms.

8.1. Prevention

Article 9 of the Palermo Protocol (United Nations, 2008) expects its signatories to develop comprehensive policies and programmes, to conduct research, to implement media campaigns and socio-economic strategies, as well as to provide information regarding human trafficking in order to deter human traffickers from committing the crime. The aim is to equip societies and countries with human trafficking knowledge. According to the Protocol, the programmes should seek to reduce factors that create vulnerability to human trafficking. Furthermore, the Protocol emphasises the establishment of regional, international and national coalitions in order to share and disseminate information. Since South Africa became a signatory to the Palermo Protocol and the publication of *'Seduction, sale and slavery'* (Mathews, 2004)) by the International Organization for Migration (IOM) in 2003, prevention services have been intensified to educate and inform the public about human trafficking.

Awareness programmes, capacity building workshops and training of civil organisations, as well as government officials in human trafficking are some of the common prevention measures aimed at reducing human trafficking of young women and girls for sexual exploitation. The IOM and its partners, the United Nations Office on Drugs and Crime (UNODC), the Department of Social Development, women's organisations, religious groups as well as sporting clubs such as Kaiser Chiefs play an instrumental role in raising awareness about human trafficking in South Africa. During these workshops, participants are introduced to the concept in all its manifestations and are informed of the legal and social resources that they could use to respond to the crime. But however diligently South Africa is working to fulfil its obligations set out in the Palermo Protocol, the filtered information may not be put to good use due to personal and socio-economic challenges faced by some South African citizens. Informal conversations with South Africans have shown that an average citizen of this country will not turn down an opportunity if it were introduced by a stranger (Le Roux, 2009b; O'Connor, 2009). This attitude is motivated by the desire to experience the world, earn more and access employment opportunities.

Socio-economic challenges are cited in most South African reports on human trafficking as fundamental reasons fuelling the occurrence of human trafficking for all purposes. The IOM has reported that 84% of documented and undocumented immigrants vulnerable to human trafficking in South Africa cited family breakdown, religious and ethnic persecution as fundamental reasons that brought them into the country (IOM, 2009). However, on arrival in South Africa, they faced socio-economic hindrances that made it difficult for them to acclimatise to the country. They may encounter xenophobic treatment whilst looking for jobs and housing. As stated elsewhere in this chapter, South Africa has its own internal economic challenges, which are difficult to eradicate. Some children reside in homes earning less than an average wage. Economic Mobilization, a new initiative facilitated by the IOM to prevent human trafficking in South Africa, seeks to mitigate the socio-economic challenges driving some young women and girls to turn to human traffickers. Economic Mobilization provides training and funds to small businesses in three impoverished provinces, namely Limpopo, Mpumalanga and the Eastern Cape. The aim is create sustainable projects that could provide employment opportunities to young women and girls in order to reduce their vulnerability to human traffickers (Eye on Human Trafficking, 2009).

8.2. Protection

Identification, reporting and referral are some of the protective measures applied by South Africa to respond to human trafficking. A designated official, such as a social worker, border official or community worker, can determine whether a child is a victim of human trafficking. Once a child has been identified as a victim of trafficking, the official is expected to report the child to the criminal justice authorities. The identified child can then be referred to a place of safety whilst waiting for her circumstances and experiences to be documented. Article 6 of the United Nations' Palermo Protocol states that on identification of a trafficked victim, each member state is required to provide privacy and confidentiality, housing, counselling, medical, psychological and material assistance to the victims. The IOM offers trafficked victims shelter, medical and psychological support, legal assistance, as well as to return them to and reintegrate them in their community. The organisation has to date assisted 300 victims of sexual exploitation and forced labour trafficking inside and outside South Africa (Eye on Human Trafficking, 2009). Molo Songololo has assisted 26 victims of child sexual exploitation and 44 rape cases, as well as provided victim empowerment services to 32 children (Tyakume, 2009). Recommendations have been made by the South African Law Reform Commission for victims of trafficking to be granted immunity from prosecution.

8.3. Prosecution

Despite the absence of a legislation to prosecute human trafficking fully, South Africa has successfully prosecuted and is currently prosecuting suspects alleged to have committed the crime. Sections from existing legislation are used to prosecute human trafficking. The Prevention of Organised Crime Act (Act 112 of 1998), the Immigration Act (Act 13 of 2002) and the Sexual Offences Act (Act 23 of 1957) are some of the Acts used to prosecute human trafficking activities ([40, 74]). Furthermore, the Children's Act (Act 38 of 2005) and the Criminal Law (Sexual Offences and Related Matters) Amendment Act (Act 32 of 2007) contain sections dedicated to combating the human trafficking of young women and girls for sexual exploitation. However, the Children's Act is not yet fully promulgated (Qaba, 2007). These efforts are not enough to prosecute and receive a conviction for the crime. Few trafficking offences have been prosecuted using parts of existing Acts in the absence of a concrete and specific trafficking legislation. The Criminal Law (Sexual Offences and Related Matters) Amendment Act (32 of 2007) and the Sexual Offences Act (23 of 1957) can only be used to prosecute sexual exploitation. Although the offenders are not convicted for human trafficking, but for sexual exploitation associated with human trafficking, the South African legal system is at least demonstrating some progress in this regard.

Two successfully prosecuted cases of human trafficking for sexual exploitation have been reported (Qaba, 2007). In the first of these, Elizabeth Maswanganye recruited, transported and lured into prostitution through false promises young women and girls looking for employment in Pretoria. She was charged with running a brothel and with soliciting girls for carnal intercourse under section 2 and 14 of the Sexual Offences Act (Act 23 of 1957). She is currently serving a five-year term of imprisonment. In the second case, Amien Andrews lured young women and girls looking for a good time at shopping malls into brothels. He was charged with kidnapping, assault to do grievous bodily harm, indecent assault and rape. He is currently serving a 17-year sentence.

Eight suspects have appeared in a criminal court in KwaZulu-Natal Durban on human trafficking charges. A woman from Thailand and a South African man recruited female prostitutes in Thailand to work in up-market establishments in South Africa. The recruits were tied into debt bondage and intense sex work on arrival in this country. The Thai recruiter and the South African male are facing charges of racketeering under the Prevention of Organised Crime Act (Act 121 of 1998: Sections 20-21) of the contravention of immigration principles under the Immigration Act (Act 13 of 2002: Sections 16-19), of keeping a brothel and facilitating prostitution under the Sexual Offences Act (Act 23 of 1957: Sections 3-15), as well as of running a business without a license under the Business Act (Act 71 of 1991) (Lutya, 2009). Furthermore, 27 Chinese female prostitutes and their recruiter were arrested and charged with contravening the Immigration Act and Labour Acts for entering and working in South Africa illegally (Kreston, 2007). It is problematic that in these cases victims are prosecuted alongside traffickers and are offered no assistance. Once the trafficking legislation comes into effect, victims will be protected instead of being treated as accomplices to the crime (Kreston, 2007; Le Roux, 2009b; SALRC, 2004; Stuurman, 2009).

8.4. Politics of legal reform in South Africa

On 26 August 2009, the South African Cabinet approved the Prevention and Combating of Human Trafficking Bill (Qaba, 2009). The next step is tabling the law in Parliament for final approval. It has taken five years for this Bill to obtain Cabinet approval, due to the number of constraints hindering the process. Divergent opinions regarding the sections contained in the Bill and the manner in which the law will be interpreted could be the reason behind the slow progress. It appears that religious, political, moral, gender and medical differences are delaying the finalisation of the Bill. The main issue of concern is the sexual exploitation of victims by human traffickers by means of forced prostitution. Organisations such as Sex Worker Education and Advocacy Taskforce (SWEAT), which are fighting for the legalisation and decriminalisation of prostitution, are of the opinion that some trafficked young women and girls exercise agency and accept offers from human traffickers knowing what will transpire at the place of destination (Harper, 2009). With this mind, they argue that such young women and girls would also be prosecuted alongside human traffickers. SWEAT is of the opinion that when some young women and girls are caught by criminal justice authorities without legal documentation – tied into debt bondage – they cry sexual exploitation (Harper, 2009). Organisations fighting to reduce violence against women such as Masimanyane Women's Support Centre, which are seeking to criminalise prostitution by arresting users of prostitutes and saving prostitutes from the business, point out that prostitutes are not free to choose this profession, but are forced by a variety of gender-related discriminatory circumstances to work as prostitutes. The Bill should render prostitution a crime instead of distinguishing between voluntary and involuntary prostitution, as is the case now. Additional political pressures from the tourism sector, the trade sector and as a result of sporting events hosted by South Africa are putting pressure on South Africa to accept and regulate the prostitution industry.

In addition to this political pressure, religious organisations are defining prostitution, voluntary and involuntary, as an abomination to God. With all these opposing and contentious opinions on the table, the South African Law Reform Commission is responsible for ensuring that all parties are satisfied with the final outcome of this Bill. Notwithstanding the fact that South Africa is a diverse country consisting of citizens adhering to differing standpoints, it may appear that the only group of persons victimised by traffickers are young women and girls trafficked for involuntary prostitution. The moral connotations associated with prostitution may be the reason that most organisations are strongly opposed to or in agreement with some sections dealing with sexual exploitation in this legalisation. According to Section 4:3 (b) of the Bill, it is no defence not to charge a trafficker if an adult has consented to exploitation or exploitation did not occur, or if human traffickers have recruited, transported and manipulated young women or girls to think that the jobs offered are financially lucrative. SWEAT argues that consent should be disregarded where children are concerned (Harper, 2009). Adults should be seen as capable of giving consent to the work of prostitution, irrespective of the coercive methods traffickers use to lure women into the trade.

8.5. What would be a more effective policy to deal with human trafficking?

The promulgation of the Prevention of Trafficking in Persons Bill may not necessarily address women's legal and social challenges, but it will ensure that legal mechanisms exist to address the legal needs of formerly trafficked young women and girls. However, it will not address the factors which have motivated the trafficked victims to accept 'assistance' from human traffickers. The same applies to other laws addressing women's issues: it could make a difference to young women and girls who have been abducted and kidnapped. This set of victims is often caught by surprise whilst either walking home from school or running an errand for a parent.

For a woman who needs better employment opportunities, it may lead to the kind of self-blame that is often observed in victims of acquaintance rape. A more effective strategy could be a combination of services provided to potential victims of human trafficking. This strategy will necessitate a change in the manner in which families, communities and the South African citizens entirely select their lifestyles.

A combined strategy includes full participation by the families of potential victims, communities, civic organisations, criminal justice authorities and former victims of human trafficking, brothel owners, clients or users of human trafficking victims, as well as the families and relatives of former victims of trafficking. This strategy should be a government-driven policy led by the Department of Social Development (DSD). It should be implemented at a primary level before victims are recruited, kidnapped or abducted. At that point, human trafficking has not yet occurred. However, owing to the increasing number of young women and girls who are falling victim to this crime, unaffected potential victims should be educated about the crime. The department is already driving many prevention and early intervention programmes aimed at addressing risk factors that could result in the victimisation of families in general.

However, human trafficking is a clandestine crime that should be addressed separately. Firstly, parenting programmes should be designed, planned and implemented. The facilitators of these parenting programmes should identify parenting deficits and behavioural factors expressed by young women and girls that could result in victimisation. The parenting programmes should be implemented at a community, school and family level. In this manner, teachers, neighbours as well as other family members are aware of the existence of the crime and can help alter young women and girls' behavioural expressions and parenting practices and styles that result in victimisation. Secondly, alongside parenting programmes civil organisations, criminal justice authorities' former victims of trafficking should be instrumental in raising awareness about the crime. Victims of human trafficking are likely to contact NGOs for assistance; formerly trafficked women are knowledgeable about the mechanisms used by traffickers to capture, confine and transfer them whilst increasing profits. Third, clients or users of prostitutes can engage with young women and girls in the business without making them feel interrogated. This information could be sent to the police who will contact brothel owners amicably and alert them to the finding before an arrest is made. Lastly, the families and relatives of trafficked young women and girls should form part of the strategy by supporting their trafficked victims in order to ensure that their reintegration is achieved with fewer challenges.

Most researchers in South Africa are advocating for the immediate promulgation of the Prevention and Combating of Trafficking in Persons legislation in order to reduce the occurrence of the crime. Gender equality can be achieved through the enactment of laws granting an opportunity for women to access justice (Ntlama, 2006). However, the introduction of this legislation is bound to be delayed, because of differing opinions pertaining to prostitution. It might be easier to separate voluntary and involuntary prostitution once the trafficking law has been promulgated (Qaba, 2009). Along with the legalisation and decriminalisation of (voluntary) prostitution, brothels will be inspected regularly, the human rights of prostitutes will be observed and prevention efforts will take cognisance of the socio-economic factors influencing young women and girls to perform the work (Khumalo, 2009; Qaba, 2009).

It is a betrayal of women's aspirations when the criminal justice system does not fulfil its obligations to improve the quality of their lives (Drakopolou, 2008). Meanwhile, owing to the diversity of young women and girls, justice may not be accessed by formerly trafficked young women and girls (Drakopolou, 2008). There are young women and girls who accept offers knowing fairly well that they will work as prostitutes, but they are not alerted to the conditions under which they will work. Once they exit the clutches of human trafficking, they do not report the violations encountered at the hands of human traffickers, but often continue to work in the prostitution industry as they were recruited to do.

8.6. Partnerships

Several partnerships have been established in South Africa to counter human trafficking for all purposes. They are situated in provinces, nationally and regionally coordinated by governmental and NGOs. The IOM, women's organisations and the National Prosecuting Authority (NPA) coordinate most partnerships against human trafficking. The Southern African Counter Trafficking Assistance Programme (SACTAP), Migration Dialogue for Southern Africa (MIDSA), the National Task Team, Mpulimo, the Southern African Network against Trafficking and Abuse of Children (SANTAC), and Activists Networking against the Exploitation of Child Domestic Labour (Anex CDW), are some of the partnerships addressing human trafficking in South Africa.

The publication of *Seduction, Sale and Slavery: Trafficking in Women and Children in Southern Africa* (Mathews et al., 2004) in 2003 resulted in the formation of SACTAP (IOM, 2009). SACTAP, coordinated by the IOM, is a regional body consisting of representatives from the South African Development Community (SADC) region. Since 2003 it has assisted 300 victims of human trafficking and trained more than 1 200 police officers, as well approximately 500 practitioners from civil organisations in victim assistance and identification (Eye on Human Trafficking, 2007). Its areas of focus are research, information dissemination, victim assistance, and capacity building (Le Roux, 2009a).

The IOM also coordinates MIDSA, which gets government officials from SADC to meet in workshops to debate matters related to migration issues three times a year (IOM, 2009). Human trafficking and human smuggling are some of the migration-related matters discussed at these workshops. Furthermore, the National Task Team, a government initiative, was formed in 2005 to monitor activities aimed at preventing human trafficking in South Africa. It is made up of government departments such as the Organised Crime Unit, the SAPS, Justice and Constitutional Development, Home Affairs, Social Development and Labour, as well as NGOs, the IOM, Molo Songololo and the UNODC. Its most important roles are to monitor strategies against human trafficking and share information pertaining to the developments in human trafficking matters (Qaba, 2009). They meet quarterly to share and disseminate information.

The Mpulimo Task Team against Human Trafficking includes government departments such as the SAPS, Health, Social Development, Home Affairs and the Vhembe District Municipality, as well as NGOs such as the SABC Polokwane branch, Terres Des Hommes Johannesburg, and Sithabile Youth and Child Care Centre (Amazing Grace, 2009). Most important among its tasks are to help the police investigate child trafficking cases and assist in the identification and assistance of victims. To date, Mpulimo has played a vital role in the prosecution of human traffickers operating around the Musina border between South Africa and Zimbabwe. They have rescued children transported to South Africa in trucks, taxis and private cars.

The Southern African Network against Trafficking and Abuse of Children (SANTAC) started in 2004 as a Norwegian-sponsored initiative aimed at creating awareness about the exploitation and abuse of children in the SADC region. The purpose of SANTAC is to collaborate and interlink with other African countries in order to fight the commercial sexual exploitation, labour, trafficking and abuse of children (Le Roux, 2009a; Le Roux, 2009b). The network lobbies African governments to formulate legal policies for the purpose of prosecuting human traffickers and providing assistance to the victims of human trafficking. Former South African first lady Graça Machel and Archbishop Emeritus Desmond Tutu are patrons of SANTAC (Le Roux, 2009a; Le Roux, 2009b). SANTAC is working towards reducing human trafficking and child abuse. SANTAC launched an anti-trafficking campaign called Red Light 2010 in preparation for the 2010 Soccer World Cup, jointly with Women in Law in South Africa and the Child Welfare Society. The aim of Red Light 2010 was to raise awareness about human trafficking and address aspects creating vulnerability of women and children to the crime (Le Roux, 2009a; Le Roux, 2009b).

Tsireledzani, a TshiVenda word meaning *'Let's protect'* (Eye on Human Trafficking, 2009), is a coordinated group of organisations, governmental and non-governmental, applying the principles of the Palermo Protocol against human trafficking by conducting research, training practitioners in the field, raising awareness about the crime and supporting governments to formulate legal and social policies to counter human trafficking (Eye on Human Trafficking, 2009). Some of its affiliates include the Human Sciences Research Council (HSRC), the University of South Africa (UNISA), the United Nations Children's Fund (UNICEF), the IOM and the UNODC. It is driven by the National Prosecuting Authority (NPA) and financially supported by the European Commission. Tsireledzani has to date held workshops with the media – journalists, editors, producers, web managers, television presenters, photographers, correspondents and press officers – as well as with police officers, investigators and other government officials, such as Home Affairs and Immigration officials, for the purpose of educating them about human trafficking (Eye on Human Trafficking, 2009).

A provincial-based partnership, Activists Networking against the Exploitation of Child Domestic Labour (Anex CDW), aims to end the exploitation of children trapped in domestic labour with special consideration of girl-children moved from urban to rural areas. They perform advocacy work, conduct research, and lobby government to create policies that may improve the situation of children, run media campaigns, as well as create support for children in domestic labour (Eye on Human Trafficking, 2007). To date, Anex CDW has released a research publication describing the profile of children vulnerable to exploitation in domestic work and the occurrence of human trafficking from rural areas to urban areas in Cape Town.

9. Conclusion

Human trafficking for sexual exploitation occurs in South Africa. For the first time since South Africa ratified the United Nations Protocol in 2004, in 2008/2009 the SAPS recorded cases of human trafficking for sexual exploitation. It appears that this crime has historical roots going back to the colonial period and slavery. Traditional cultural practices are also driving the occurrence of the crime. In addition, socio-economic conditions, gender violence, violent cultural practices, as well as dislocated and displaced children, form part of the context within which the crime occurs. Although the legislation to prosecute the crime has not yet been fully promulgated, sections of existing legislation are used to prosecute trafficking for sexual exploitation only. That presents some challenges, in the sense that most efforts to address the crime are geared towards reducing sex trafficking, despite the occurrences of other forms of trafficking. Differing opinions about the legalisation, decriminalisation or criminalisation of prostitution are delaying the process, because human trafficking for sexual exploitation and prostitution intersects to some extent. Nevertheless, legislation alone cannot be the only mechanism with which to deal effectively with the crime: primary prevention programmes should play a central role. The family, the community and criminal justice agents should collaborate to prevent human trafficking. Moreover, once human traffickers are caught, effective legislation should be in place to prosecute the crime fully.

Author details

Thozama Mandisa Lutya
Department of Social Work and Criminology, University of Pretoria, South Africa

10. References

Amazing Grace. (2009). *Mpulimo Task Team against human trafficking launching in Limpopo.* (Available online: http://www.agch.org.za, accessed 24 March 2009).

Bermudez L.G. (2008). *'No experience necessary': The internal trafficking of persons in South Africa.* Pretoria: International Organisation for Migration (IOM).

Bernat, P.F., & Zhilina, T. (2010). Human trafficking: the local becomes global. *Women and Justice, 20*(10), 2-9.

Bernat, P.F., & Winkeler, H.C. (2010). Human sex trafficking: the global becomes local. *Women and Justice, 20*(1), 186-190.

Bolowana, A. (2004). *40 000 child prostitutes: street children vulnerable to sex trade.* (Available online: http://www.iol.co.za, accessed 5October 2009.

Bruce, D., Dissel, A., & Menziwa, M. (2007). *The violent nature of crime in South Africa: a concept paper for the Justice, Crime Prevention and Security Cluster.* Braamfontein: Centre for the Study of Violence and Reconciliation (CSVR).

Burton, P. (2008). *Merchants, skollies and stones: experiences of school violence in South Africa.* Claremont: Centre for the Justice and Crime Prevention (CJCP).

Chetty, R. (2009). An investigation of the treatment and protection of child refugees in the Durban Metropolitan area. *Crimsa Bi-annual Conference* 28-30 September, Pretoria.

Children's Institute. (2009). *Children count: Abantwana babalulekile.* Cape Town: University of Cape Town.

Clark, D. (2005). Socio-political context of vulnerable victims in South Africa. In Davis, L. & Snyman, R. *Victimology in South Africa.* (171-173). Pretoria: Van Schaik.

CSVR. (2008). *Conference Report: the South African Domestic Violence Act: lessons from a decade of legislation and implementation.* Johannesburg, 26-28 November.

Community Law Centre. (2006). *Children used by adults to commit crime: children's perceptions of their use by adults in the commission of offences.* Cape Town: Bellville.

Daems, T. (2005). Repeat victimisation and the study of social control. *International Journal of the Sociology of Law, 33,* 85-100.

Dawes, A., De Sas Kropiwnicki, Z., Kafaar, Z., & Richter, L. (2005). *Corporal punishment of children: a South African national survey.* Cape Town: Human Sciences Research Council (HSRC).

Delport, E., Koen, K., & MacKay, A. (2007). *Human trafficking in South Africa: root causes and recommendations.* Paris: United Nations Educational Scientific and Cultural Organization (UNESCO).

Drakopoulou, M. (2008). Feminism, governability and the politics of legal reform. *Griffith Law Review, 17*(1), 1-16.

Dunkle, K.L., Jewkes, R., Nduna, M., Jama, N., Levin. J., Sikweyiya, N., & Koss, M.P. (2007). Transactional sex with casual and main partners among young South African men in the rural Eastern Cape: prevalence, predictors and associations with gender-based violence. *Social Science and Medicine, 65,* 1235-1248.

Dyantyi, C.N., & Pritz, E. (2009). The vulnerable child in the face of 2010: child headed households. *Towards multi-disciplinary expertise in handling child abuse – A focus on trafficking.* Pretoria: 4-6 May

Eye on Human Trafficking. (2007). Issue 1. Pretoria: International Organization for Migration (IOM).

Eye on Human Trafficking. (2009). Issue 21. Pretoria: International Organization for Migration.

Fick, N. (2007). *Policing sex workers: A violation of rights.* Cape Town: SWEAT.

Fitzgibbon, K. (2003). Modern day slavery? The scope of trafficking in person in Africa. *African Security Review, 12*(1), 81-89.

Frank, S., Esterhuizen, T., Jinabhai, C.C., Sullivan, K., & Taylor, M. (2008). Risky behaviours of high school pupils in an era of HIV and Aids. *South African Medical Journal, 98*, 394-398.

Frank, C., & Muntingh, L. (2006). *Children used by adults to commit crime: children's perceptions of their use by adults in the commission of offences*. Cape Town: Community Law and Child Justice Alliance.

Gould, C. (2005). Cheap lives, countering human trafficking: considerations and constraints. *SA Crime Quarterly, 16*, June, 19-25.

Gould, C., & Fick, N. (2008). *Selling sex in Cape Town: Sex work and trafficking in a South African city*. Cape Town: Institute of Security Studies and SWEAT.

Govender, S. (2008). Girl gangsters flex their muscles. *The Times*, 10 February, 1.

Hargreaves, S., Vetten, L., Scheineder, V., Malepe, L., & Fuller, R. (2006). *'Marriage is like sitting on red coals': a case of domestic violence in four villages of the Moretele District, Tshwane Metropole*. Braamfontein: Centre for the Study of Violence and Reconciliation.

Harper, E., Massawe, D., & Mentor-Lalu, V. (2009). *Project 107 Sexual Offences: Adult Prostitution (Submission to the South African Law Reform Commission)*. Cape Town: SWEAT.

Human Sciences Research Council (HSRC). (2009). *South African National HIV Prevalence, Incidence, Behaviour and Communication Survey 2008: A turning tide among teenagers*. Cape Town: HSRC Publishers.

International Organisation for Migration. (2009). *IOM's Counter Trafficking Statement*. (Available online:
http://www.iom.org.za/site/indexphp?option=com_content&task=view&id=15&Itemid=4, accessed 14 October .2010

Irish, J. (2005). *Illicit trafficking of vehicles across Beit Bridge border pass*. Institute of Security Studies Occasional Paper, 109, June.

Khumalo, N. (2009). *In support of submissions advocating decriminalization of sex work: Submission to SALRC*. Pretoria: South African National Aids Council (SANAC).

Kreston, S. (2007). Trafficking in children in South Africa: an analysis of pending legislation. *Child Abuse Research in South Africa, 8*(1), 35-50.

Leclerc-Madlala, S. (2003). Transactional sex and the pursuit of modernity. *Social Dynamics 29*(2), 213-233.

Leoschut, L. (2008). *School violence: What makes learners vulnerable?* Claremont: Centre for Justice and Crime Prevention.

Le Roux, S. (2009a). Human trafficking: A practical perspective. *Research Seminar: A Multi-Disciplinary approach to Human Trafficking*, Pretoria, 16 September.

Le Roux, S. (2009b). Trafficking: incidence, trauma and caretaking of the trafficked child in Southern Africa. *Towards multi-disciplinary expertise in handling child abuse – A focus on trafficking* – Pretoria: 4-6 May.

Lutya, T.M. (2007). Home and family circumstances of young offenders. An examination of social workers' view. *British Journal of Community Justice, 5*(3), 63-80.

Lutya, T.M. (2009). An overview of human trafficking in South Africa. *Research Seminar: A Multi-Disciplinary approach to Human Trafficking,* Pretoria, 16 September.

Lutya, T.M. (2010a). Lifestyles and routine activities of South African adolescents at risk of being trafficked for involuntary prostitution. *Academy of Criminal Justice Sciences 47th Annual Meeting 'Beyond our boundaries': The Inclusivity of Criminal Justice Sciences,* 23-27 February: San Diego, CA.

Lutya, T.M. (2010b). The importance of a stable home and family environment in the prevention of youth offending in South Africa. *Association of Psychology & Psychiatry for Adults & Children (A.P.P.A.C.) 'Neuropsychiatric, Psychological & Social Sciences Today'*. 4-7 May: Athens, Greece.

Malapa, A. (2008). Young women immigrants. In Gorton, J., & Geffen, N. *Equal treatment: Welcome to South Africa? A special report n the systematic abuse of immigrants* (16-17). Cape Town: Treatment Action Campaign.

Mashaba, S. (2009). Shocking child abuse statistics. *Sowetan,* 17 September, 1.

Martens, J. (2003). *'Seduced, imported and sold': Trafficking in women and children in Africa.* Pretoria: International Organization for Migration (IOM).

Martens, J., Pieczkowski, M., & Van Vuuren-Smyth, B. (2003). *Seduction, sale and slavery: trafficking in women and children in Southern Africa.* Pretoria: International Organization for Migration (IOM).

Mathews, S., Abrahams, N., Martin, L.J., Vetten, L., Van der Merwe, L., & Jewkes, R. (2004). *'Every six hours a woman is killed by her intimate partner': a national study of female homicide in South Africa.* Pretoria and Johannesburg: Medical Research Council and Centre for the Study of Violence and Reconciliation.

Minnaar, A. (2009). Multiple victimisation: refugees, asylum seekers, foreign migrants and xenophobic violence in South Africa: May 2008. *Crimsa Bi-annual Conference,* 28-30 September, Pretoria.

Mistry, D., Snyman, R., & Van Zyl, M. (2001). *Social fabric crime in the Northern Cape.* Johannesburg: Institute for Human Rights and Criminal Justice Studies.

Mokwena, S. 1991. *The era of jackrollers: Contextualizing the rise of youth gangs in Soweto.* Braamfontein: Centre for the Study of Violence and Reconciliation (CSVR).

Molo Songololo. (2005). *Trafficking in children in the Western Cape Province.* Cape Town: Molo Songololo.

Muftić, L.R., Bouffard, L.A., & Bouffard, J.A. (2007). An exploratory analysis of victim precipitation among men and women arrested for intimate partner violence. *Feminist Criminology, 2*(4), 327-346.

Muller, K., & Holley, K. (2009). 'I want to be a different person'. The impact of trafficking on children: the story of Elsie. *Towards multi-disciplinary expertise in handling child abuse – a focus on trafficking* – Pretoria: 4-6 May.

Mutongwizo, T. (2009). Foreign fears? An exploratory study of perceptions and fear of crime in South Africa amongst international students at the University of Cape Town. *Crimsa Bi-Annual Conference,* 29-30 September, Pretoria.

Naidoo, Y. (2007). Addiction fuels boom in teen prostitution. *Cape Argus,* 11 March, 19.

Naidoo, Y. (2008). Tik epidemic sparks rise of girl gangs. *Cape Argus,* 26 January, 11.

Nettlebeck, T., Wilson, C., Potter, R. & Perry, C. (2000). The influence of interpersonal competence on personal vulnerability of person with mental retardation. *Journal of Interpersonal Violence*, 15(1), 46-62.

Ntlama, N. (2006). Equality: A tool for social change in promoting gender equality. *The improvement of the quality of life, status, justice and Constitutional development of women.* 1-2 August: South African Reserve Bank Conference, Pretoria.

O'Connor, M. 2009. *Human trafficking and child prostitution on the rise for 2010 FIFA Soccer World Cup*. (Available online:

http://fromtheold.com/opinion/human-trafficking-child-prostitution-rise-2010-fifa-soccer-world-cup-2009110115679.html, accessed 10 November 2010).

Oliphant, L. (2009). *Marriages made in Hell.* City Press, 12 April, 25.

Palmary, I. (2005). *Engendering wartime conflict: women and war trauma*. Braamfontein: Centre for the Study of Violence and Reconciliation.

Parker, S. (2008). *Will the 2010 World Cup increase modern day slavery?* (Available online:

http://www.iss.co.za/static/templates, accessed 18 September 2009).

Prince, C. (2009). Parents sell girls as child brides. *Sunday Times*, 31 May, 1.

Qaba, N. (2007). Prosecuting trafficking without trafficking laws. *Trafficking in human beings: National and International perspectives*, 17 August, Bloemfontein.

Qaba, N. (2009). *Human trafficking strategy: South Africa's response to trafficking in persons.* (Available online:

http://www.gov.za, accessed 5 October 2009).

Reuters. (1998). Thai women lured to South Africa as sex slaves. (Available online:

http://www.catinternational.org/factbook/South%20Africa.php. Accessed 19/01/1999

Richter, M. (2009). Pimp my ride for 2010: Sex work, legal reform and HIV/Aids. *"Score a goal for Gender Equality: Getting the Ball Rolling: Multimedia Launch Event.* Bedfordview, Johannesburg, 10 December.

Russell, R., & Tyler, M. (2002). Thank heaven for little girls: girl heaven and the commercial context of feminine childhood. *Sociology*, *36*(3), 620-637.

SALRC. (2004). Issue Paper 25, Project 131: Trafficking in persons. Pretoria: SALRC.

SALRC. (2008). *Project 131: Report on trafficking in persons.* Pretoria: SALRC.

SAPS. (2010). *Crime Statistics*. Pretoria: South African Police Service.

Sigsworth, R. (2008). *The promulgation of the Criminal Law (Sexual Offences and Related Matters) Amendment Act: Bureaucracy versus Democratization*. Braamfontein: CSVR.

Statistics South Africa. (2009). *Quarterly Labour Force*. Pretoria: Stats SA.

Stuurman, L. (2009). Trafficking: The child and the South African legal framework. *Towards multi-disciplinary expertise in handling child abuse – A focus on Trafficking* – Pretoria: 4-6 May.

Tshwane Alliance for Street Children. (2009). (Available online:

http//www.tasc.org.za, accessed 26 September 2009).

Tyakume, V. (2009). *Child protection, violence and abuse against children, ukuthwala practices, virginity testing, initiation: Department of Justice and Molo Songololo briefings*. Pretoria: Parliamentary Monitoring Group.

United Nations Children's Fund (UNICEF). (2003). *Trafficking in human beings especially women and children in Africa*. Italy: UNICEF Innocenti Research Centre.

United Nations. 2000. *Protocol to prevent, suppress and punish trafficking in persons, especially women and children, supplementing the United Nations Convention against Transnational Organised Crime*. United Nations: Geneva.

United Nations Office on Drugs and Crime (UNODC). (2007). *Situational assessment of human trafficking: a 2005 situational assessment of human trafficking in the SADC region, a survey of South Africa, Zimbabwe and Mozambique*. Hatfield: UNODC.

Van der Hoven, A., & Maree, A. (2005). Victimisation risk factors, repeat victimisation and victim profiling. In Davis, L., & Snyman, R. (Eds). *Victimology in South Africa* (55-71). Pretoria: Van Schaik.

Van der Merwe, N. (2009). A quantitative study on the pro-violence attitudes among learners in South Africa. *Crimsa Bi-annual Conference* 28-30 September, Pretoria.

Van Onselen, C. 1984. *The small matter of a horse: the life of Nongoloza Mathebula 1867-1948*. Johannesburg: Jonathan Ball.

Van der Watt, M. (2009). Trafficking: best practices, a case illustration. *Towards multi-disciplinary expertise in handling child abuse – A focus on trafficking* – Pretoria: 4-6 May.

Wambugu, L. (2003). Searching for sanctuary: refugee women in South Africa. *Agenda, 55*, 27-36.

Chapter 6

Increasing Awareness of Brazilian Family Health Team Professionals on Reporting Child Abuse: A Case Study

Thais H. Bannwart and Lúcia C.A. Williams

Additional information is available at the end of the chapter

http://dx.doi.org/10.5772/48219

1. Introduction

There are diverse and countless cases of child abuse reported by the media, giving the general public the impression that its number has drastically increased. We know that is not the case. Child abuse is, unfortunately, a very old habit in need of change, and it is, in fact being changed. Many cases come to health professionals in the very beginning, such as when a nurse witnesses a mother humiliating a child who refuses to eat. Unfortunately, many cases also appear only when it is too late, as when a physician signs a death certificate in a child abuse fatality.

This paper aims at pointing out the need for changes in health professional training regarding child abuse - a public health issue which directly affects individual and collective health. Preventing and coping with abuse demands the formulation of specific policies and organizational practices and services for the sector [1]. The World Report on Violence and the World Health Organization [2] mention that psychiatric disorders, depression, anxiety, substance abuse, and aggression, feelings of shame or cognitive disorders, posttraumatic stress, sleep disorders, thoughts and suicidal behavior, as potential consequences of child abuse. In addition, adult diseases, such as ischemic heart disease, cancer, chronic lung disease, irritable bowel syndrome and fibromyalgia may be intensified due to child abuse experiences.

A considerable amount of money is spent on treating cases related to child abuse. This includes: a) offender arrests and subsequent court issues, b) abuse investigation reports, c) mental health services for adults with a child abuse history; d) especial educational support; e) expenses associated with foster care and adoption; and f) costs in the employment sector due to absenteeism and low productivity [2]. In the health system, child abuse is responsible for increases in emergency assistance, and rehabilitation expenses, the latter more costly than most conventional medical procedures [1].

Due to the complexity of child abuse, its close link with Public Health and the fact that mandated reporting is regulated in many countries, health professionals involvement with the topic has been the focus of several studies. In Brazil, the Child and Adolescent ACT (ECA – *Estatuto da Criança e do Adolescente* 1990) ,in Article 245, [3] regulates mandated reporting to proper authorities of any suspected or confirmed child abuse case. Failure to do so may receive a penalty involving from 3-20 minimal wage fines.

The Child and Adolescent Act was implemented in Brazil in 1990, guarantying special rights and full protection of children. In addition, the Ministry of Health developed guidelines in the document "*National Policy for Reduction of Morbidity and Mortality from Accidents and Violence",* in existence since 1998. Later, with the publication of another document ("*National Policy for Reduction of Morbidity and Mortality from Accidents and Violence in Childhood and Adolescence*"), in 2001, child abuse mandated report by Unified Health System professionals was enforced [4]. Despite this requirement, violence underreporting in all areas is a reality in Brazil. It is estimated that for every reported case, at least two others exist which have not been reported [5].

1.1. Health professionals' role in dealing with child abuse

Health professionals are under-qualified to deal with child abuse, in part due to a lack of awareness on how to proceed when cases arise. There is lack of regulations to guarantee appropriate technical procedures to deal with abuse cases in Brazil. In addition, there is an absence of legal mechanisms to protect those who do report cases. Failure in child abuse identification by health professionals, and fear of breaching client confidentiality, are barriers that also contribute to under–reporting [6]. Additionally, the difficulties may include lack of basic information to identify abuse, a topic not been addressed in undergraduate or graduate curricula. Lack of infrastructure and an excessive workload by Child Protection Services (CPS), and even its non-existence in some counties are also barriers to be mentioned. Another peculiarity is a culture which values family privacy and, Finally, threats made to professionals by abusers are also arguments responsible for non-reporting [6].

Child abuse reporting is extremely important because it is a tool to curb and prevent maltreatment, allowing interventions to take place at various levels. When child abuse becomes public, one may see that it is more common than expected. Needless to say that no type of violence should be considered ordinary or normal [7].

In spite of Brazil's mandatory reporting laws, there is a large gap between legislation and reality. Iossi [8] conducted interviews and document analysis in the municipality of Guarulhos, in the greater São Paulo area, observing that 23% of child abuse referrals health professionals made to treatment centers were made without the awareness of CPS, that is, without proper reporting. This situation may result in duplication of referrals to health services, resulting in false demands, illustrating , thus, the need for effective communication among different stakeholders of the child protection network.

A survey [9] analyzed the child abuse reporting process with 359 family health team professionals in the city of Fortaleza, Northeast Brazil, showing that reporting by professionals happens sporadically, rather than systematically. In that sense, the development of programs for continuing education and the increase of professional network support may reduce insecurity, and increase the number of child abuse reported cases.

Insecurity and difficulties faced by health professionals in identifying and reporting cases of child abuse were also addressed in other Brazilian studies. Health professionals' perception of child abuse, and responsibility to report cases according to past experience were analyzed through interviews (n=10) [10]. All professionals said that they discard organic hypothesis by examining the victims, and only then investigate "external causes". A third of interviewees said that when there are injuries suggesting abuse (such as bruises in a child admitted to the Hospital), it is difficult to confirm this diagnosis, as they fear committing "injustices". Whether or not the reporting occurred, feelings of frustration, powerlessness, and immobility were recurrent. In addition, in two reported cases, the police advised professionals to withdraw the notification. Psychological abuse was less valued than physical violence; as such acts were viewed as natural forms of child rearing. The study reports that mental health professionals tend to be silent about abuse, because "their training involves understanding and treating offenders and therefore do not consider reporting as their responsibility " (p.23).

The perception of 17 health professionals was analyzed [11] in relation to attitudes regarding child abuse, by means of semi-structured interviews. A swing between belief and disbelief of solving cases was noticed by researchers, as well as fear and emotional insecurity. Problems associated to lack of professional training, and the reproduction of cultural patterns of non-involvement beliefs regarding family issues were also identified. The study also highlighted the disbelief in the effective action of Child Protection Services, and previous negative experiences as reasons for not getting involved in child abuse cases.

Studies in the U.S. [12] also indicate difficulties professionals face in reporting abuse, as well as negative experiences with the legal system, contributing to non-reporting. Another study in Australia identifies problems with services available to children and families where child abuse reporting is made, indicating the need for continuing education of health professionals to identify symptoms and signs of physical abuse, as well as the physicians' role in multidisciplinary efforts to address child abuse [13].

This first author [14] sought to investigate problems found by pediatricians in identifying and reporting cases of abuse in a mid-size city of the State of São Paulo, Brazil. Main results pointed out that difficulties were related to lack of training, disbelief and doubts about CPS, fear of possible legal consequences, and fear of causing further trauma or discomfort in the family and/or the child. The study detected a general belief in the need to confirm the suspicion of abuse as a prerequisite to reporting.

Difficulties in dealing with child abuse are present in other health related areas besides medicine: 84% of dentists (n = 70) in the city of Blumenau, Southern Brazil, [15] reported feeling unprepared to deal with child abuse. Difficulties associated in reporting were related to not being sure about confirming the abuse (42%), lack of knowledge, (32%), and fear of consequences (6%). Likewise, Australian dentists were unaware about child abuse issues, as shown by the high frequency of "*I don't know*" answers, when asked about procedures to be followed in child abuse cases [16].

1.2. Brazil's Family Health Program

The *Family Health Program* (*Programa Saúde da Família* or PSF), was initiated, in Brazil, in 1994, as a strategy for reorienting the healthcare model, through the implementation of multidisciplinary teams in primary healthcare units. These teams are responsible for monitoring a number of families (up to 4.500 persons) located in a defined geographical area. The teams act on health recovery, health promotion, disease rehabilitation, and more frequent disorders, as well as maintaining the community's health level [17].

Each team is responsible for becoming aware of family demographics by taking pertinent data from each family, filling out information on different diagnoses for all individuals in a given family. Health professionals and the families create bonds, which in turn, facilitates the identification and assistance to community health problems [18].

The Family Health Program in the city of San Carlos, where this study was conducted, was established in 2001 with four Teams. Currently this program benefits 64.000 people, and 16 teams are in operation. The municipality has a goal of reaching 50% of the population by the end of 2012, as the city undergoes a health service remodeling process.

Another peculiarity about this city is the fact that the Medicine Faculty from *Universidade Federal de São Carlos* (Federal University of São Carlos) has partnered with the municipality in terms of developing an innovative project geared towards family health care. The project involves adopting a model with a strong interaction between the public healthcare system in which the medical student starts his/her practice in the Family Health Program.

Working in the Family Health Program exposes professionals to various types of violence, such as family and urban violence which may affect professionals' mental health [19]. In addition to violence, through home visitation, professionals notice other adversities, such as extreme poverty, which in its turn, may trigger feelings of helplessness. Other potential problems are the non-recognition of efforts, no delimitation between professional and personal boundaries; fear of exposure to risks; feelings of moral and physical integrity threats, and fear of retaliation. All this context and challenges must be considered when proposing any intervention with such professionals [19].

1.3. The training of health professionals on child abuse

For Brazil's Ministry of Health [20], the development of a child abuse reporting system must overcome three challenges: 1) incorporating the reporting process in the healthcare activities routine, and in the organizational framework of welfare and educational services; 2) raising awareness and training health professionals and educators to understand the consequences of abuse to children's development, teaching professionals how to diagnose child abuse, how to report cases and make referrals when problems are found; and 3) building partnerships and alliances to ensure that reporting is only a first step of a much broader activity to support children, adolescents, their families or institutions working with them, and not simply an obligation as an end in itself.

Researchers agree on the need to train professionals on child abuse, and to systematically evaluate such trainings in studies in order to overcome the difficulties mentioned [4,13,15-16]. In addition, there is a need to insert the topic into curricula, as knowledge of child abuse is essential for healhcare [21]. The literature indicates that for physicians already in practice, training is more relevant in terms of case variables which are more difficult to observe, such as: a) the explanation given for the injury in case of physical abuse; and b) the time taken to bring the child for medical care, instead of restricting training to injury severity and its relationship to child abuse exclusively [21]. For medical students, it is necessary to develop skills of information gathering, and case deductions, and from the onset of training, students should actively be involved in the process of identification and child abuse reporting, working with experienced professionals as role models [22].

Moreover, it is important for professionals to become familiar with epidemiological data on child abuse, as this helps in making decisions to evaluate the information collected, especially in relation to the explanation given when child abuse is suspected, or in differential diagnosis [13, 21]. The literature also indicates that the difficulties in identification and reporting child abuse are found in several health related areas [14], thus it would be possible to start training from a broader topic such as what is child abuse, and subsequently direct the training to specific areas, such as types of treatment that a physician and a dentist may have to perform with an abused child [14].

The literature [22] has also recommended that for the training to be appropriate it should consider the ecological context of child maltreatment to understand risk factors present in the child, the family, the community and society. Researchers also say that the disparity in knowledge of health professionals who work at the same institution should be reduced by training all staff, with emphasis in the need for continuing education. The same conclusion was reached by scholars [23] who found an increase in the number of reported cases after training, but a decrease in subsequent months, indicating the need for ongoing education. Additionally, it is suggested [13] having regular case discussion meetings, stressing the investigative nature of protective services, and to educate physicians in the multidisciplinary aspects of child abuse.

Furthermore, it is recommended [24] that challenges faced by pediatricians in dealing with child abuse cases may be inserted into the training, such as: having the families, not just the children and mothers as the focus of attention; assessing routinely risk and protective factors associated with the child and the family; strengthening protective factors; and working to minimize or eliminate the risk factors.

Experiences with training other professionals on child abuse prevention are also worth mentioning. A quasi-experimental study was conducted by the second author to train pre-school educators [25] to act as child sexual abuse primary prevention agents. 101 pre-school teachers, 2.918 children, and 2.732 family members of these children took part of the program, which was developed in partnership with the city of São Carlos' Board of Education. Teachers participated of 12 weekly meetings, for three months, in which they learned to develop practical activities with the children, and their family members on child sexual abuse prevention. The program had a very positive impact in all involved, and the sexual abuse cases reported in the community nearly doubled at the program's end.

Training teachers in child abuse prevention is highly recommended. Hazzard and Rupp [26] compared child abuse-related knowledge and attitudes of pediatricians, mental health professionals (social workers, psychiatrists and psychologists), teachers and University students who completed a questionnaire on definitions, characteristics, causes and effects of child abuse. Mental health professionals were better informed than pediatricians. In contrast, teachers and University students were the least knowledgeable. On the basis of this study results, additional abuse-related education was recommended for pediatricians and, particularly, for teachers.

The training of health professionals should aim at increasing awareness of children's rights and needs, in ways to also increase the skills in identifying child abuse, maximizing the commitment to child abuse notification to ensure compliance with the law [7]. Thus, the aim of this study was to increase awareness of Family Health Program professionals in preventing child abuse, by evaluating a training course to identify and report abuse. Professional child abuse awareness was here defined in terms of the ability to identify child abuse cases, as well as specifying its different modalities, and to comply with legal requirement of case notification, when child abuse is suspected or confirmed.

2. Method

2.1. Participants

Two Family Health Unit teams (Group A and B) of the mid-size city of São Carlos, in the State of São Paulo, Southeast Brazil, took part of the study, encompassing a total of 22 health professionals. Group A consisted of one physician, a nurse, two nursing aids, a dentist, a dental assistant and six community health agents. Group B had similar members, minus the dentist and dental assistant, as configuration of the teams varies according to practical demands. The groups were similar regarding the number of participants, gender distribution, average age and average length of professional experience. Table 1 below presents a description of both family health teams.

The teams were chosen based in communities with higher prevalence of child abuse in the year of 2008, as reported to CPS. The Protection Service had only started to have reports with number of reported cases per neighborhood as of the year 2008.

		Group A	Group B	Total
Number of participants		11	11	22
Sex	Female	8	9	17
	Male	3	2	5
Age (years)		23 – 41 M = 29	24 – 47 M = 33	23-47 M= 31
Length of professional experience		10 months – 18 years M = 7.6 years	16 months – 21 years M = 6.4 years	10 months – 21 years M= 6.9 years

Table 1. Demographic characteristics of participants in Groups A and B.

2.2. Instruments used in data collection

a) *Questionnaire on Hypothetical Cases,* [14] containing two vignettes with the aim of verifying which procedures the professional would adopt in the process of child abuse identification and reporting. The instrument was originally developed by the first author to pediatricians, and the vignettes were written based on reports from health professionals who had contact with suspected child maltreatment. For the present study, the instrument was adapted adding the context and routine of the Family Health Program. The first vignette involved a possible neglect case, and the second a suspected sexual abuse case. The choice of these two types of violence refers to the difficulty in identifying negligence by health professionals, in spite of being the most common type of abuse reported to CPS; as well as the fact that sexual abuse is still considered by many a taboo, and often, a family secret.

b) *Child Maltreatment in Pediatric Primary Care Evaluations* by Lane and Dubowitz [27].The instrument contains three parts: the first being a survey of cases of physical, sexual abuse and neglect reported or not reported; the second part is made of 38 sentences in which the professional responds according to a five point Likert Scale of agreement, where 1 corresponds to *strongly disagree* with the statement, and 5 with *strongly agree* with the statement. The statements address reporting consequences to the professional, evaluate need for training and support in making decisions, and assess knowledge on the subject. The third part of the instrument characterizes the professional (giving information on age, gender, ethnicity, work experience, number of courses on the subject). For the present study only 37 sentences of the second part of the instrument were used. The authors gave authorization to the translation and adaptation of this instrument to Portuguese for this study.

c) *Questionnaire on Family Violence against Children and Adolescents,* developed by Rossi [28] whose definitions of types of violence were adapted by Giusto [29]. This questionnaire aimed at investigating whether reporting was a procedure adopted by health professionals working in the public sector. In addition, the instrument was designed to assess the knowledge of professionals about the signs of abuse, to identify if there are personal and professional consequences to child abuse reporting, and to identify whether discussion of family violence was part of the professionals' training. The instrument provides a definition of each type of Violence (physical, sexual, psychological abuse and neglect,), giving information on professional demographic characteristics; on identification of signs and symptoms of child abuse; knowledge of laws; aspects of personal consequences of reporting child abuse; knowledge of the professional ethics code; training on child abuse and the responsibility to report.

Data collection also involved monitoring child abuse reporting behavior to CPS by each team participant, prior to the training program (for one year) and afterwards.

2.3. Procedure

The project was approved by the University's Ethics Committee, and participants signed Informed Consent explaining the study's objectives, risks and benefits associated with the research, and guarantee of anonymity. The initial contact with the health teams was made by telephone, followed by a letter sent by email, with the course proposal attached. After interest in participation was expressed, a meeting was held with the first author to provide further explanations.

The intervention initially took place exclusively with Group A, and two pre-intervention assessments were done with Group B prior to their respective training. The training took place at each Family Health Unit's office, in rooms designated for staff meetings. Each Unit office was located in different geographical areas.

Before starting training with Group A, the *Questionnaire on Family Violence against Children and Adolescents* was administered to both groups to evaluate the initial repertoire on the subject and previous group experience. The instruments *Questionnaire on Hypothetical Cases* and *Child Maltreatment in Pediatric Primary Care Evaluations* were applied at pre-test to evaluate the course, as well as at post-test for comparison.

2.4. The training procedure

The training was aimed at overcoming the second challenge indicated by Brazil's Ministry of Health [20] which is to raise awareness, and train health professionals to understand the consequences of abuse to children's development, teaching professionals how to diagnose child abuse, how to report cases, and make referrals when problems are found.

The training contents were divided into four main themes:

1. Definition of child abuse according to Brazilian law, Brazil's Ministry of Health and the World Health Organization;
2. What is mandated reporting and its importance to society;
3. How do Child Protection Services, the Judiciary System and the Protection Support Network operate and some of the difficulties they face;
4. Proper use of the child abuse mandated reporting form to health professionals;

The training relied on LAPREV's (The Laboratory for Analysis and Prevention of Violence) past experience in teaching the topic of child abuse to different professionals, such as, teachers [25], police [30], CPS [31] and institutional staff [32].

The specific training involved that by the end of the course professionals should be able to: a) identify family violence as a phenomenon, b) identify different modalities of child abuse; c) identify the signs and symptoms associated with such violence; d) identify risk and protective factors for child abuse; e) analyze myths surrounding the subject; f) analyze appropriate ways to approach victimized children; g) identify the protective network in their community; h) identify and analyze factors that promote resilience; i) establish a dialogue with CPS, and j) correctly complete the mandated child abuse health professional reporting form.

Training lasted 15 hours in total, divided into 10 biweekly meetings, lasting one and a half hour each, inserted into their regular four-hour staff meetings. Different activities to increase participation were used throughout.

Different activities to increase participation were used throughout the training. In meetings 2 and 6 there were discussions about written material compiled by the first author. In meetings 3 and 7 excerpts from the film "*Bastard Out of Carolina*" [33] were shown, as well as an animation "*Once upon a family*" [34] to facilitate group discussion. In addition, at meeting 7, local and national newspaper clippings on child abuse cases were given for analysis of risk factors and procedures involved. At meeting 4 there was role-playing of a fatal child abuse hypothetical case by participants, who were divided into pairs, and given different roles. In the meeting 9, two reporting forms were analyzed: one used by the State Department of Health and another by the Ministry of Health. In meeting 5, a representative of the local Child Protection Service made a presentation, and answered questions, and in meeting 8 a forensic psychologist working in the Judiciary system made, likewise, a presentation.

After each meeting, the first author took records of the main procedures and verbalizations. At the end of the training course, a questionnaire was administered to assess the degree of participant satisfaction.

2.5. Data analysis

This case study had a pre-experimental A-B design which allowed comparing differences in scores on the pre-test and post-test in both groups [35].

In the *Questionnaire on Hypothetical Case* [14] data analysis is based on categories established by questions. The answers were analyzed qualitatively, enabling the creation of subcategories, and a descriptive analysis of the responses was performed.

The *Child Maltreatment Evaluations in Pediatric Primary Care* [27] uses a Likert scale of 5 points: *strongly disagree* (SD), *disagree* (D), *neutral* (N), *agree* (A) and *strongly agree* (SA). To verify if there were changes of opinion between the steps, the Wilcoxon test was used. The level of significance was set at 5%. Thus, the p-value obtained in each test rejected the hypothesis of equality groups and no change of opinion when the p-value is greater than 0.05. Data analyzes were performed using SPSS statistical software.

The *Questionnaire on Family Violence against Children and Adolescents* [29] has a predetermined set of response categories for each variable, thus the final score involved the frequency responses of presented options.

3. Results and discussion

We will initially present data on participant's previous experience with child abuse cases, for both groups. In sequence we will present the quantitative data from the instruments regarding pre and post measures, and lastly qualitative data will also be presented to compare changes in participants' views.

3.1. Previous experience with child abuse

Table 2 presents the distribution of participants who had contact with suspected or confirmed cases of physical abuse, sexual abuse, psychological abuse, and neglect, illustrating participants' previous experience.

	Physical Abuse	Sexual Abuse	Psychological Abuse	Negligence
Yes, once	6	4	7	5
Yes, more than once	4	0	5	7
No, never	10	16	8	7
No answer	1	1	1	2

Table 2. Previous experience of suspected or confirmed child abuse cases in frequency per modality of abuse (n=21, both groups combined).

The data indicates that at least once a particular health team member had previous contact with a child abuse case. Lack of previous involvement with sexual abuse cases was high (76% of participants), which may indicate difficulty or uncertainty in identifying such cases, as well as how under-reported this type of violence still is in this country. Although there were two different teams in different geographical areas, previous experience was similar among the groups.

Figure 1 illustrates how many participants had reported child abuse cases in the past, and how many would hypothetically report if a child abuse case occurred. Previously reported cases involved discussing the issue with the immediate boss or with colleagues. Most of the reported cases involved physical violence for both groups. Sexual violence cases were the most frequently reported in supposition.

The large difference between actual reported cases and intention of reporting may indicate socially acceptable answers to the instrument. Nevertheless, one has to consider the possibility that it may also reflect a genuine intention or high motivation to report, if they were to identify a child abuse case. Unfortunately, we were unable to verify if professionals past reporting experience did in fact take place, as CPS data was only gathered after the year 2008.

Among reasons given by participants not to report previously, "*not knowing how to do* it" was noteworthy. In addition, there were written comments on the instrument suggesting a new category "*the problem was solved in the workplace*", which seems to indicate that the professional found a temporary solution, instead of fulfilling the reporting law.

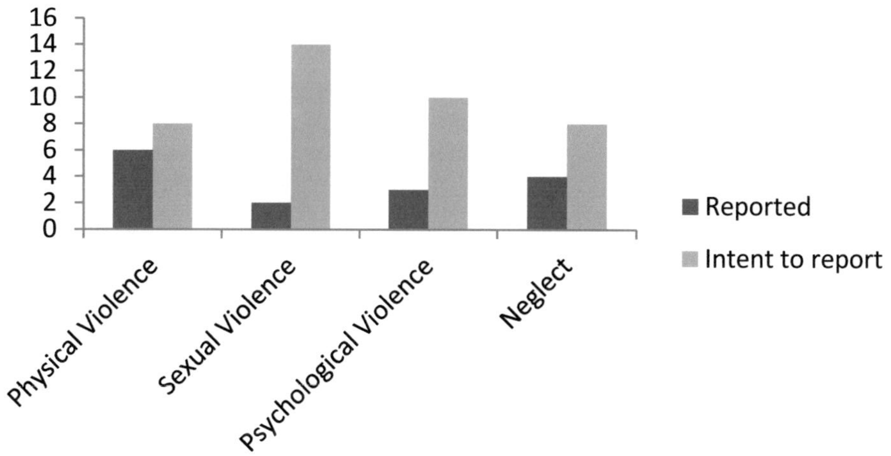

Figure 1. Frequency of participants who had previously reported child abuse and who would report, if needed.

In summary, both groups had contact with child abuse cases, but there was a low frequency of reporting to Child Protection Services. Although several participants stated that they would indeed report child abuse if needed, they also said that lack of knowledge about the correct procedure or by difficulties in identifying these cases were barriers to be faced. This entry data reinforces the need for training to reduce misunderstandings and comply with current legislation, ensuring the protection of children.

3.2. Evaluation of the training course

Table 3 presents frequency of responses given by participants in the *Questionnaire on Hypothetical Cases* [14] about which procedures would be adopted in a hypothetical situation of suspected negligence.

Procedures	Before training (n=19)	After training (n=18)
Call Child Protection	4	12
Request assistance from the team	8	7
Make home visits	9	2
Speak to parents or neighbors	7	2
Confirm the suspicion	3	1

Note: more than one answer may be given

Table 3. Frequency and types of procedures given to a hypothetical situation of suspected neglect.

After the training, there was a marked increase in the decision to involve the Child Protection Services, as required by law. The category *"request assistance from the team"* maintained approximately the same level,, although the procedure is considered suitable for such situation.

The procedure "*speaking to parents/neighbors*" had an expressive change, decreasing the frequency as indicated. Similar to speaking with parents, home visitation is a common procedure in the Family Health Program. Nevertheless, the professional role in this case involves speaking to the family, but not conducting an investigative interview, as this would not be appropriate. One of the training course topics was how should the professional behave if child abuse is suspected, without doing an investigation or adopting different professional boundaries.

Table 4 presents the procedures that would be adopted in a hypothetical situation involving suspected sexual abuse. The data illustrates that after the intervention, most participants would call Child Protection Services.

Procedure	Before training (n=19)	After training (n=18)
Request assistance from team	10	6
Call Child Protection/Police	6	12
Refer to a psychologist	0	1
Visit/communicate school	2	4
Speak to parents/neighbors	5	4
Speak to the victim (child)	2	2
Making home visits	2	1

Note: more than one answer may be given

Table 4. Frequency and types of procedures given to a hypothetical situation of child sexual abuse.

More participants reported that they would call CPS, doubling before training data. However, the category "*speak to parents*" and "*speak to the child*" remained unchanged, and this may be an artifact of the vignette involved in the instrument.

The difficulties encountered by participants to the situations of neglect and sexual abuse presented in instrument [14] were similar for both groups, namely: possible resistance from the family to take responsibility for the abuse, fear of retaliation from the abuser, lack of experience with these cases, fear that CPS would not handle appropriately the reported case, fear of exposing the child and not knowing how to speak with the child. After the training, the most frequently cited difficulty was "*possible resistance from the family to take responsibility for the abuse and to receive help*".

Previous contact with the theme of child abuse during professional training was classified as "*none*", except for two participants (a Community Health Agent and a nurse) who had "*little*" experience and had attended talks about child abuse.

3.3. Professionals 'opinions about personal and work-related aspects of child abuse

Child Maltreatment Evaluations in Pediatric Primary Care [27] responses were analyzed to see if the training had been responsible to change professionals 'opinions. The Wilcoxon test was conducted and significant changes of opinion between pre and post training (using both groups together) were seen for four instrument's questions (question 19 "*I feel competent to give a definitive opinion about physical abuse*" p = 0.027; question 25 "*I Know the law involved in the reporting child abuse/neglect"* p = 0.005; question 26 "*I know how to report a case of child who is being abused*" p = 0.013 and question 27 "*I feel comfortable in talking with families about child abuse"* p = 0.031).

It is somewhat frustrating that out of 32 questions, only 4 showed significant differences comparing pre-post results, suggesting that the training had little influence. However one must not discard the small size of the sample, difficulties answering the instrument, and the fact that participants may have given socially accepted answers.

The reasons provided in the instruments in general for not reporting child abuse corroborated the literature regarding the disbelief in CPS [10], lack of knowledge about activities of the Judiciary [12], lack of basic information to identify violence, peculiarities of each case which are influenced by professionals 'personal factors or by the structure of mostly insufficient services, [11], insufficient infrastructure and excessive workload of staff, and threats from the abuser to professionals, as well as fear of retaliation for living in the same community [6].

After the training, some of these factors did not change (nor could they have been changed), such as the excessive workload, and lack of infrastructure, but the positive assessment made by participants following the visit from Child Protection and the Forensic Psychologist may have been responsible to improve the image of this institutions as being inoperative. Participants gave testimonials regarding the changes in receiving information: "*The training was invaluable for learning and knowledge. It was a great achievement for the team.* "(PA11 – Participant 11 from Group A), and" *The course we had was very satisfactory; it has given us a new view of things, which sometimes, we passed unnoticed* "(PA7).

3.4. Effect of reporting behavior by participants

Monitoring of reporting behavior to Child Protection Services by health teams in the year preceding the training and afterwards was conducted. Group A reported *one* case to CPS after training and this same group had not reported *any* cases in the previous year. The report made by Group A employed the proper health notification form for child abuse, which was introduced in the training and it involved a sexual abuse case of 5 year old girl. The girl's mother who was pregnant had arrived for a routine check-up, and told the nurse that her daughter was *different* and that she thought her uncle might be doing "*the same thing to her daughter that he had done with her as a child*". Medical examination of the girl revealed a ruptured hymen. The team's nurse phoned the University, to confirm with the first author that all the necessary steps had been taken, and indeed the suggested procedure (reporting to CPS) had been adopted by the team.

Group B began the study without a history of reporting to CPS, but just before their training (while Group A had started to receive training), Group B made a report of a suspected case of sexual abuse. One may speculate if this reporting behavior was prompted by familiarity with the topic provided by the instruments. The reported case involved a 9 month-child, female, who was taken to Family Health Unit by her aunt because the baby had a rash in the genital area. Two professionals examined the child separately and found that the genital region did not have a rash, but was indeed, edematous and red, signaling possible sexual abuse. The girl's aunt told both professionals that she suspected sexual abuse by the child's stepfather. CPS was, then, called and a letter by the physician indicating possible sexual abuse was forwarded as well. When the first author examined this case at CPS, there was also a letter from the child's mother among the documentation, registering a complaint against the physician, as she felt that the reporting was aimed at harming her family.

According to staff reports, the child was sent for an exam at the city's Legal Medical Institute, but supposedly the expert had written that that "*because there is no hymen rupture one cannot claim that there was sexual abuse*". The family moved away from the neighborhood, and no longer visited that particular health unit. During the first training meeting with Group B, the case was narrated, and assessed by the team as an example of failure from the protection network. The general opinion was that even when the professional fulfilled his/her role, there were no guarantees that the case would have a proper resolution, point that was often discussed throughout the course.

This case illustrates the difficulties and shortcomings of the Protection Network and how difficult it is to prosecute child sexual abuse cases in the city [36]. The case also illustrates the need for ongoing training of all agencies involved, including experts from the Forensic Institute, who conduct medical examinations of children who may have been sexually abused.

After training, one more report record was observed by Group B, which may indicate that the intervention helped to overcome the initial negative experience. There is however another complication concerning notifications to CPS by Group B. At the fifth meeting in which a CPS staff made a presentation to the group, health participants reported five cases during this visit (two cases involving adolescents with drug involvement, a case of suspected neglect and two cases of physical violence). CPS staff wrote down names and addresses of the five children, explaining that he would refer them to other staff members of CPS. Nevertheless, no such records existed when the first author examined CPS data, but one cannot say that the reporting steps were not taken because the cases could have been "old" in the sense of previously reported, and therefore inaccessible in their data base.

Despite the low number of reporting done by the groups after the training, the fact that they existed may be considered an important step and positive result, given the very low contact staff reported having had previously with sexual abuse cases.

To Brazil's Ministry of Health [37] the main consequences of notification are: facilitating a registration system with trusted information and to ensure that victims are receiving support in institutional routines [20]. In spite of this assertion, systematic record keeping is no guarantee of its proper use or potential. The data itself is not useful if it does not help to support concrete public policies and actions at the local level. Reporting per se does not warrant that proper service is incorporated into the routine of the unit. There is a risk that a professional may fill out a reporting form and subsequently feel that his/her responsibility is over. However, it is felt that continuing education on child abuse prevention may reduce this risk by empowering professionals and adding new elements for case analysis, such as identifying risk and protective factors.

4. Conclusions

The goal of this study was to to increase awareness of Family Health Program professionals for preventing child abuse, by evaluating a training course to identify and report abuse. The choice of these professionals was based on the literature that indicates that training the team as a whole is more efficient than just training professionals individually [22].

Results indicated that there were positive changes of opinion and attitudes facing the topic of child abuse. From a quantitative point of view, results were not as robust as expected. Perhaps the instruments used in the study were not sensitive enough to observe changes, which would require investment in the construction of questionnaires with proper psychometric data, tested in large scale. Additionally, the reduced sample may have hampered the detection of quantitative improvements. From a qualitative viewpoint, on the basis of consumer satisfaction, the results were very encouraging. Additionally, there seems to have been initiated a systematic engagement with Child Protection Services, which did not exist before.

The prompt acceptability by staff, with which the teams agreed to take part of this training, reflects an interested and motivated attitude to learn about child abuse. However, because we provided training to a team in operation, many challenges had to be overcome as, for example, the insertion of a researcher in the teams and the floating of professionals during meetings for various reasons, hindering attendance. Initial questionnaire data confirmed that there was a lack of familiarity with the topic and, this way, basic concepts such as the fact that humiliating a child corresponds to psychological violence, had to be discussed with the teams.

One aspect that may have contributed to participants' positive course evaluation were the visits from CPS staff and the forensic psychologist, which helped to provide a realistic picture of the work involved, diminishing negative impressions. Some of the comments professionals made after such visits were: "*now I understand how Child Protection Services work, it was very enlightening*" (PA1), and "*It was enough to get a sense of how difficult it is to work there*" (PA6).

Authors [22] indicate that one should work with the team as a whole in order to reduce the disparity of knowledge of health professionals from the same institution. We could see that this was indeed possible and that it strengthened the bonds amongst teams.

Another point observed was the influence of health professionals own personal history of abuse as in the example of one team staff who said that: "*the last meeting* (about different types of violence*) made me reflect on the way I was raised, always with slaps and screams and that this was not necessary*" (PA12). Another participant disclosed to the team that when she was young, the aunt who raised her used to bang her head against the wall, if the child did not do house chores properly, and in addition, her cousins had attempted to rape her. It was agreed that these disclosures reflected confidence in the group as a team, and should remain confidential. A third participant disclosed privately to the researcher that she had been sexually abused as a child by and uncle, and a fourth professional told the researcher privately about what it was like to grow in a home with domestic violence, and how much she strived to provide a different environment to her children.

Yoshihama and Mills [37] examined the personal history of professionals and their influence on the professional responses to allegations of family violence. They found that about half of professionals (n = 303) reported having suffered physical and/or sexual violence by an intimate partner; one-third of respondents reported physical abuse in their childhood, and 22% had suffered sexual abuse as a child. Professionals who had an abuse history identified more with abused cases encountered, and offered greater support to victims, making more protective decisions. This aspect was not explored in the present questionnaires, but participants' accounts in each group with a history of corporal punishment, sexual and psychological violence indicate that there were indeed previous abuse histories. In future research it would be interesting to investigate this variable and match them to their respective opinions about the role of health professionals.

The emphasis given to the need of a training program rather than a single lecture [22] seems to be valid. The training in the present study lasted five months, enabling reflection among participants and a change of verbalizations, beliefs and attitudes about child abuse, which would have been difficult to observe in a shorter period of time. In addition, the inclusion of the training course in the work routine encouraged discussion of several potential or real child abuse cases.

Lane and Dubowitz [27] stated that clinical experience is essential for the development of skills and comfort level regarding assessments of child abuse Thus, a brief training may not be suitable to create the knowledge needed to assess and treat children suspected of abuse. Additionally, Lane and Dubowitz [27] verified the need for expert assistance, which is also relevant to this study, as after the training, the team pointed out that an interdisciplinary group would be ideal in terms of assessment of child sexual abuse and neglect cases.

Another possibility of course expansion would be to include in-depth encounters for each type of violence, as was proposal by the second author [25] after giving a specific training course on sexual sexual abuse, as each violence modality leads to specific demands. The training program recommendation on the ecological context of child abuse to understand risk and protective factors [22] was well suited to the context of the Family Health Program, which aims to meet individuals and family needs fully and continuously, developing actions to promote and restore health [38].

In conclusion, the training of health professionals to identify and report to competent authorities cases of child abuse, may be instrumental to Brazil's Family Health Program. It would be important to incorporate this approach, once tested in large scale, as public policy aimed at training professionals to improve the general care of the population, and especially to prevent violence.

Author details

Thais H. Bannwar
Federal University of São Carlos, Department of Psychology,
LAPREV (The Laboratory of Violence Analysis and Prevention), São Carlos, São Paulo, Brazil

Lúcia C.A. Williams
Federal University of São Carlos, Department of Psychology,
LAPREV (The Laboratory of Violence Analysis and Prevention).São Carlos, São Paulo, Brazil

5. Acknowledgement

This paper is part of the M.A. thesis conducted by the first author with a fellowship from FAPESP (Federation of Research Support from the State of São Paulo), supervised by the second author.

6. References

[1] Minayo, MCS. The inclusion of violence in the health agenda: historical trajectory. Cien Saude Colet. 2006 April/June;11(2): 1250-67.
[2] Krug EG, Linda LD, Mercy JA, Zwi AB, Lozan R. World report on violence and health. Geneva, World Health Organization; 2002.
[3] Brazil, Congress. [Statute of Child and Adolescent]. São Paulo, Editora Escala; 1990. Portuguese.
[4] Pires ALD, Miyazaki MCOS. [Children and adolescents maltreatment: a literature review for health professionals]. Arq de Cienc Saude. 2005 Jan-Mar; 12 (1): 42 – 9. Portuguese.
[5] Pascolat G, Santos CFL, Campos ECR, Valdez LCO, Busato D, Marinho DH. [Physical abuse: the profile of aggressor and child victim]. J Pediatr (Rio J). 2001 Feb; 77(1): 35-40. Portuguese.
[6] Gonçalves H, Ferreira AL. [Health professionals' reporting of family violence against children and adolescents]. Cad Saude Publica. 2002 Jan/Feb; 18 (1): 315-19. Portuguese.

[7] Deslandes S. [Medical care for victims of violence in emergency room: is it time for prevention?] Cien Saude Colet. 1999; 4(1): 81-93. Portuguese.

[8] Iossi MA. [The involvement of health professionals from Guarulhos in care the children who are victims of domestic violence: a necessary trajectory]. [dissertation]. Ribeirão Preto: University of São Paulo; 2004. Portuguese.

[9] Luna GLM, Ferreira RC, Vieira LJES. [Mandatory reporting of child abuse by professionals of Family Health Teams]. Cien Saude Colet. 2010 Mar; 15(2): 481-91. Portuguese.

[10] Braz M, Cardoso MHCA. [In contact with the violence – The health care professionals and their patients victims of abuse]. Rev Lat Am Enfermagem. 2000 Jan; 8 (1): 91-7. Portuguese.

[11] Gomes R, Junqueira MFPS, Silva CO, Junger WL. [The approach to bad treatment against children and teenagers in a public health-care unit]. Cien Saude Colet. 2002; 6(2): 275-83. Portuguese.

[12] Theodore AD, Runyan DK. A survey of pediatricians' attitudes and experiences with court in cases of child maltreatment. Child Abuse Negl. 2006 Dec; 30 (12): 1353-63.

[13] Haeringen, A.R.V., Dadds, M. & Armstrong, K. L. (1998). The child abuse lottery: will the doctor suspect and report? Physician attitudes towards and reporting of suspected child abuse and neglect. Child Abuse Negl. 1998 Mar; 22 (3): 159-69.

[14] Bannwart TH, Brino RF. (2011) Difficulties to identify and report cases of abuse against children and adolescents from the viewpoint of pediatricians. Rev. paul. pediatr. 2011 June; 29 (2): 138-45.

[15] Silveira JLGC, Mayrink S, Nétto OBS. [Child abuse: cases, knowledge and pratice among dentists in Blumenau – SC]. Pesq Bras Odontoped Clín Integr. 2005; 5(2): 119-26. Portuguese.

[16] John V, Messer LB, Aurora R, Fung S, Hatzis E, Nguyen T, San A, Thomas K. Child abuse and dentistry: a study of knowledge and attitudes among dentists in Victoria, Australia. Aust Dent J. 1999 Dec; 44(4): 259-67.

[17] Souza RA, Carvalho AM. Health Care Family Program and quality of life: a view from Psychology. Estud. psicol. (Natal). 2003 Sep/Dec; 8(3): 515-23.

[18] Andrade LOM, Barreto ICH, Bezerra RC. [Primary attention in health and the Family Health Program's strategy] "In": Campos GWS, Minayo MCS, Akerman M, Drumond Júnior M, Carvalho YM. Tratado de Saúde Coletiva. Rio de Janeiro: Hucitec; 2006. 783-836. Portuguese.

[19] Lancman S, Ghirardi MIG, Castro ED, Tuacek TA. [Repercussions of violence on the mental health of workers of the Family Health Program] Rev Saude Publica. 2009 June; 43(4): 682-88. Portuguese.

[20] Ministry of Health - Brazil. [Child maltreatment reporting by health professionals: one more step towards a socially responsible healthcare]. Brasília: Ministério da Saúde/ Secretaria de Assistência à Saúde; 2002. Portuguese.

[21] Warner-Rogers JE, Hansen DJ, Spieth LE. The influence of case and professional variables on identification and reporting of physical abuse: a study with medical students. Child Abuse Negl. 1996 Sep; 20 (9): 851-66.

[22] Reece RM, Jenny C. Medical training in child maltreatment. Am J Prev Med. 2005 Dec; 29 (5 Supplement 2): 266-71.

[23] Cerezo MA, Pons-Salvador G. Improving child maltreatment detection systems: a large-scale case study involving health, social services, and school professionals. Child Abuse Negl. 2004 Nov; 28 (11): 1153–69.

[24] Ferreira AL. Follow-up of child abuse victims: challenges for the pediatrician. J Pediatr (Rio J). 2005 Nov; 81 (5): 173-80.

[25] Brino RF, Williams LCA. Brazilian teachers as agents to prevent child abuse: an intervention assessment. "In": Daro D. World Perspectives on Child Abuse. 7ª. Ed. Chicago: ISPCAN – International Socitety for Prevention of Child Abuse and Neglect. 2006. 75-8.

[26] Hazzard A, Rupp G. A note on the knowledge and attitudes of professional groups toward child abuse. J Community Psychol. 1986 Apr; 14(2): 219-23.

[27] Lane W, Dubowitz H. Primary care pediatricians' experience, comfort and competence in the evaluation and management of child maltreatment: Do we need child abuse experts? Child Abuse Negl. 2009 Feb; 33 (2): 76-83.

[28] Rossi D. [Child abuse reporting: Health Professional procedures in the public sector of Campinas, SP]. [Dissertation] Campinas: Universidade Estadual de Campinas; 2004. Portuguese.

[29] Giusto RO. [Community health agents and their views on family and family violence.] [MA thesis] São Carlos: Universidade Federal de São Carlos; 2011. Portuguese.

[30] Williams LCA, Gallo AE, Maldonado DA, Brino RF, Basso AFT. [A workshop on psychology to Police officers from the Women's Police station]. Psi: Teo e Prá. 2000 ; 2 (2): 103-19.

[31] Maia JMD, Williams LCA. [Analysis of a training proposal to child protection agents]. "In": Williams LCA, Maia JMD, Rios KSA. Aspectos psicológicos da violência: Pesquisa e intervenção cognitivo-comportamental. Santo André: ESETec; 2010. 501-25. Portuguese.

[32] Prada CG, Williams LCA. [Effects of a behavior management intervention program for caregivers of foster care victimized children]. Rev. bras.ter. comport. cogn. 2007 June; 9 (1): 63-80. Portuguese.

[33] DiGiulio A/Huston A. Bastard Out of Carolina [DVD]. EUA: PlayArte Home Video; 1996. 97 min.

[34] Bianco R. Once up a family. [DVD]. Rio de Janeiro: Promundo/ Save the Children; 2007. 22 min.

[35] Cozby PC. Methods in Behavioral Research. California: Mayfield Publishing Co; 2001.

[36] Williams LCA, Padovani RC, Brino RF. Empowering families to face domestic violence. São Carlos: EDUFSCar/PAHO; 2009.

[37] Yoshihama M, Mills LG. When is the personal professional in public child welfare practice? The influence of intimate partner and child abuse histories on workers in domestic violence cases. Child Abuse Negl. 2003 Mar; 27 (3): 319–36.
[38] Ministry of Health - Brazil. [Family Health: a strategy to reorganize the healthcare system]. Brasília: Ministério da Saúde; 1997. Portuguese.

Chapter 7

Residential Care as a Resource of the Childhood Welfare System: Current Strengths and Future Challenges

Eduardo Martín

Additional information is available at the end of the chapter

http://dx.doi.org/10.5772/46402

1. Introduction

The aim of this chapter is to analyze the role played by residential care (hereafter, RC) within the childhood welfare systems, acknowledging its strengths, but also its weaknesses. The historical evolution and the changes made in the model to adapt it to current legislation are briefly analyzed. The model is currently set in Spain, where it is still more relevant than in other European countries, where other alternatives—such as placement with foster families—are more developed for children and adolescents who must be separated from their biological families. This resource attends a large number of children. According to the data of Save the Children (2011), worldwide, 8 million children are living in some RC modality, of whom 15000 live in Spain (Observatorio de la Infancia [Children's Observatory], 2011).

Throughout the long history of this resource, research on RC has mainly focused on the negative effects it may have on children. The results of the investigations conducted from a clinical and psychopathological approach are critically reviewed and analyzed, because research usually employs normalized comparison groups. Further, no pre-post measures are taken in order to reliably appraise the effects that living in RC has on these children, and, in many cases, a lot of the developmental problems detected may be due to the prior situation of maltreatment that led to separating the child from the family. The results of some studies with pre-post measures performed in Spain are presented, and they show that living in RC can be beneficial, although not in all cases, but only for certain profiles. Moreover, they belie the idea that the more time children spend in these resources, the worse effect they have on them. It is shown that very short stays can be as harmful as long stays, and that the most important aspect is to adjust the time to the characteristics of each case.

Subsequently, the research currently carried out in Spain on the integration in school of children and adolescents who live in RC is analyzed. The results reveal that they have many difficulties to integrate at school and their academic achievements are far below average, and a considerable percentage of these residential children do not even finish compulsory education, and only a token number of them continue post-compulsory education. As will be discussed, education for these children is important for several reasons: 1) Family and school are the two most important contexts for children's development. When one of them is lacking, such as the case of the family for these children, the school should reinforce its compensating role. 2) The school is the main normalized context that allows these children to establish relations of friendship and to enrich their social support networks, both with peers and with adults. 3) Finishing their studies and achieving adequate formation and qualification will allow for better socio-work insertion, once they come of age. This, in turn, will allow them to break out of the vicious circle of social exclusion, because most of the youngsters who drop out of the welfare system when they come of age return to the family from which they had to be separated for their own protection.

I will conclude by underlining the strengths and future challenges of RC as one more resource within the childhood welfare system. With regard to the strengths, I underscore its modernization, the professionalized care provided to the children, the positive effects it has in many cases and with certain profiles, being able to work with the families so as not to break the family bonds, as well as its flexibility to combine with other resources.

The challenges of the future involve the capacity to improve these children's academic adjustment—which is usually already impaired when they reach the residential homes—and their socio-work insertion when they come of age. One of the topics in RC research that has recently awakened much interest is the transition to adult life, where not all the results of the investigations carried out are positive. Some reflections are made about how to improve these processes. Among other aspects, other administrations, such as the educational administration, should take on a more active role within the childhood welfare system. Only by means of inter-administrative coordination can we provide effective solutions to these future challenges to RC. We shall also address the topic of care for the mental health problems of this population. The studies carried out on this aspect indicate that the prevalence of mental health problems in this collective is much higher than that of the population of children and adolescents who live with their families.

2. Residential care: Evolution of the models and typology

RC has a long history as a resource to attend children and adolescents who, for whatever reason, have no family to protect them. Both the old-fashioned orphanages and the current supervised homes have helped a considerable percentage of minors who were in a situation of vulnerability. With the change of the model of the childhood welfare system that takes place in Europe in the second half of the 20th century, we abandoned the notion that the only possible intervention for unprotected childhood was the charity-based one, where practically the only resource was the enormous residences in which boys and girls were interned because their parents could not (or did not want to) attend their needs. At that not too distant time, children were admitted so that their basic needs would be taken care of within the residences, because they even studied and received medical care without leaving the enclosure. Most of the boys and girls who entered these residences did not leave them until they were of age and, in many cases, they were all alone in a society they were unfamiliar with, because they had grown up within the walls of the institution. Until the first half of the 20th century, the socially constructed image of these children was that of victims of a traumatic situation, and it was thought that they would not be able to develop normally because they had no family, so most of them were predestined to poverty, delinquency, or prostitution. The future granted to these children was social margination. Therefore, there was no social pressure to change the care and opportunities provided to these children, because most of the population had ambivalent feelings towards them, a mixture of compassion and fear. A famous refrain says *"ojos que no ven, corazón que no siente"* [out of sight, out of mind], so it was considered appropriate for these children to be practically locked up in these large residences, concealing them from the public opinion, which did not accept any responsibility for this population other than some beneficial gesture. Thus, there was at this time no kind of external control or supervision of what went on within these institutions, and over time, too many cases of maltreatment and even indiscriminate adoptions, under the suspicion of commercial transactions, have come to light. The characteristics of these large institutions, according to Del Valle and Fuertes (2000), are shown in Table 1.

Indiscriminate admittance criterion	The children were often collected directly from the parents, and cases of maltreatment, abandonment, or simply of poverty were indiscriminately mixed together. The treatment received by the children did not respond to their peculiarities, but instead all were treated equally.
Self-sufficiency and institutionalization	All the children's needs were met within the institution: medical care, feeding, hygiene, education, leisure, etc., so the children did not need to leave the enclosure and could not relate to other people except for the staff and the other children who lived in the institution. Thus, they were deprived of basic aspects for their development, such as the establishment of social networks and physical and social experiences.
Basic care	The care provided to the children was essentially meeting their most basic needs, without attending the possible problems they had due to their prior experiences of maltreatment or poverty and social margination.
Lack of staff training	The staff that attended the children was not required to have any kind of training. Most of these institutions were of a religious nature, and the way they dealt with the children was based more on doctrinal aspects than on scientific knowledge.

Table 1. Common characteristics of the charity-model institutions for children

World War II, the most destructive and atrocious war suffered by humanity throughout its history, led to the generalized realization of the rights of human beings. In 1948, the recently created General Assembly of the United Nations approved the Universal Declaration of Human Rights, although it took more than 40 years to approve the Convention on Rights of the Child. This delay is not casual. Childhood was never granted a voice to claim its rights, easily trampled by adults due to children's inability to assert them and defend themselves from all kinds of aggressions suffered, and which many children still currently suffer. This is vitally important in order to understand that the evolution of modern childhood welfare systems (among which is RC, as it is understood nowadays) has been relatively slow, which is why they are not yet fully developed. Moreover, the adequate social construction of childhood and our responsibility towards children who are not our blood relations are still far from ideal. As noted by Garrido (2001), legislators not only make decisions as a function of research, but particularly, depending on whether their decisions make sense to society and are demanded by it. We should therefore appraise the development of the childhood welfare systems that currently exist from this perspective.

As a result of the adherence by most countries to the Convention of Rights of the Child(although there are still a few that have not yet signed it, some of them really surprising), the charity model of children's welfare is beginning to be abandoned. In developed countries, this adherence led to legislative development that provided the foundations of the welfare systems as they are currently known. In the case of Spain, this transition was delayed due to the military dictatorship, which lasted until almost the end of the 1970s. The model sustained by this change disrupted the charity model. Firstly, RC went from being almost the only resource for the welfare of childhood to becoming just one more resource. Adoption and foster care become alternative and preferential measures for children who had to be separated from their families. Moreover, family intervention programs were promoted, which sought to strengthen families so that the children would not have to be separated (Rodrigo, Máiquez, Martín & Byrne, 2008), because one of children's essential rights was established by consensus: the right to grow up in a family, if possible, the family of origin. Nevertheless, in spite of these good intentions and the consensus about the priority that all children grow up in a family setting, in Spain, the implementation of protective measures, such as foster care, developed slower than in other countries like the UK (Colton & Hellinckx, 1995). Although things are changing, and the number of available families is increasing, the number of children who live in RC and the new cases that are admitted each year are surprisingly stable. Figure 1 shows the evolution of RC in Spain during the past few years. Each year, an average of 9000 children enters RC, with a yearly total approximately 15000.

The principle of normalization is established for those cases that must be admitted into RC. The aim is that the lives of children who live in RC should be as similar as possible to the lives of children who live with their families. However, this principle is currently the subject of some debate because, for some authors, to consider normal a situation that should be exceptional can lead to institutionalization (Campos, 2011). Due to the implementation of this principle, the large residences have been turned into small homes, with a reduced group of children who carry out many activities outside of the home, thus promoting community integration; and where all the children have a work plan: to return to their families or to another foster family, adoption, or preparation for the transition to adult life in those cases in which they cannot or do not want to return to a family environment. Moreover, in most cases, the staff that works in these resources has adequate training (Del Valle & Fuertes, 2000).

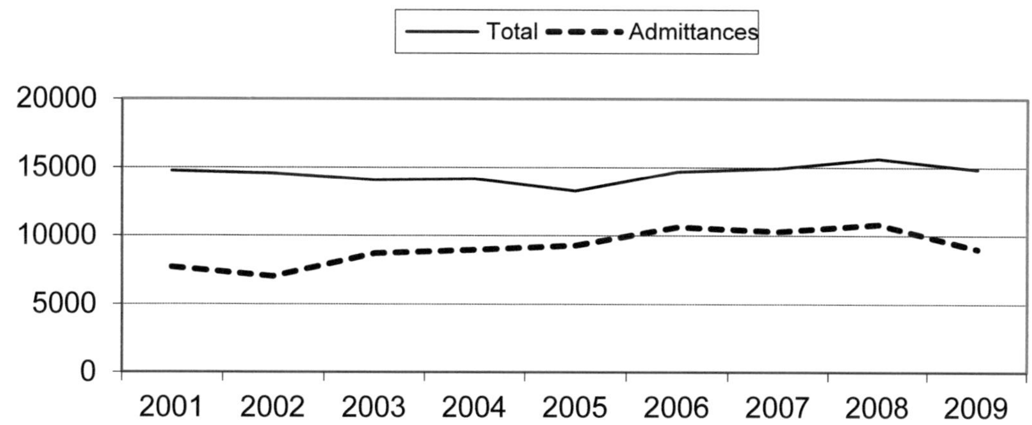

Figure 1. Evolution of yearly admittances and the total number of children in RC in Spain (Source: Observatorio de la Infancia, 2011).

The concern to provide adequate care to this population of children led to the elaboration of quality standards to appraise the work carried out in RC (General Assembly of the United Nations, 2009; Child Welfare League of America, 1991; Del Valle & Bravo, 2007; Redondo, Muñoz & Torres, 1998; Fedération Internationale des Communautés Educatives [FICE], International Foster Care Organisation [IFCO] & Children's Villages, SOS, 2007).

One of the recommendations of these standards is to provide individualized treatment in all cases and, in this regard, the existence of very diverse profiles has made it necessary to create centers specialized by profiles, which, moreover, vary according to the country. This leads to the need to define what we mean by RC and what are the modalities. When performing a bibliographic search of the topic children's residential care, studies about boarding schools, centers for children with special educational needs, or even centers for young offenders may be found. We shall use RC to refer to the resources provided for children and adolescents who must be separated from their families for their own protection, because their families cannot meet their basic needs. And we shall only refer to those resources where the children carry out their entire daily activity, excluding day centers in which the children only spend a few hours a day with very clear goals of meeting some specific needs, but from which the children return to their family home every day (Svenlin, 2010). In the case of Spain, according to classification of Bravo and Del Valle (2009), we can find the following types of RC:

- *Immediate Shelter Centers*: These are centers aimed at attending cases of urgent separation from the family, where the child's status and case are appraised, to be subsequently referred to the most appropriate resource for that case. The stay in these centers should be short, a few months at most, although in many cases the stays are unduly prolonged.
- *RCs for children under 3 years of age*: Although there is a legislative initiative aimed at preventing small children from living in centers, until this intention becomes a reality, the RC network includes this type of children's center because children of these ages have different needs of attention and care from those of older children.
- *Supervised Children's Homes*: Herein are included all the resources in which children of different ages live in a home that is an attempt to imitate a family environment. Within this category are diverse resources, such as those in which the staff work in shifts and those with fixed 24-hour staff.
- *Homes to prepare adolescents for independence*: Although the legislation obliges the state to protect minors until they are of age (in Spain, this is 18 years), it is necessary to prepare them for emancipation in all cases in which family reunification is not foreseen. Skills to facilitate social and occupational integration are taught so the adolescents can be independent when they leave the welfare system. As in contemporary society, and more so due to the economic crisis, being economically independent at 18 years of age is practically impossible, resources to attend to youngsters over 18 who have no resources are beginning to appear, so they can continue with their studies. These resources could be included within this category.
- *Homes and centers for adolescents with emotional and behavioral problems*: A change that has recently been observed is the increase in cases of children over 12 years old who enter the welfare system at their parents' request because their parents cannot control their behavior. Although most of the cases occur due to lacks in the parents' educational styles—which indicates enormous lacks in prevention—in many cases, these minors require specialized attention because some of them have even developed mental health problems. These centers are an attempt to respond to this profile with specialized attention.
- *Homes for unaccompanied alien minors*: Due to the economic bonanza in Europe during the years before the current crisis, the phenomenon of immigration emerged, and it was especially visible in frontier countries like Spain. In addition to adults and families, unaccompanied minors with no family references began to arrive. As they were minors in Spanish territory, the law considered them to be the object of protection, but their profile is very different culturally and religiously, and also with regard to language and even to their life goals, so they require special handling. Nevertheless, the crisis has led to a decrease in the migratory flow and the current situation is therefore not as chaotic as it was at the beginning of the 21st century.

As can be seen, there are very diverse profiles, and RC childhood is a very heterogeneous population, but they have one thing in common: they are all neglected minors who have no family setting, and for whom special children's homes are the only available alternative in order to live together with other people. The question is: does RC protect them or does it do more harm? This leads us to review the results of the scientific research on this resource of the welfare system.

3. Research of residential care

The charity-based past of this resource, as well as the lack of research until not long ago, has led to the appraisal of RC and its effect on children more as a function of beliefs than of knowledge. In many cases, this resource has been satanized, even by legislators, and we hear cries advocating the disappearance of RC and its replacement by other measures, such as foster homes, which are considered, per se, to be better than RC. Therefore, it is essential to collect data about the research developed in this field. Given its long past, the research of RC has changed, even as a function of the paradigms and predominant theories of each epoch. Towards the mid 20th century, the works of Spitz on the hospitalism syndrome of institutionalized children and the works of Bowlby about the negative effects of maternal deprivation began to generate a bad image of RC after World War II, a time when society began to be more sensitive about these children. A first effect of these early studies was, on the one hand, to initiate a line of research based on the problems developed by children in RC, and, on the other hand, as a consequence of the former, to generate a psychological intervention model based on an eminently clinical and psychiatric approach. This model was based on the idea that the child was the problem, so the intervention had to focus on the child. The line of research on all the kinds of problems produced by RC generated an enormous quantity of literature. The research method used was mainly to compare children raised in RC with groups of children who had always been with their family, or who had been adopted after living in RC (Chisholm, 1998; Han & Choi, 2006; Harden, 2002; Hodges & Tizard, 1989; Kaler & Freeman, 1994; O'Connor, Rutter & the ERA Team, 2000; Sloutsky, 1997; Tizard & Hodges, 1978; Vorria, Rutter, Pickles, Wolkind, & Hobsbaum, 1998). All these studies coincide that children raised in RC have more emotional, cognitive, social, and even physical problems than children who live with their families or who were sent to foster families or adopted by another family. A review of these studies carried out by Johnson, Browne, and Hamilton-Giachritsis (2006) concludes that, especially for smaller children, spending more than 6 months in RC can have severe consequences for their development. These results have helped to firmly fix the bad image of RC in the political and public opinion. Nevertheless, these results have been questioned mainly due to methodological defects, because they do not differentiate the effects of the prior situation that led the minor to be admitted in RC, nor are there any works that compare the status of the minor upon admittance and at some later date (Del Valle, 2003; Martín, Rodríguez & Torbay, 2007). Although some studies try to identify the problems caused by the prior family situation before the problems produced by the stay in RC (Knuston, 1995; Roy, Rutter, & Pickles, 2000), poorer results are still found in children raised in RC. But in spite of these attempts, there are still shortcomings in the research designs. Firstly, the children's opinion about their stay is not taken into account, and the situation is appraised exclusively from the adults' viewpoint. Secondly, the samples of children in RC came from orphanages of countries that are not particularly distinguished for the quality of their protective systems. And thirdly, a relevant fact that usually goes unnoticed was not taken into account: the children who enter RC are the ones who, because of their age or their problems, or simply because they have no extended family, have no other alternative, and they are the most difficult cases and the ones that usually develop more problems at all levels.

With the change of model produced at the end of the past century, the work has become professionalized, making it possible to achieve a series of assessable goals. Thus, as there were now recoding and assessment instruments, a line of research based on the assessment of the RC programs appeared (Bullock, Little & Milham, 1993; Skinner, 1992). In Spain, some works based on one of these systems was developed: the "Sistema de evaluación y registro en acogimiento residencial" ([System of assessment and recording of RC]; Del Valle & Bravo, 2007). Del Valle and Bravo (2001) found that aspects such as family involvement in the work carried out in the residence or social integration within the community were the most difficult goals to achieve. Martín, Torbay, and Rodríguez (2008) and Martín *et al.* (2007) used this assessment and recording system to conduct a study with repeated measures. They analyzed the degree of goal achievement of the programs at two moments with a 9-month interval. They found that some children improved, others worsened, and others maintained their scores over time (see Figure 2). When analyzing which children improved, they found that the ones who had experienced a situation of more severe maltreatment and who remained in RC for over one year and less than three years obtained the highest benefits. Moreover, if the professionals worked with the family, and the family cooperated with the home in educational tasks, the children obtained more benefits, which no doubt facilitated a possible family reunification. From the above, various aspects are derived that should be underlined. Firstly, when children have been the victims of severe maltreatment, and urgent separation from the family is required, RC can provide them with an adequate and stable setting to recover from some of the negative effects suffered. These effects, which are often emotional instability and behavior problems, impair their good adjustment to foster care. Admittance of these cases in RC would forestall a possible interruption of foster care, thus preventing yet one more separation; we know that the greater the number of changes and interruptions suffered by the children from the time of their admittance into the welfare system, the more emotional sequelae they display.

Secondly, we must qualify the effects of the stay in RC on these children. The results of these studies show that very short and very long stays are the most harmful. If a child enters into RC, it is with one aim, and to achieve it requires a certain time, which is usually not very long. Trying by any means to minimize the time spent by children in RC, independently of whether or not the goals were met, can be harmful, because it could hinder a subsequent family reunification or being admitted into a foster home.

Thirdly, when working coordinately with a family, and the family cooperates with the residence (naturally, in those cases in which it is foreseen that the child will return to the family), the children improve very much, which increases the likelihood of successful reunification. Goals, such as the family's involvement in the children's education and learning educational and care tools, can also be worked on with the family.

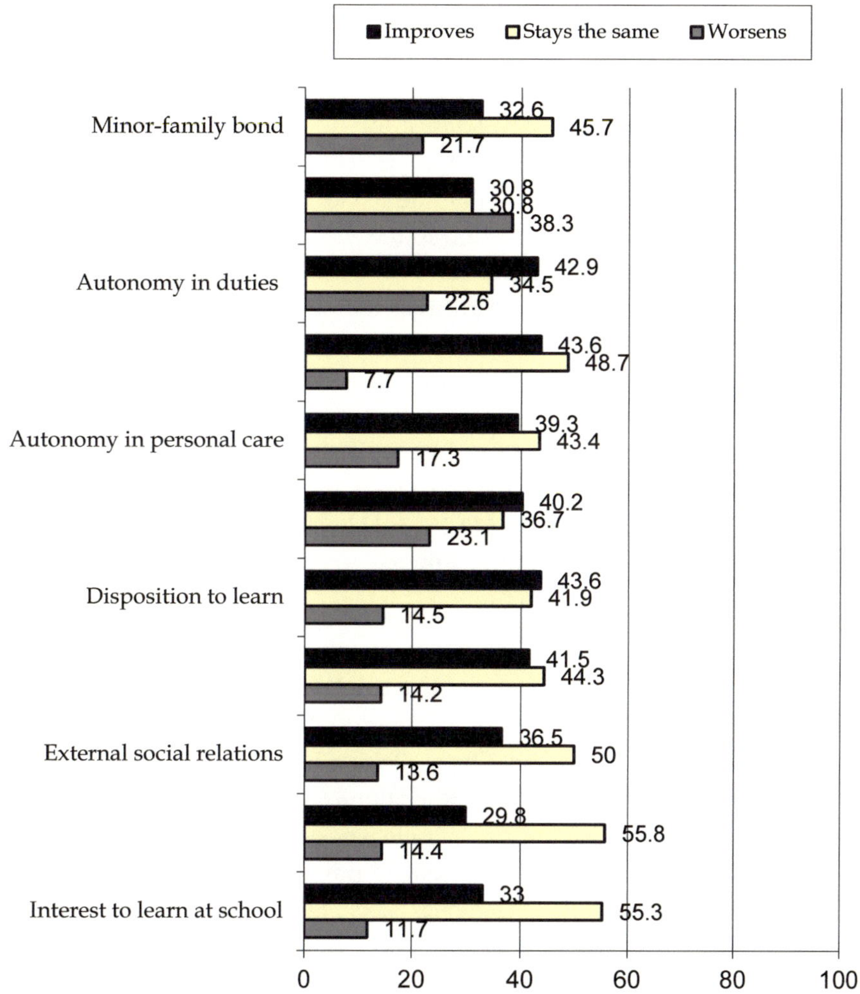

Figure 2. Percentage of minors as a function of the change observed in the diverse dimensions assessed (Reproduced from "Evaluación diferencial de los programas de acogimiento residencial para menores" of E. Martín, T. Rodríguez and A. Torbay, 2007, Psicothema 19(3), 406-412. Copyright: Colegio Oficial de Psicólogos del Principado de Asturias. Reproduced from "Cooperación familiar y vinculación del menor con la familia en los programas de acogimiento residencial"of E. Martín, A. Torbay and T. Rodríguez, 2008, Anales de Psicología 24(1), 25-32. Copyright: Servicio de Publicaciones de la Universidad de Murcia).

4. Adaptation and academic achievements of children and adolescents in RC

The legislative changes that modernized the RC model near the end of the 20th century granted special relevance to children's and adolescents' social integration as a means to achieve the normalization of this collective and to prevent the perverse effects of institutionalization and stigmatization that were produced in the past. Thus, the children began to go to the schools of the area with other boys and girls. This evidently had a positive effect on the normalization process. Thus, the school became the main normalized context for their development, of vital importance for the collective of children in RC (Berridge, 2007; Brodie, 2005; Goddard, 2000; Maclean & Connely, 2005; Martín, Muñoz & Pérez, 2011), and this is essentially due to the fact that the school can fulfill a large number of the needs of these minors. Firstly, a good adaptation to the school and good academic achievement will allow them to improve their qualifications, which will facilitate their social integration through the work market, thus interrupting the cycle of intergenerational reproduction of social exclusion that occurs in many cases (Vacca, 2008). On the other hand, as the school is a normalized context of formal and normative development, this offers the opportunity to learn to get on well both with adults and with peers, respecting the established rules. And lastly, it leads to the establishment of bonds, both with prosocial adults and providers of support—which has proven to be a key factor for socially disadvantaged minors (Baker, 2006; Cyrulnik, 2002; Lázaro, 2009; Martín & Dávila, 2008; Masten & Reed, 2002)—and also with peers—whose role in these minors' cognitive, emotional, social, and moral development is extremely important.

The studies that have analyzed the academic situation of minors in RC show that this collective has higher rates of failure, academic delay, and school dropout than the rest of the population (Berridge, 2007; Cameron, Hollingworth & Jackson, 2011; Casas & Montserrat, 2009; Stone, 2007; Trout, Hagaman, Casey, Reid & Epstein, 2008). This problem is attributed to three main causes (Martín, Muñoz, Rodríguez & Pérez, 2008). Firstly, the prior situation of maltreatment can provoke a series of deficiencies in the cognitive, emotional, and social development that hinders their adjustment to the academic and relational demands of the school (Anthonysamy & Zimmer-Gembeck, 2007; Leiter, 2007). Martín *et al.* (2008) analyzed 60 classrooms in which children in RC were studying. They used a scale of perceptive attribute assignation and found that the children in RC were perceived by their classmates as not getting on well with the teachers, being more aggressive, and calling attention to themselves more often (see Figure 3). This behavioral profile impairs relations both with peers and with teachers, and therefore it becomes a risk factor that can cause maladjustment and school dropout (Martín & Muñoz de Bustillo, 2009; Martín *et al.* (2011).

Secondly, the frequent changes of locations that usually occur while the minor is under the guardianship of public administrations also involve changing schools, which does not facilitate a good academic adjustment (Trout *et al.*, 2008). And lastly, the RC programs prioritize therapeutic goals over educational goals, which, in many cases, means they cannot dedicate the necessary resources (time, personnel, materials, coordination with tutors, etc.) that are required to improve the academic situation of minors in RC (Harker, Dobel-Ober, Lawrence, Berridge & Sinclair, 2003; Linsey & Foley, 1999).

These problems have gone unnoticed until a very short time ago, when studies that analyze the transition from the welfare system to independence have begun to appear (Stein, Ward

& Courtney, 2011). The reason is that this population has been an invisible collective for society (Casas & Montserrat, 2009), so no attention has been paid to these worrisome data. Moreover, it has never been entirely clear which entity is responsible for all this: the educational administrations, those in charge of the childhood welfare system, or their coordination. Some positive experiences in the UK seem to show that, when working coordinately from both systems, the academic results of children and young people in RC improve (Cameron *et al.*, 2011; Maclean & Connelly, 2005).

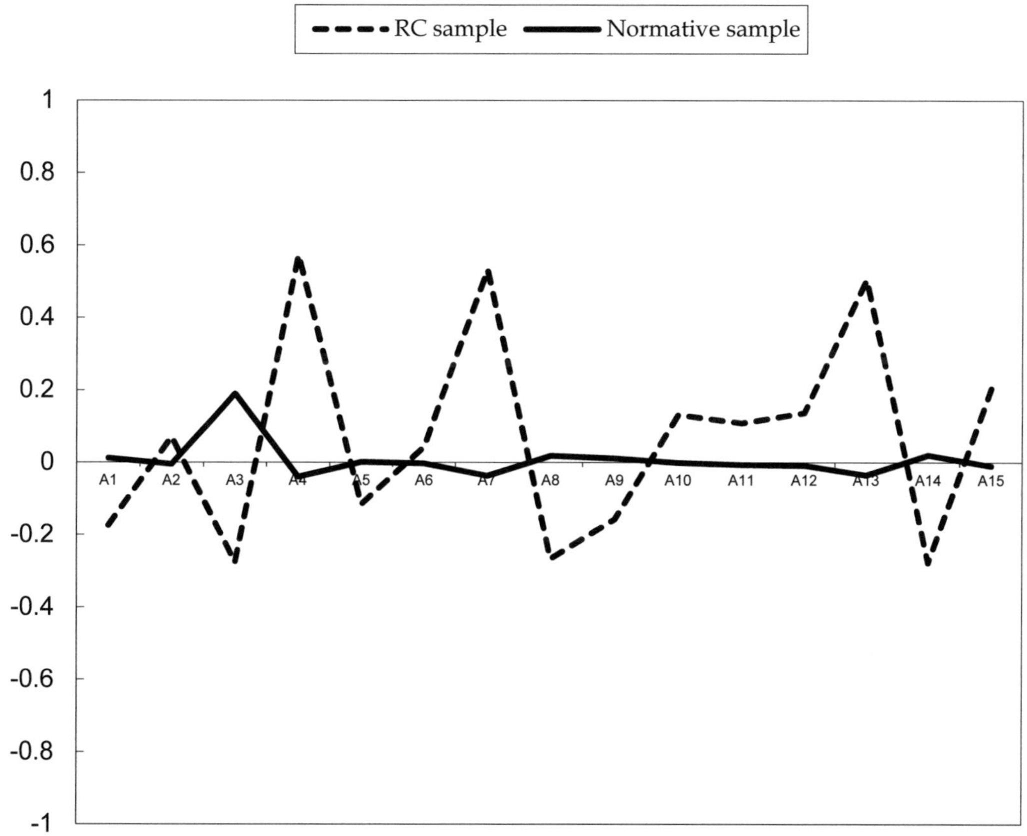

Note: A1: Having many friends; A2: Having few friends; A3: Getting on well with the teachers; A4: Not getting on well with the teachers; A5: Being nice to classmates; A6: Being nasty to classmates; A7: Being aggressive; A8: Being able to solve conflicts; A9: Knowing how to communicate with others; A10: Not knowing how to communicate with others; A11: Feeling superior to others; A12: Feeling inferior to others; A13: Always wanting to call attention; A14: Being a mature person; A15: Being an immature person

Figure 3. Behavioral profile of children in RC and children from a normative sample. ((Reproduced from "De la residencia a la escuela: la integración social de los menores en acogimiento residencial con el grupo de iguales en el contexto escolar" of E. Martín, M. C. Muñoz, T. Rodríguez and Y. Pérez, Psicothema 20(3), 376-382. Copyright: Colegio Oficial de Psicólogos del Principado de Asturias)

But we must not only consider the merely curricular and qualification aspects that the educational system can provide to these children. This can help them achieve a good occupational insertion, and, thereby, socioeconomic integration when they leave the childhood welfare system, as most of them will either have to become independent or else return to the family from which they had to be separated for their own protection. School can also play an essential role in the compensating intervention that must be carried out with these children. Firstly, the school enables better cognitive development, which can help the children to understand their personal situation and to integrate it adaptively into their life story (Cyrulnik, 2002). Sometimes, the adults in charge are unaware of children's difficulties to understand and interpret the experiences—many of them terrible—that they have undergone. The fact that children do not ask questions about it or show signs of being upset does not mean that they are not suffering.

Secondly, school enables the children in RC to relate to prosocial adults who can become their reference adults. Martín and Dávila (2008) found that the affective bond with adults outside of the family setting has a positive impact on the adaptation and adjustment of children who were in RC. The need for unconditional support from an adult is acknowledged from developmental psychology, and all the more so for these children, who were deprived of adult figures in the family setting. The same can be said about their peers. Their contribution to the cognitive, affective, social, and moral development is essential for these children due to the important compensatory role they play (Gauze, Bukowski, Aquan-Asse & Sippola, 1996; Masten & Reed, 2002).

5. Strengths of RC as a resource of the childhood welfare system

Being the resource of childhood welfare that has attended the greatest number of children and adolescents in a situation of vulnerability, and perhaps precisely because of this, RC is habitually questioned both from academic and political spheres. A social discourse has emerged that argues the need for RC to disappear for two essential reasons. One is that all children in a situation of vulnerability should be provided with a family that protects them and cares for them. The other is that to grow up within RC resources can have sequelae on the children's development, especially in the younger children. The latter argument has already been discussed in previous sections and, although it is true that there have been many such cases—especially in the past—if RC currently works well, this should not occur. In fact, RC can become a therapeutic setting in which to work on the problems that caused the family situation and the neglect in the first place. The former argument, that all children should grow up in a family, is a consensus we have all reached: politicians, professionals, and investigators. But this is not enough to close down all the supervised homes. In Spain, we have legislative initiatives of this sort that, if not accompanied with other resources, such as the creation of a good pool of foster families, will only reflect good intentions.

But the fact that we all reached this consensus and that we should begin to set the foundations so this can happen in the future does not necessarily mean that RC should disappear as a welfare resource. This "satanization" to which it is so often submitted should not conceal its many strengths and the solutions it provides to many children and adolescents. The first aspect that must be clarified is that, nowadays, RC is necessary because there are not enough foster families available, and because the preventive work carried out is not enough to prevent situations of vulnerability. The term "last resort" has been used to refer to the last alternative to which one turns (Hellinckx, 2002). The reality is that it is very often not the last resort but the only one, and it is therefore necessary to analyze its possibilities. These strengths are:

1.- One of the arguments habitually heard is that the educators and other workers in RC cannot fulfill functions that correspond to the children's' parents. This is true; foster parents do not take the place of the biological parents if work is being carried out with the children and the family in a family reunification program. The most we could say is that RC will never be a family home, although it can be very similar. The principle of normalization facilitated the integration of supervised homes in the community, and currently, many of them are flats in residential buildings. The educators cannot and should not be parents, but they can become reference adults for the children, giving them what their own parents could not give them, at least temporarily. This is important because it can become a factor that promotes resilience in these children. Martín and González (2007) studied the quality of the care that the children received in supervised homes by interviewing the children. They discovered that the factor with the highest association to quality care was the relation established with the educators. Allusions such as *the educators love me, the educators help me, they listen to me*, etc. indicate that, for the children in RC, having the educators as reference adults is of vital importance for their quality of life. The professionalization and technicality of the figure of the educators, which has been positive, should not be incompatible with their establishing affective bonds with the children. This is necessary and it is very often not promoted, erroneously thinking that this could cause some kind of conflict of loyalty and role confusion in the children about the adults who are a part of their lives. If one is clear when informing the child, there should be no conflict or confusion. Also, the more extensive the child's network of adults, the better (Martín & Dávila, 2008).

2.- We would like to emphasize that entering RC can also be an opportunity to enrich the children's social support network Not only because the children relate to other RC children and to the staff, but also because the promotion of out-of-school and community activities—which many of their biological families could not afford—help the children to get to know their peers in diverse settings, and adults who will become part of their social network. This variable is recognized as one of the most important to improve the quality of life of these children, as it has a direct impact on their adaptation (Martín & Dávila, 2008). Such aspects should not go unnoticed, and we must work towards the achievement of these goals, taking the differences as a function of the children's developmental stage into account. For instance, it is more important for the smaller children to have available adults than for the adolescents, for whom the peer network is more relevant (Del Valle, Bravo & López, 2010; Martín, 2011). In the same vein, the creation of emancipation flats and residences for adolescents who are almost of age, where several of them could live together, not only facilitates their acquisition of the basic skills for independence, but also allows them to strengthen their peer support network, which they can retain when leaving the welfare system.

3.- With regard to the above, we must analyze the role played by groups of siblings. The proportion of children who enter the welfare system alone is relatively low, and it is more habitual to declare groups of siblings—sometimes quite numerous—to be in a situation of vulnerability. The diverse handbooks of quality standards and legislative proposals defend the idea of keeping groups of siblings together while they are under the guardianship of the competent administrations. This allows maintaining the bonds among them and facilitates the work of family reunification programs, as it allows them to organize family visits and meetings of the children with their families and with the family intervention teams. Although the results of the research analyzing the benefits of living with their siblings for RC children's development are neither overwhelming nor very clear (Davidson & Klein, 2011), it is nevertheless the most logical and desirable option. And it must be acknowledged that, in most of these cases, RC is the only available resource. The larger the number of siblings, the more difficult it is to find a foster home, or even an adoptive home, because the groups of siblings may comprise small children and adolescents, which makes it economically costly and complicates adjusting well to a new family. Therefore, it must be admitted that if siblings should remain together in RC, then it is necessary and even recommendable to maintain this resource.

4.- One advantage of RC that it is more widely acknowledged is that it allows the children who have lived in destructured families, where there was no schedule and no rules, to live in a structured setting. The same can be said about a foster family. One of the basic needs of childhood is the acquisition of a system of rules and values. The RC fulfills these needs adequately, and even allows intensive and therapeutic work that may offset this developmental deficit of the children who are admitted into RC. In the cases of children who have suffered greater emotional, cognitive, and behavioral sequelae, this intensive work is essential, even before the first step towards foster care or adoption can be taken. If these children go directly to another family without prior work in RC, the foster care is considerably more likely to fail. This is related to the fact that RC has become increasingly specialized in caring for specific collectives: minors with behavioral and mental health problems, unaccompanied immigrant minors, etc., profiles that are very difficult to accommodate in foster families.

5.- One of the erroneous ideas that persists in many sectors of society is that children's admittance into RC implies their total separation from the family. This is only true in those cases in which contact with the family implies considerable risk for the minor. Fortunately, this does not occur in most cases. The goal of separation is to protect the children and fulfill their needs, but not to break bonds. In many cases, the goal is family reunification, and in the meantime, the children are in RC and the professionals work with the families. In these cases, there is a visiting schedule, either in the RC itself or in other specified places, or the children even spend the weekends with their families. These programs are not only to maintain family bonds but also so that the family intervention professionals can work with the families, teaching them how to take on parental responsibilities, and learn educational skills and childhood care. Martín, Torbay *et al*. (2008) found that, in many cases, separation not only did not harm the minor's bond to the family, but it even strengthened it. Let us not forget that there are cases in which a short "breathing space" of separation is necessary, especially concerning adolescents, in which RC is valid. These authors also found that, when the RC professionals work cooperatively with the family, there is a considerable increase in the benefits for the children's development produced by their stay in RC. We underline that RC and family are not incompatible concepts. On the contrary, if one works adequately, they provide mutual support in benefit of the child.

6. Current and future challenges for the improvement of residential care

Till now, we have seen the role played by RC within the childhood welfare system. This resource—criticized and questioned for a long time from diverse instances, usually because of erroneous beliefs and ignorance— has an unfair negative image, because it has many strengths to attend childhood, especially certain collectives and in certain cases. In the former section, we briefly mentioned these strengths. But there are also a series of deficiencies, which should become challenges for improvement, and which we cannot ignore or adopt a complacent position in the face of the aforementioned critical current. Without meaning to be exhaustive, these challenges are as follows:

1.- As commented upon above, the problems of adaptation and academic performance of the children and adolescents in RC. In this collective, many of the children reach RC after long periods of truancy, due to the sequelae of maltreatment, or because their parents were uninterested in their children's education. That is, the children already arrive at RC with academic delay. What is really worrisome is that the welfare system does not offset this delay, or it actually impairs its compensation. Firstly, it is not always possible for the children to remain in their original schools, and, moreover, they sometimes change schools several times, as often as the measures adopted for their cases are changed. Thus, sadly enough, some children go to various schools, undergoing changes that do not always coincide with the end and the beginning of the school year. We must find formulas within the welfare system to minimize this harm caused by the welfare system itself. However, there are few experiences of coordination between the welfare and the educational systems, beyond the tutorship visits, which are also attended by the educators who are in charge of the children. Not only the welfare system, but the entire society is responsible for childhood protection. It is necessary for other administrations to take responsibility in order to efficiently deal with the academic problems of children and adolescents in RC. Secondly, the history of RC has made it a context in which therapeutic features have priority over the psychoeducational ones, so that, in many cases, the RC staff does not correctly value the academic aspect. Although therapeutic intervention is necessary, and daily life often makes it impossible to dedicate time to educational goals, a change in this direction is nevertheless necessary. Moreover, from psychology educational, it has been proved that children's motivation for school increases if their parents value it and show interest We must assume that the same thing would apply for RC educators. A last aspect to underline is determined by the fact that childhood is legally protected until the child comes of age. This means that, in those cases where reunification or foster care are impossible, the children are referred to technical schools so they can learn a trade that will support them when they are of age. For this purpose, their academic trajectory is rerouted, even in youngsters with good academic adjustment and performance, who have expectations of continuing their studies beyond compulsory education. This fact shows that RC is still not completely prepared to fulfill such a basic and necessary need for a good sociocommunity integration as education.

2.- Adopting the principle of normalization, in some cases, led to generating erroneous beliefs, thinking that the children and adolescents in RC were exactly the same as those who live with their families, thus relaxing the mechanisms to detect certain problems, such as academic failure and mental health problems. In the latter case, in Spain, the line of thought that criticized research based on a psychopathological approach because it confused the effects of RC with those of the prior situation of maltreatment did not take into consideration the mental health problems of this collective, whatever their causes. The lack of studies may have contributed to this, as there is only one (Del Valle, Sainero & Bravo, 2011). Nevertheless, international research has contributed contrasted evidence that children and adolescents have more mental health problems than the general population (Clausen, Landsverk, Ganger, Chadwick & Litrownik, 1998; EUROARC, 1998; Ford, Vostanis, Meltzer & Goodman, 2007; Heflinger, Simpkins & Combs-Orme, 2000; Pecora, Jensen, Romanelli, Jackson & Ortiz, 2009; Sempik, Ward & Darker, 2008). The results of these studies show relevant data in this sense: the percentage of children and adolescents with some mental health problem is somewhere between 48 and 89%, depending on the studies. That is, the prevalence of mental health problems in this population is four times higher than in the general childhood and adolescent population.

Therefore, one cannot just look away. As occurred with educational care, the principle of normalization externalized RC children's physical and mental care, to some extent, ignoring these problems. Moreover, health resources are designed, at most, for the prevalence of disorders in the general population, so there are not enough external resources to attend to this problem. Admitting these problems does not mean attributing them to the stay of these children and adolescents in RC, but of adequately attending to the sequelae that their family situation may have caused.

3.- Another challenge of RC is to adequately deal with the processes of transition to adult life of the adolescents who live in these facilities (Stein *et al.*, 2011). The youngsters must often face independence at the age of 18, because they have no family or because their family is not able to take charge of them—something that is currently not demanded of the majority of the juvenile population. In other cases, although they return to their families, they must contribute their own economic resources to help out in a precarious family situation. Knowing what RC can contribute to guarantee the success of this process of transition to adult life is a priority of the childhood welfare system. Till now, due to the fact that the legislation only obliges their protection until the age of 18, the problems faced by 18-year-old adolescents were not perceived as a responsibility of the welfare system. However, they are now perceived as such, because this is an indicator of the results of the work carried out while the adolescent lived in RC. Del Valle, Bravo, Álvarez, and Fernanz (2008) found that the situation of emancipated youngsters from RC was better the older they were when the follow-up was performed. This indicates that it is very difficult at such early ages for these youngsters to achieve the personal, social, and economic resources that facilitate a good socio-work integration. The proliferation of homes for youngsters over 18 in which those who are old enough to leave the RC can live together and continue studying and preparing for adult life provides them with opportunities similar to those of youngsters who can count on powerful family support in their transition to adult life. This flexibilizes the time needed to ensure that this process will be successful. Although still scarce, these resources are a first step to adequately attend the needs of this collective.

Dumaret, Donati, and Crost (2011) analyzed the factors that facilitate a good transition to adult life and found that the above-mentioned factors were essential to guarantee this process. On the one hand, adequately attending the education of the children and adolescents in RC helps them in the sense that higher qualification means a more likely socio-work insertion, without forgetting all the opportunities to strengthen the support social network provided by the educational system. However, efficiently attending the mental health problems while they are still in RC would place them in a better condition to become integrated into society as personally and socially adapted adults. And lastly, the authors emphasize the importance of reinforcing the resources for emancipation, providing these youngsters with emancipation homes and other support resources beyond their majority of age (18 years). Applying pure logic, we cannot demand from these young people more than we ask from the rest of the boys and girls of the same age. It is simply unfair, because, having received much less, they should not have to give more.

7. Conclusions

In this chapter, we carried out a review of the historical evolution and the current reality of RC, an important resource for the childhood welfare system. The enormous number of children and adolescents who are admitted to this resource worldwide requires us to analyze it from objective, evidence-based criteria contributed by research. Unfortunately, this does not usually occur, because from political, professional, and even academic instances, the discourse is based more on ideological proposals and beliefs than on facts.

As in almost all social topics, we must come to a consensus about what should be done. In childhood protection, we reached the agreement that growing up in a family is not only a right of children, but also a need for their emotional, social, cognitive, and moral development. Therefore, measures are promoted for alternatives to RC, such as foster care and adoption, which are much more important for small children. We all agree about this, but some people, many in the legislative spheres, take advantage of this consensus to demonize RC and propose its elimination. Such harassing can even give rise to the error of trying to turn RC into a family. There are examples of homes where children of different ages live together, in many cases, groups of siblings, with two resident educators, a man and a woman, trying to turn a professional resource for living together into a family. A welfare home will never be family, and the educators will never be the parents. Nor should they. The children already have a family, although they cannot live with it.

A welfare home is a resource that tries to fulfill all the needs of the children and adolescents as normally as possible. And the educators are adults who are responsible for this, and who can become important figures in the social support network of children and adolescents who are separated from their families. In fact, they should not be seen as opposite resources from the families. Living in a welfare home does not imply total separation from the family. There are visits, weekends, working together with the family, the minor, and the technical teams, always depending on the goals to be achieved in each case. When children are separated from their families, it is to protect them from the family situation, not to shut them up in any center. That is, we must dismantle the social consensus that RC is a resource to separate children from their families, and build the idea that RC is a resource of support for the families.

The results of current research must be made visible, as they show that RC can have beneficial effects in certain cases, that the stays should not be too short for fear of negative effects on the children, but instead their duration should depend on the goals aimed at for each child and each family. Day-care centers in which children return to spend the night with their families must be promoted, for those cases in which aspects concerning hygiene, feeding, and academic support are the main needs to be fulfilled. And, particularly, other alternative resources must be promoted, such as foster care, increasing the pool of available families. And we must not only increase their quantity, but also their quality. The scarce number of available families and the satanization of RC frequently leads to the selection of families considered suitable as foster homes (thus, preventing the child from going into RC), when we know that foster care can also fail, producing unnecessary break-ups for the children (López, Del Valle, Montserrat & Bravo, 2011). Foster care is positive, but only when the families are selected adequately for each particular case.

However, collectives like adolescents with emotional or behavioral problems, unaccompanied immigrant minors, or large groups of siblings find in RC the only available resource for living together within the welfare system. For most of these cases, there is no other alternative. The voices that propose the elimination of RC should change their discourse and, in any event, demand its specialization to attend to these special groups. For all these reasons, we must consider RC a flexible resource, compatible with others, which can become specialized and deal with problems that other resources cannot reach.

Another important aspect we should not ignore is the visibilization of protected children in general, and the RC children in particular. With the pretext of protecting the identity and intimacy of this collective, we have sometimes overdone it, and they have been concealed from the public opinion. This has perverse effects, because it does not facilitate the social awareness of such a severe problem as that of the children and adolescents living in RC. Knowledge of a problem is the first step to take on the responsibility of coping with it. Children separated from their families are not perceived as a social problem. Moreover, such ignorance provokes fear and rejection. Thus, when an organization tries to rent or buy a flat to turn it into a welfare home, they usually encounter the neighbors' rejection, because they do not know the difference between a welfare home and a reformatory for adolescents with judicial measures. This produces stigmatization and rejection of a population as vulnerable as this one. In addition, this concealment from the public opinion even deprives these youngsters, who cannot publicize themselves, of even reclaiming their rights.

Nor can we forget that we should definitely promote prevention programs to avoid separating children from their families. Only the most severe cases should have to go into RC.

Ultimately, RC should be seen from the perspective of its historical evolution, acknowledging the advances produced in this resource. We must value its contribution to children and adolescents who are separated from their families, and realize its limitations and the improvements still pending. And all of this should be considered according to the evidence contributed by research in this field, not to beliefs and assumptions.

Only this way can we have one more adequate and efficient resource within the childhood welfare system, to respond adequately to the needs of the boys and girls who, unfortunately, must be separated from their natural growth setting, which is their family.

Author details

Eduardo Martín
Senior Lecturer of Developmental and Educational Psychology, University of La Laguna, Spain

8. References

Anthonysamy, A. & Zimmer-Gembeck, M. J. (2007). Peer status and behaviors of maltreated children and their classmates in the early years of school. *Child Abuse and Neglect, 31*, 971-991.

Backer, J. A. (2006). Contributions of teacher-child relationship to positive school adjustment during elementary school. *Journal of School Psychology, 44*, 211-229.

Berridge, D. (2007). Theory and explanation in child welfare: education and looked-after children. *Child and Family Social Work, 12*, 1-10.

Bravo, A. & Del Valle, J. F. (2001). Evaluación de la integración social en acogimiento residencial. *Psicothema, 13*(2), 197-204.

Bravo, A. & Del Valle, J. F. (2009). Crisis y revisión del acogimiento residencial. Su papel en la protección infantil. *Papeles del Psicólogo, 30*(1), 42-52.

Brodie, I. (2005). Education and residential child care in England: A research perspective. In D. Crimmens & I. Milligan (Eds.), *Facing forward: Residential child care: in the 21st century* (pp. 163-171). Dorset: Russell House Publishing.

Bullock, R., Little, M. & Millham, S. (1993). *Going home: the return of children separated from their familias*. London: Dartmouth.

Cameron, C., Hollingworth, K. & Jackson, S. (eds.) (2011). *Secondary analysis of national statistics on educational participation. The YIPPEE Project*. Date of access: 26-5-2011, Available from: http://tcru.ioe.ac.uk/yippee

Campos, G. (2011). ¿Cómo se percibe a la infancia protegida? De la normalización a la institucionalización. En M. I. Jociles, A. Franzé y D. Poveda (Eds.), *Etnografías de la infancia y la adolescencia*. Madrid: Los libros de la Catarata.

Casas, F. & Montserrat, C. (2009). Sistema educativo e igualdad de oportunidades entre los jóvenes tutelados: estudios recientes en el Reino Unido. *Psicothema, 21*(4), 543-547.

Child Welfare League of America. (1991). *Standard of excellence for residential group care services*. Washington: CWLA.

Chisholm, K. (1998). A three year follow-up of attachment and indiscriminate friendliness in children adopted from Romanian orphanages. *Child Development, 69*, 1092-116.

Clausen, J. M., Landsverk, J., Ganger, W., Chadwick, D. & Litrownik, A. (1998). Mental health problems of children in foster care. *Journal of Child and Family Studies, 7*, 283-296.

Colton, M. J. & Hellinckx, W. (1995). *La atención residencial a la infancia en la Unión Europea. Guía por países sobre acogimiento familiar y atención residencial*. Madrid: Ministerio de Asuntos Sociales.

Cyrulnik, B. (2002). *Los patitos feos. La resiliencia: una infancia infeliz no determina la vida*. Barcelona: Gedisa.

Davidson-Arad B. & Klein, A. (2011). Comparative well being of Israeli youngsters in residential care with and without sibilings. *Children and Youth Services Review, 33*, 2152-2159.

Del Valle, J. F. (2003). Acogimiento residencial: ¿innovación o resignación? *Infancia y Aprendizaje, 26*(3), 365-379.

Del Valle, J. F. & Bravo, A. (2007). *SERAR: Sistema de evaluación y registro en acogimiento residencial*. Oviedo: Nieru.

Del Valle, J. F., Bravo, A. & López, M. (2010). Parents and peers as providers of support in adolescents' social network: a developmental perspective. *Journal of Community Psychology, 38*, 16-27.

Del Valle, J. F., Bravo, A., Álvarez, E. & Fernanz, A. (2008). Adult Self-sufficiency and social adjustment in care leavers from children's homes: a long-term assessment. *Child and Family Social Work, 13*, 12-22.

Del Valle, J. F. & Fuertes, J. (2000). *El acogimiento residencial en la protección a la infancia*. Madrid: Pirámide.

Del Valle, J. F., Sainero, A., & Bravo, A. (2011). *Salud mental de menores en acogimiento residencial*. Badajoz: Junta de Extremadura.

Dumaret, A. C., Donati, P. & Cross, M. (2011). After a long-term placement: investigating educational achievement, behaviour and transition to independent living. *Children and Society, 25*, 215-227.

EUROARC. (1998). *Care to listen: A report of residential child care in four european countries.* Glasgow: The Center for Residential Child Care.

FICE, IFCO & Aldeas Infantiles SOS. (2007). *Quality4Children: Estándares para el cuidado de niños fuera de su familia biológica en Europa*. [Standards for the care of children outside of their biological family in Europe]. Date of Access: 13-03-2010. Available at: http://www.aldeasinfantiles.es/Conocenos/publicaciones/otras-publicaciones/pages/default.aspx

Ford, T., Vostanis, P., Meltzer, H. & Goodman, R. (2007). Psychiatric disorder among British children looked after by Local Authorities: A comparison with children living in private households. *British Journal of Psychiatry, 190*, 319-325.

Garrido, V. (2001). Tres pilares en la pedagogía de la delincuencia: el apoyo social, la justicia de la restauración y la prevención familiar. En E. López y A. Ripio (Coords.), *Justicia de menores e intervención socioeducativa* (pp. 221-243). Murcia: Consejería de Trabajo y Política Social.

Gauze, C., Bukowski, W. M., Aquan-Assee, J. & Sippola. L. K. (1996). Interactions between family environment and friendship and associations with self perceived well-being during adolescence. *Child Development, 67*, 2201-2216.

General Assembly of the United Nations (2009). *Resolution 64/142: Guidelines for the Alternative Care of Children.* New York: UN.

Goddard, J. (2000). The education of looked after children. *Child and Family Social Work, 5*, 79-86.

Han, E. & Choi, N. (2006). Korean institutionalized adolescents' attributions of success and failure in interpersonal relations and perceived loneliness. *Children and Youth Services Review, 28*, 535-547.

Harden, B. (2002). Congregate care for infants and toddlers: Shedding new light on an old question. *Infant Mental Health Journal, 23*, 476-495.

Harker, R. M., Dobel-Ober, D., Lawrence, J., Berridge, D. & Sinclair, R. (2003). Who takes care of education? Looked after children's perceptions of support for educational progress. *Child and Family Social Work, 8*, 89-100.

Heflinger, C. A., Simpkins, C. G. & Combs-Orme, T. (2000). Using the CBCL to determine the clinical status of children in state custody. *Children and Youth Services Review, 22*, 55-73.

Hellinckx, W. (2002). Residential care: last resort or vital link in child welfare. *International Journal of Child and Family Welfare, 5*(3), 75-83.

Hodges, J. & Tizard, B. (1989). IQ and behavioural adjustment of ex-institutional adolescents. *Journal of Child Psychology and Psychiatric, 30*, 53-75.

Jonhson, R., Browne, K. & Hamilton-Giachritsis, C. (2006). Young children in institutional care at risk of harm. *Trauma, Violence and Abuse, 7*, 34-60.

Kaler, S. R. & Freeman, B. J. (1994). An analysis of environment deprivation: cognitive and social development in Romanian orphans. *Journal of Child Psychology and Psychiatric, 35*, 769-781.

Knuston, J. F. (1995). Psychological characteristics of maltreated children: putative risk factors and consequences. *Annual Review of Psychology, 45*, 401-431.

Lázaro, S. (2009). Resiliencia en niños y adolescentes: revisión teórica e implicaciones para la intervención psicoeducativa en situaciones de maltrato familiar. *Estudios de Psicología, 30*(1), 89-104.

Leiter, J. (2007). School performances trajectories after the advent of reported maltreatment. *Children and Youth Services Review, 29*, 363-382.

Linsey, M. & Foley, T. (1999). Getting them back to school: Touchstones of good practice in the residential care of young people. *Children and Society, 13*, 192-202.

López, M., Del Valle, J. F., Montserrat, C. & Bravo, A. (2011). Factors affecting foster care breakdown in Spain. *The Spanish Journal of Psychology, 14*(1), 111-122.

Maclean, K. & Connely, G. (2005). Still room for improvement? The educational experiences of looked after children in Scotland. In D. Crimmens & I. Milligan (Eds.), *Facing forward: Residential child care in the 21st century* (pp. 173-183). Dorset: Russell House Publishing.

Martín, E. (2011). Apoyo social percibido en niños y adolescentes en acogimiento residencial. *International Journal of Psychology and Psychological Therapy, 11*(1), 107-120.

Martín, E. & Dávila, L. M. (2008). Redes de apoyo social y adaptación de los menores en acogimiento residencial. *Psicothema, 20*(2), 229-235.

Martín, E. & González, M. S. (2007). La calidad del acogimiento residencial desde la perspectiva de los menores. *Infancia y Aprendizaje, 30*(1), 25-38.

Martín, E. & Muñoz de Bustillo, M. C. (2009). School adjustment of children in residential care: a multi-source analysis. *The Spanish Journal of Psychology, 12*(2), 462-470.

Martín, E., Muñoz de Bustillo, M. C. & Pérez, N. (2011). Las relaciones de amistad en la escuela de los menores en acogimiento residencial. *Revista de Psicodidáctica, 16*(2), 351-366.

Martín, E., Muñoz de Bustillo, M. C., Rodríguez, T. & Pérez, Y. (2008). De la residencia a la escuela: la integración social de los menores en acogimiento residencial con el grupo de iguales en el contexto escolar. *Psicothema, 20*(3), 376-382.

Martín, E., Rodríguez, T. & Torbay, Á. (2007). Evaluación diferencial de los programas de acogimiento residencial de menores. *Psicothema, 19*(3), 406-412.

Martín, E., Torbay, Á. & Rodríguez, T. (2008). Cooperación familiar y vinculación del menor con la familia en los programas de acogimiento residencial. *Anales de Psicología, 24*(1), 25-32.

Masten, A. S. & Reed, M. G. (2002). Resilience in development. In C. R. Snyder & S. J. López (Eds.), *Handbook of positive psychology* (pp. 74-88). New York: Oxford University Press.

O'Connor, T. G., Rutter, M. & the ERA Team (2000). Attachment disorder behaviour following early severe deprivation: Extension and longitudinal follow-up. *Journal of the American Academy of Child and Adolescent Psychiatry, 39*, 703-712.

Observatorio de la Infancia (2011). *Estadística básica de protección a la infancia*. Madrid: Ministerio de Sanidad, Política Social e Igualdad.

Pecora, P. J., Jensen, P. S., Romanelli, L. H., Jackson, L. & Ortiz, A. (2009). Mental Health Services for Children Placed in Foster Care: An Overview of Current Challenges. *Child Welfare, 88*, 1-25.

Redondo, E., Muñoz, R. & Torres, B. (1998). *Manual de buena práctica para la atención residencia a la infancia y adolescencia*. Madrid: Federación de Asociaciones para la Prevención del Maltrato Infantil.

Rodrigo, M. J., Máiquez, M. L., Martín, J. C. & Byrne, S. (2008). *Preservación familiar: Un enfoque positivo para la intervención con familias*. Madrid: Pirámide.

Roy, P., Rutter, M. & Pickles, A. (2000). Institutional care: risk from family background or pattern of rearing? *Journal of Child Psychology and Psychiatry, 41*, 139-149.

Save the Children (2011). *Agenda de Infancia 2012-2015*. Madrid: Save the Children España.

Sempik, J., Ward, H. & Darker, I. (2008). Emotional and behavioural difficulties of children and young people at entry into care. *Clinical Child Psychology and Psychiatry, 13*(2), 221-233.

Skinner, A. (1992). *Another kind of home*. Edinbourgh: HMSO.

Sloutsky, V. M. (1997). Institutional care and developmental outcomes of 6 and 7-year-old children: A contextualist perspective. *International Journal of Behavioral Development, 20*, 131-151.

Stein, M., Ward, H. & Courtney, M. (2011). Editorial: International perspectives on young people´s transitions from care to adulthood. *Children and Youth Services Review, 33*, 2049-2411.

Stone, S. (2007). Child maltreatment, out-of-home placement and academic vulnerability: a fifteen-year review of evidence and future directions. *Children and Youth Services Review, 29*, 139-161.

Svenlin, A. R. (2010). What we know and what should we know about short-term fostering?. In E. J. Knorth, M. E. Kalverboer & J. Knot-Dickscheit (Eds.), *Inside out: How interventions in child and family care work. An international source book* (pp. 229-231). Antwerp-Apeldoorn: Grarant Publishers.

Tizard, B. & Hodges, J. (1978). The effect of early institutional rearing on the development of eight year old children. *Journal of Child Psychology and Psychiatric, 19*, 99-118.

Trout, A. L., Hagaman, J., Casey, K., Reid, R. & Epstein, M. H. (2008). The academic status of children and youth in out-of-home care: a review of the literature. *Children and Youth Services Review, 30*, 979-994.

Vacca, J. S. (2008). Breaking the cycle of academic failure for foster children-What can the schools do to help? *Children and Youth Services Review, 30*, 1081-1087.

Vorria, P., Rutter, M., Pickles, A., Wolkind, S. & Hobsbaum, A. (1998). A comparative study of Greek children in long-term residential group care and in two-parent families: I. Social, emotional and behavioural differences. *Journal of Child Psychology and Psychiatry, 39*, 225-245.

Chapter 8

Interaction Design for Preventing Child Abuse

Euichul Jung and Joonbin Im

Additional information is available at the end of the chapter

http://dx.doi.org/10.5772/48130

1. Introduction

The chapter aims to share various approaches to prevent crimes against children with students and professionals interested in developing and designing interactions. Accordingly, it is focused on discussing various examples and features of current interaction designs based on a diversified examination of designed products, services, and social systems. It also aims to understand and analyze characteristics of crimes against children from a designer's perspective and suggest a new direction for design while discussing basic suggestions on crimes against children and examining design methods with regard to crimes against children.

1.1. How to study

Firstly, what are the characteristics of children? Secondly, what are the characteristics of crimes against children? Thirdly, what is the current prevention system for against crimes and the advantages and disadvantages of such as system? Fourthly, what technologies could complement the disadvantages? The current study discusses interaction designs aimed to prevent crimes against children based on service designs through resolutions to suggested problems.

Researchers have revealed that more practical preventive measures can be taken when a protector – the government (the police) or private companies (security providers) – communicate with children to prevent crimes. The protector must immediately estimate the situation on behalf of children and a government agency or a private security service provider serves as a linking device and intervenes to protect children.

From examining the current products on the market as available devices, smart phones have been deemed appropriate; however separate development guidelines are needed given that users are children.

2. Theoretical background

This chapter analyzes children's performances and circumstantial judgments through literature and studies on preventing methods through understanding the procedure and characteristics of precedents of crimes against child over the past seven years.

2.1. Characteristics of a child

A child refers to the ages between 6 and 12. During this period, a child learns similar tasks that he or she must perform once they become an adult[1]. Child development is often discussed from the perspective of developmental psychology and paediatrics and is defined from biological and psychological perspectives. Child development is believed to have characteristics of dependency, continuous development, susceptibleness, demand, and adaptability[2]. Table 1 summarizes research conducted Sigmund Freud, Erick Erikson and Jean Piaget with regard to the psychological cognitive development of children.

Psychologists	Development	Stages	Characteristics
Freud	**Psychosexual Development**	Latency Stage 6-11 year old	Libido is repressed and the child develops superego.the child acquires social value through playing with same age group with same sex and adults other than family members.
Erikson	**Psychosocial Development**	Industry vs. Inferiority Latency Stage 6-11 year old	Children develop competence and cooperation skills in school. Complex develop through negative experiences in the family or when experiencing incompetence in school or among same age group.
Piaget	**Stages of Development**	Concrete Operations Stage 7-11 year old	A child can conduct logical reasoning what regard to specific cases and is able to divide objects into different categories (i.e., children can conduct operation). In this stage, the child which performs concrete operational reasoning, but cannot perform reasoning that requires algebraic equations because it require advanced abstract thinking.

Table 1. Characteristics of child by Freud, Erikson, and Piaget

Jean Piaget's "concrete operations stage," which is third of four stages of development applies to 7-11-year-old children. Children in this stage can perform simple operations and logical reasoning replaces intuitive thinking, which means that children can operate a mobile phone. However, how well a child can operate a mobile phone in case of an emergency must be carefully examined.

Therefore, the following needs to be considered when designing a device for kids. Although child in the concrete operations stage can perform operations that requires quite

[1] Laura E. Berk, translated by Nang Ja Park, Infants & Children.

[2] Sung Sim Han, Joo Mi Song, 'Child Welfare', Chang Ji, 2003, page 12.

complicated and logical thinking, it must be designed so a child can operate quickly in case of emergency. Table 2 shows a list to consider in accordance with the characteristics of children.

Items	Contents
General Characteristics	• should be able to get attention from same age group • should seek for a way to educate children about utilization in case of emergency through game • should prepare for malfunction caused by shock • should educate children to avoid unintended operation out of curiosity • child should be familiarized with operation
Physical Characteristics	• design should consider physical development of childhood • design should consider safety of a child so he/she does not get injured from unintended operation due to physical development
Cognitive Characteristics	• cognition of age of 6, 9, and 12 is different and should have flexible structure or icon design for respective ages. • not only a button but also a variety of methods need to be considered to respond in case of emergency • circumstantial judgment and discernment may insufficient compare to an adult

Table 2. List of considered device designs in accordance with the characteristics of a child

2.2. Characteristics of Child Abuse

Based on the analysis of precedents, what marks the child abuse is that most crimes involve sexual motivation, although some lead to the murder of a child. For the crime from occuring, there must be three prerequisites: (1) crime will, (2) victim, and (3) crime scene.

Once these are satisfied, there are five phases to commit a crime; crime prerequisite → approaching → luring and kidnapping → movement → committing the crime.

Step 1		Step 2	Step 3	Step 4
Crime prerequisite	Approaching	Luring and Kidnapping	Movement	Committing the crime

Table 3. Process of Crime

The intention of classification of a crime is to extract the Design Specification of the device for children to respond to each phase of the crime and prevent it the crime from occuring.

First the prevention of the first phase, crime prerequisite, has been conducted in the West in various ways.

Nevertheless, criminals continue to approach victims, wearing electronic Tagging. Criminals lure victims using feigned identity or by asking for directions. Criminals may also capture victims by force and move to a certain spot to commit the crime.

In the Kim Kil-Tae case, the preschool, the crime scene, and the criminal's house were located within 300m. This shows that many crimes are committed within the child's home environment. On study showed that the luring point and crime scene are only 30 min. away (i.e. within 2km).

Phase	Counter Measures
Crime prerequisite	Need for systematic measures to block any attempts for crime will, victim, crime scene.
Approaching	Alert the child's parent by receiving signals from the Electronic Tagging of recidivism through a device for children.
Luring	Educating the child about the action guide and letting them avoid the crime scene.
Kidnapping	Informing the third party about the danger using an emergency button or strap when captured by force.
Movement	Collecting all data about a child's routine pattern and alerting the parents when their child strays from the routine.

Table 4. Counter measures for each crime phases

According to a survey, cases where the victim's house, crime scene, lure place, victim's school and perpetrator's house were located within 2 km and accounted for 50% or more of crimes. Findings also revealed that a perpetrator searched for the subject of the crime in surrounding areas and the crime scene was a familiar environment. In addition, the lure place was not the same as the crime scene, and a perpetrator lured the child to another place to commit the crime. In these cases, it is the only time when a child can be rescued. Of note, 2 km takes up to 30 minutes to traverse on foot.

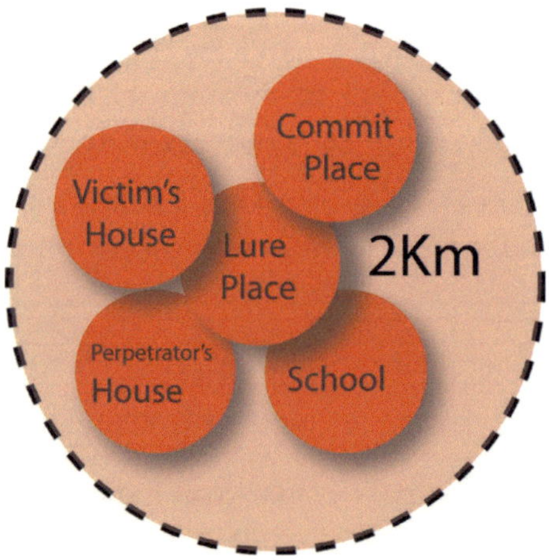

Figure 1. Distance from victim's house, crime scene, lure place, victim's school, and perpetrator's house.

A main characteristic of crimes against children is that it is impossible for children to protect themselves or ask for help when they perceive a crime because of physical differences between the child and perpetrator. Accordingly, it has been perceived that the intervention of a third party, who can immediately extend a helping hand to children, is desperately needed. Therefore, this study focuses on determining measures to achieve such an intervention.

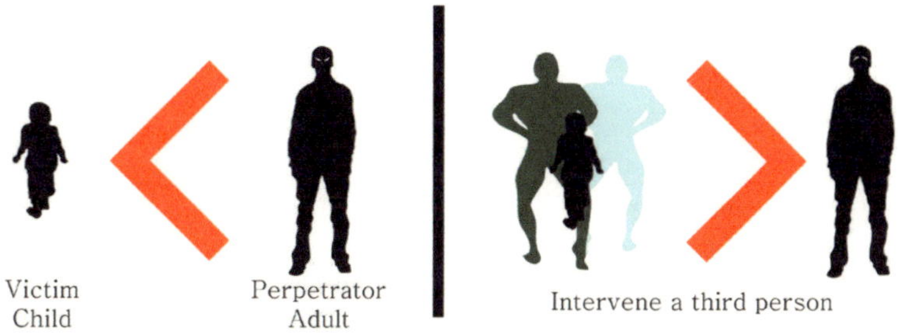

Figure 2. Physical differences between a victim and a pertpetrator

2.3. Prevention system and current technologies

Preventive means can be divided into individual and social means. As seen in the Figure 3, the social means are characterized by handling a situation after the fact. As it is difficult to protect many and unspecified persons, an emphasis is placed on preventing the recurrence of crimes that center on ex-cons. However, it is difficult to protect victims prior to a crime. Individual means are characterized by prevention that is focused on self-protective instincts aimed to protect oneself and one's family from many and unspecified persons.

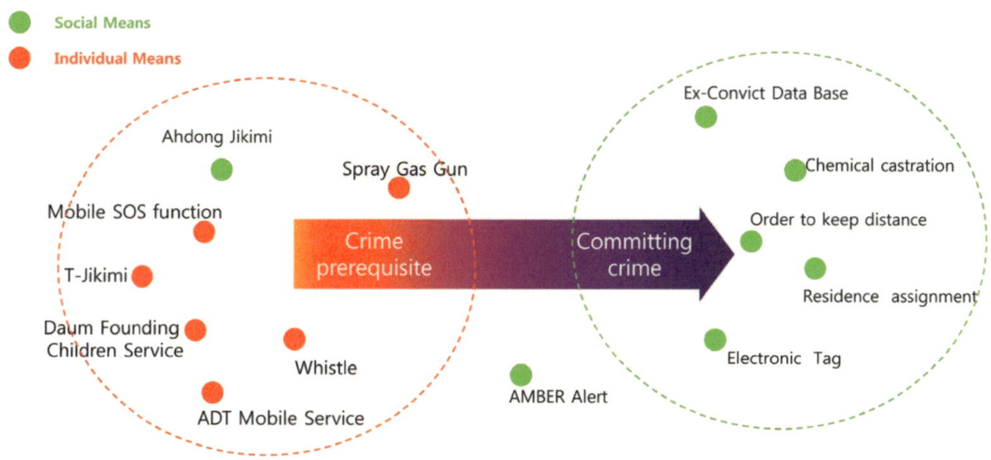

Figure 3. Characteristics of individual and social means

According to Table 5, which compares the domestic and foreign prevention system, the domestic system shows more favor to the rights of the criminal than those of the victims or the many and unspecified possible victims. Under certain circumstances, prevention becomes essential.

type	Measures	Comparison
Domestic System	• Child safety guards • Amber alert • Electronic Tagging • Posting identities of sexual offenders	Victim's human right < perpetrator's human right
Foreign System	• Isolation policy of the sexual offenders (U.S) • Amber alert • Posting sexual abuse record/ identities(U.S.) • Surgical or drug castration of sexual offenders(U.S.) • Genetic database (U.K.)	Victim's human right > perpetrator's human right

Table 5. Comparison of domestic and foreign systems and victims' and perpetrators' human rights

The followings are current technologies used for crime prevention.

1. SOS feature on mobile phones: Transmits the signal to five or six people who are registered by users in case of emergency and are available for only limited mobile phones.
2. LBS (Location Based Service): Electronic Tagging of ex-convicts; this has been adopted in many different fields. The security company ADT uses LBS-based mobile service for crime prevention. Users can set up an ETA (Estimated Time of Arrival) and if the users do not arrive on time, the company dispatched their men. If users enter the plate number of a taxi, the company will do the background check. However, as seen from the Fig. 2, this is problematic because it is not a kid friendly interface.

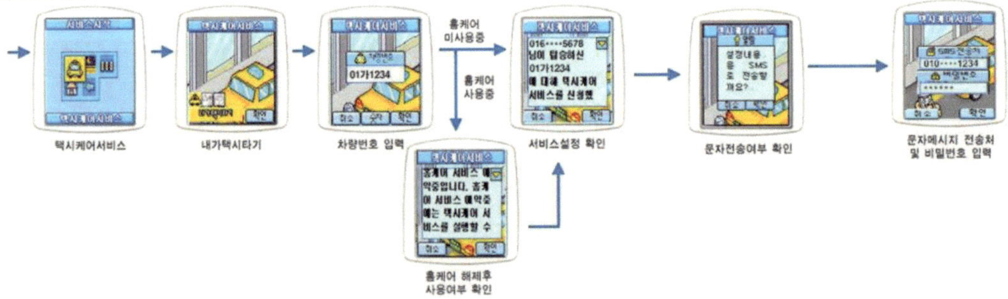

Figure 4. Example of setting up an ADT mobile phone - service name : Taxi care

3. Electronic Tagging: Domestically, electronic tagging of ex-convicts uses an LBS system. Legislation regarding adherence to Electronic Tagging for specific sexual offenders was enacted in April, 2007. After its revision in May 2008, electronic tagging was effective starting September 1st, which is an another use of LBS. Thus, if inspectors and mobile phones for children can detect the signal of the Electronic Tagging, it would provide a significant solution for preventing crimes against child.

Table 6. summarizes the results of the analysis of utilization of applicable systems and technologies through an assessment of effectiveness of each crime phase.

Phases	SOS feature of Mobile phone	LBS	Electronic positioning system /Electronic Tagging
Phase 1 : approaching	-	-	-
Phase 2 : luring and kidnapping	○ (when kidnapped)	○ (when kidnapped)	○ (when kidnapped)
Phase 3: movement	○	○	○
Post crime phase	○	○	○
Characteristics	Informs guardians in case of an emergency. Frequently unintended operation causes loss of reliability	Not a user friendly interface when using the service through a mobile phone; requires frequently resetting the settings. High cost for extra device and fees can be a burden on users when using a satellite-based system	It is a current measure that is systematically utilized. There is limits to prevention of crimes against people with no criminal records. May not expect any prevention when intentionally detached and committing a crime

Table 6. Assessment of effectiveness of prevention technologies regarding each crime phase.

It is concluded that mobile phone SOS features, LBS, Electronic Tagging are ineffective for luring and kidnapping because a child is not aware of it; however, it is effective for movement after kidnapping. In addition, to find a solution for preventing crimes against children, it is necessary to integrate mobile phone ubiquitous and LBS.

2.4. The current design of mobile phones for kids

The evaluation of precedents of existing mobile phones for kids was conducted to analyze features that are needed for this population of users.

Company model	Image	Characteristics
Verizon Migo		-emergency use for kids/elders, -minimum capacity that allows only five limited numbers be saved including emergency number (911) -no texting
Kyocera Mamorino cell phone for kids		-only available in Japan, can locate child's position and sounds alarm in emergency to inform -limited texting available through preregistered texts -there is a strap besides an emergency button and when pulled, it sounds an alarm and transmits signal to security company -when there is no light based on the setting, the lights will be turned on

Cingular Firefly		-private button for mom and dad -can save up to 20 numbers -emergency call button and designed to prevent mal-manipulation -suggests that child can be protected from harmful materials becuace there is no internet or email connection
Willcom Nico		-arrangement of large buttons/buttons with enlarged dome design -positioning system that can inform parents of child's location -parents can learn child's location by calling or through a computer at any time -high quality audio with low electromagnetic waves, which ensures safe use for kids
Gigabyte Sergeant Keroro, Doraemon	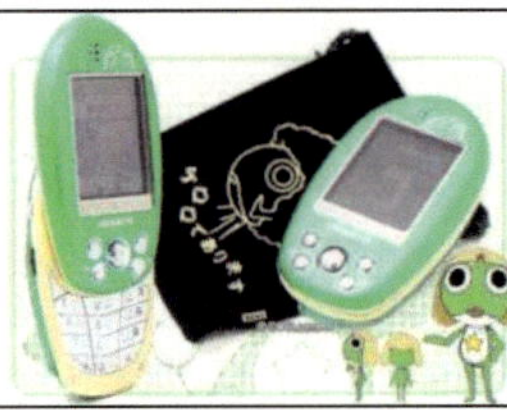	-Keroro and Doraemon version released by Taiwanese company Gigabyte -no specific features for child safety
au A5520SA		-provides location of child in real-time using GPS and informs when a child approaches specific location -pressing # for several seconds sounds an alarm and transmits current location through GPS mail to registered number and simultaneously informs the security company -can contact fire department or hospital in emergency of fire or illness -informs the child's location in time intervals, even if the power is off -wireless internet NTT Tokomo arranged 'Kids I menu' and prevents child from harmful internet content
Hop-on chitterchatter		-mobile phone that can frequently connect family with child under 10 or person with disability -comprises five (mom, dad, home, 911, Track Me) buttons with total of seven emergency numbers -child can inform parents of their location -can be put in backpack, wallet, pocket, etc, or can hang on neck or worn on the wrist

Willcom Papipo		-Papipo, released by Willcom, is manufactured by plastic model company Bandai -produced in Blue, Damogochi, Chao version and has meticulous UI design -once connected to kids studio, a database for children, a child can download wallpaper, games, ring tones and even raising Damagochi (function of fun) -provides positioning system using PHS base station, and emergency button
Dmodo M900		-manufactured by Hong Kong mobile phone handsets company -uses Walt Disney's Mickey-Mouse design -popular among kids and young women, also uses Disney characters for integrated programs such as wall papers, animation, icon, button sound.

Table 7. Precedents of existing mobile phone for kids

The precedent analysis showed that it is not easy for a child to control the device in an emergency and protecting a child through third party involvement seems an easy task. However, some features of these devices were useful such as A5520SA from AU, which informs parents when a child is approaching a specific location and informs the child's location at specific time intervals, even if the power is off. Additionally, Chitterchatter's wearing method was found useful. Table 8 summarizes useful features for preventing crimes against children.

Categories	Functions	Contents
Button	Specified Key	Easy operation for various ages and children with disabilities. Can maximize battery by allowing limited number of phone numbers to be saved and prevent unnecessary calls and harmful content.
	Emergency Button	Informs the current situation and self location to the preregistered person in case of an emergency
	Notifying Self Location Button	Can inform self location at any time
Power	Battery Cover	When the battery cover is forcibly removed, a warning sign will be sent out to preregistered numbers
	Powerless Positioning Signal	Can notify one's location without any power in certain time intervals
Lamp	Lamp	When a child is trapped in dark area, the lights will be turned on based on the settings
Emergency	Strap	If a situation doesn't allow a child to a press button, he/she can pull the strap, which will sound the alarm and send out a text message to the preregistered numbers
App.	GPS	Parents can confirm their child's location any time and will be notified when the child approaches a specific location
	DB	Parents can protect their child from harmful content and decorate the mobile phone using DB for kids.

Table 8. Useful current technologies to prevent crimes against children

The users have a need for normalization and avoiding admitting that they are special[3]. Thus, mobile phones for kids that are currently available have very small LCDs or none at all; nevertheless, designs for both specified-key mode and 10-key mode would be viable by parents setting up the key-type screens based on the Full Touch Technology and adjusted for their children's age-specific cognition levels.

2.5. Summary

- Children aged 7 to 11 experience concrete operational stage as mentioned by Piaget with regard to characteristics of children who can deal with simplified manipulation and logical inference, which suggests that children have no problem manipulating a device.
- With regard to characteristics of crimes against children, a perpetrator commits a crime if three conditions, crime will, victim, and crime scene are met and the crime goes through the stages Approaching→ Luring and Kidnapping →Movement→ Committing Crime.
- Cases where victim's house, commit place, lure place, victim's school, and perpetrator's house are located within 2 km account for 50% or more; therefore, crimes are committed near routing of children.
- As it is deemed impossible for children to protect themselves due to physical differences between the child and perpetrator, it is perceived that intervention by a third party is essential and many thoughts have been given to intervention by a third party.
- There are various methods to prevent crimes, which are divided into individual and social means. Individual means are preventive measures to protect oneself and family from many and unspecified perpetrators; however, few methods have been found to enable children to protect themselves. On the other hand, social means are related to ex-cons and are characterized by prevention after the fact; therefore, they are less often characterized by prevention prior to a crime.

According to an inquiry into preventive technologies, many useful technologies and functions have been found with mobile phones and include such diversified technologies as LBS and SOS functions. However, they may have problems because children are unable to perceive situations where they are exposed to crimes or there are difficulties in helping them directly or indirectly when they ask for help even thought they have perceived a crime.

3. Design concept of device for preventing child crime

As the study aims to prevent crimes, it is focused on suggesting the direction of design so that children can be protected from a crime through a device one way or another. Accordingly, it has designated a scenario to extract factors according to situations while suggesting guidelines needed for a device from the extracted factors.

---

[3] Shin Ah Jo, 'Research on Designing Customized Menu for Users in Mobile Phone', Dept. of Digital Design, Kyung Sung Univ.

3.1. Categories of scenario for child crimes

The following scenario was written based on crime categorization of Table 9 and was used to support reasons for necessary device features.

Criminal records	Methods	Cognition	Categories
Less than two previous conviction	Luring	does not perceive danger	category 1
	Kidnapping	recognize danger	category 2
More than two previous conviction	Luring	does not perceive danger	category 3
	Kidnapping	recognize danger	category 4

Table 9. Setting up four categories

This scenario was established based on a previous research and has the following conditions. It has been sub-divided into the following crime stages: crime prerequisite → approaching → luring and kidnapping → movement → committing crime before suggestion.

First, perpetrators are divided into ex-cons and first offenders and this scenario is related to the application of electric tagging. Some criminals attempt to commit a crime after removing electronic tagging; these are regarded as first offenders. These criminals are divided into luring and kidnapping and luring refers to as a situation where a child is unable to be exposed to a crime; kidnapping refers to as a circumstance where a child perceives that he or she is in danger.

Category 1 : Without Electronic Tagging and Luring

Category 1 of Table 10 describes the role of mobile phone for each phase under the premises that a 40-year-old man with less than two previous convictions targets a 12-year-old female victim.

Category 1	Setting	Phase 1	Phase 2	Phase 3	Phase 4
Perpetrator	40 year old, less than two previous convictions	Approaching	Luring	Movement	Commit a crime
Victim	6-12 year old girl / playground	Does not Perceive /wariness	Does not perceive	Does not perceive	Recognize
Function of mobile phone	Detecting any abnormal activities (route, speed, etc.)	-	-	Detecting any abnormal activities (route, speed, etc.)	Emergency button / Alarm/ lighting

Table 10. Category 1: Criminal without Electronic Tagging and Luring

The worst case is Category 1 because the perpetrator can hide intention and the child may never recognize the danger until right before the crime. In such a case, parents can be informed about abnormal activity of their child such as different routine pattern or sudden acceleration of speed and detect changes in mode of transportation; they can also confirm the situation of their child. In many cases, the child does not recognize danger until right before a crime, thus, active involvement of third party is necessary.

Category 2 : Without Electronic Tagging and Kidnapping

Category 2, seen in Table 11, shows a case of threatening and forcible kidnapping by a criminal with a similar previous conviction. Here, the child does not recognize danger until the criminal approaches; however, is aware of that the situation is threatening

Category 2	Setting	Phase 1	Phase 2	Phase 3	Phase 4
Perpetrator	40 year old, less than two previous convictions	Approaching	Kidnapping (threatening)	Movement	Commit a crime
Victim	6-12 year old girl / playground	Does not recognize/ wariness	Recognize	Recognize danger	Recognize danger
Function of mobile phone	Detecting any abnormal activities (route, speed, etc.)	-	Emergency button / Alarm/ lighting	Emergency button / Alarm/ lighting	Emergency button / Alarm/ lighting

Table 11. Category 2: Criminal without Electronic Tagging and Kidnapping

While the mobile phone detects routine pattern and speed, it can also alert a nearby third party by sounding an alarm or informing the child's parents and police when he or she presses the emergency button. However, when the child is being kidnapped forcibly or too nervous to control the device, the mobile phone's secondary function activates through LBS and informs guardians of abnormal activities.

Category 3 : With Electronic Tagging and Luring

Category 3, seen in Table 12, shows crimes committed by 40-year-old man with more than one previous conviction, wearing Electronic Tagging. Proposed mobile phone receives signals from Electronic Tagging; however, does not inform the child to avoid the human rights violation of the ex-convict.

Category 3	Setting	Phase 1	Phase 2	Phase 3	Phase 4
Perpetrator	40 year old, more than one previous conviction	Approaching	Luring	Movement	Commit a crime
Victim	6-12 year old girl / road	Does not recognize/ wariness	Does not recognize	Does not recognize	Does not recognize
Function of mobile phone	Detecting any abnormal activities (route, speed, etc.)	receives signals from Electronic Tagging, transmits warning message to guardians	check with guardian's remote camera, sound the emergency alarm, report to the police	Emergency button / Alarm/ Lighting	Emergency button / Alarm/ Lighting

Table 12. Category 3: Criminal with Electronic Tagging and Luring

The signal received from the Electronic Tagging transmits a warning message, such as "exposed to possible threat," to the child's guardian so they can determine whether their child is exposed to the actual threat or not. Additionally, if the guardian believes there is an actual threat, they can remotely sound the alarm on the child's mobile phone regardless of the child's will.

Category 4 : With Electronic Tagging and Kidnapping

Category 4, as seen in Table 13, is criminal wearing Electronic Tagging and kidnapping a child by threatening. In such a case, the child recognizes a danger and may take immediate action to notify a third party by pressing the emergency button. Even if the child fails to press button, he or she still can get help because the guardians are being notified by signals from Electronic Tagging device.

Category 4	Setting	Phase 1	Phase 2	Phase 3	Phase 4
Perpetrator	40 year old, more than one previous conviction	Approaching	Kidnapping (threatening)	Movement	Commit a crime
Victim	6-12 year old girl / Apartment entrance	Does not recognize/ wariness	Recognize	Recognize	Recognize
Function of mobile phone	Detecting any abnormal activities (route, speed, etc.)	receives signals from Electronic Tagging, transmits warning message to guardians	check with guardian's remote camera, sound the emergency alarm, report to the police	Emergency button / Alarm/ Lighting	Emergency button / Alarm/ Lighting

Table 13. Category 4: Criminal with Electronic Tagging and Kidnapping

Although it was impossible to consider every circumstance, this chapter has discussed the most common circumstances to conduct a study on children's perceptions of crimes and devices that can be helpful in such situations. This discussion has led to the understanding that devices require the LBS function to locate a child, a child's action radius and progress needed to be recorded and designated and a remotely controlled camera and microphone are required to help a protector judge the situation. It has also helped better understand that it is necessary to be able to communicate with parents or a guard.

3.2. Model for device system

Research was conducted to determine how devices sense abnormal movement by situation and how to deliver the information to a third party via logical operational device systems.

For the purpose of the operational system, routing, the rate of movement and location of a child, needs to be collected as data in advance for a certain period to be patternized. If the patternization is completed, the movement deviating from it, which is abnormal speed or change in rout, is considered abnormal movement of a child and is primarily reported to a protector. The following figure provides a detailed explanation.

As seen in Figure 5, a model for device function has been proposed based on the analysis of the above stated categories.

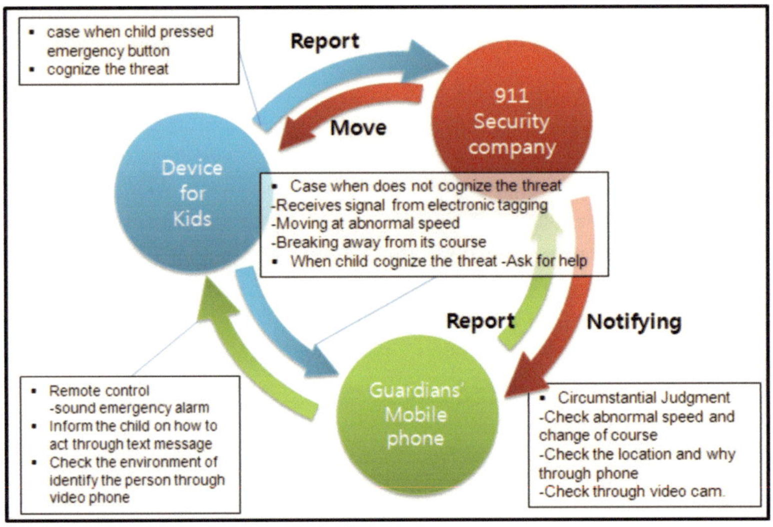

Figure 5. Model showing function of child protection device

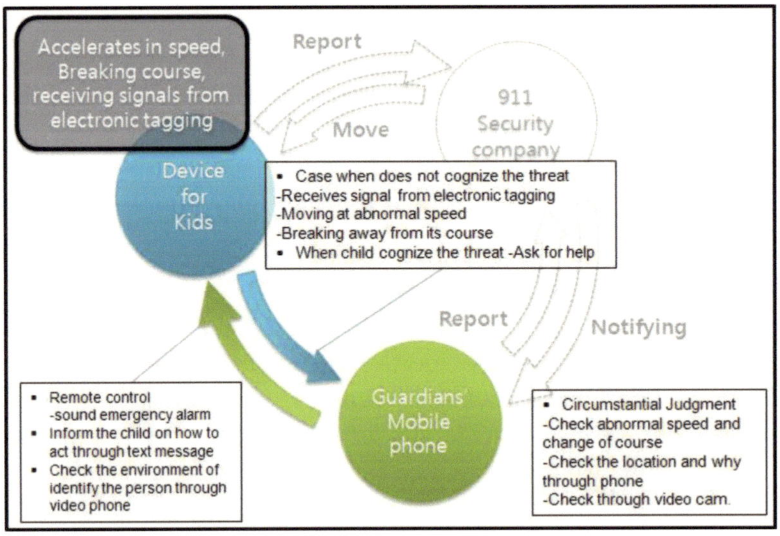

Figure 6. Model showing function of device when abnormal activities are detected

Based on the model illustrated on Fig. 5, Fig. 6 explains how a device for kids uses data on a child's routine pattern, moving speed, and signal from the Electronic Tagging and transmits information to a child's guardian when it detects abnormal activities

Fig. 7 shows how parents can explain to a child how to act through texting or calling based on the level of the threat. If a serious threat is determined, parents can sound the alarm and notify people nearby or contact a preregistered 911(US), 119(Korea), 112(Korea), or security company.

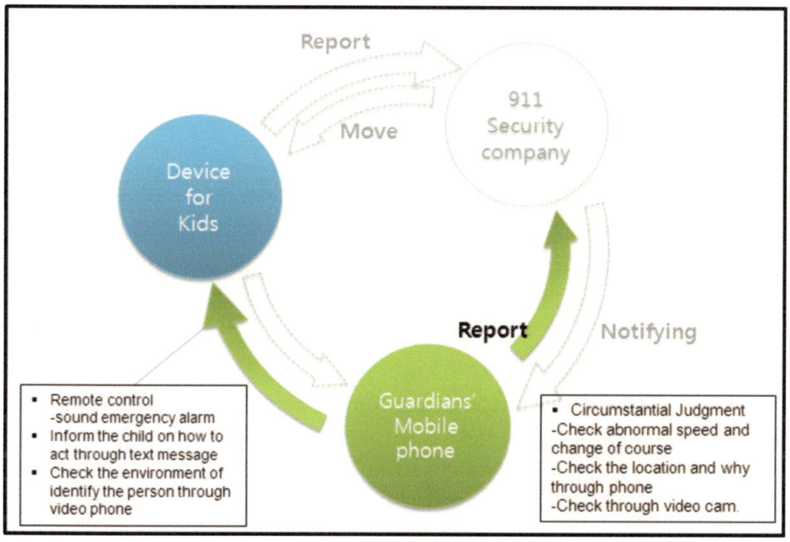

Figure 7. Role of guardians through understanding the situation

Fig. 8 shows how a system can automatically be activated and reported to the police when the device is damaged, the battery is forcibly removed, or the child presses the emergency button.

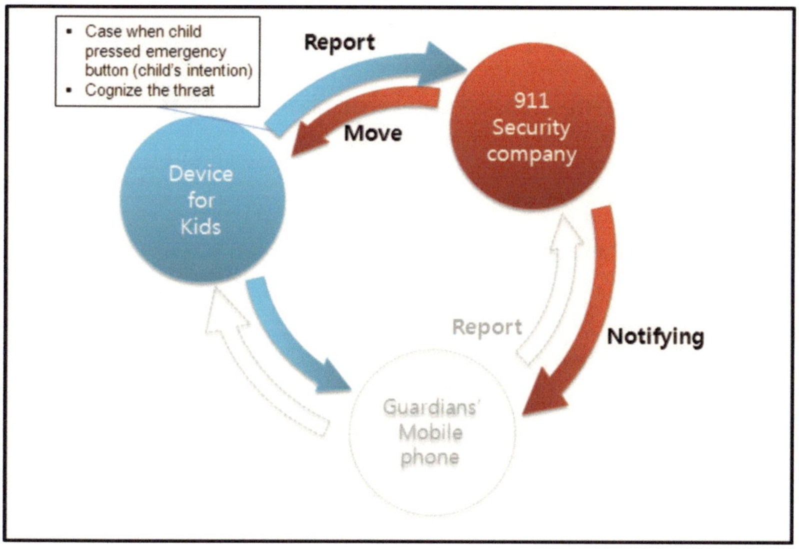

Figure 8. Model showing how children can report.

Findings suggest that a government agency (the police or a private company), a protector, and a child need to be linked to one another for cooperation when equipped with the system above as the device acts as a link. From examining products with similar or available functions among those on the market, smart phones are the technologies that best meet these requirements. However, given children aged 6 to 12 and such peripheral functions as an emergency button, it is difficult to apply existing smart phones as they are, and guidelines are deemed necessary for developing beneficial devices.

3.3. Summary

- Ex-cons, first offenders, luring and kidnapping have been mixed to categorize four scenarios based on four stages of a crime as extracted from the study: crime prerequisite → approaching → luring and kidnapping → movement → committing crime. Research has been conducted to determine the status of a child and the role of a device in each phase.
- Research has been conducted to comprehend the role of a device through these scenarios. Toward this end, research has been conducted on detailed functions of a device through a systematic diagram.
- This process revealed that practical preventive measures can be generated when a protector – the government (the police) or a private company (a security service provider) and a child communicate with one another to effectively prevent crimes. A protector can immediately estimate the situation on behalf of a child and a government agency or a private security service provider must intervene to protect a child while the device acts as a link.
- From examining products on the market with regard to a device that can fulfill such a role, smart phones are deemed the closest ones and, given that users are children, separate developmental guidelines are needed.

4. Drawing mobile phone design and demanding app

The chapter suggests guidelines for developing a device for children so that crimes can be prevented.

Information herein has been established based on useful factors on previous research, technologies, and services.

4.1. Guideline for figure design

Categories		Types	Contents
LCD Screen	Without	-	May be limited as it allows only text informing
	With	-	Informs a child of how to respond through various information
	Type	Window	Provides information through text or illustrations
		Full touch	Button type (Hotkey & 10-key) can be jointly used and age-specific usage is possible
	Size	-	Should not be larger than 5x9cm for usage by children aged over 6
Button	Number of buttons	6-9 year old	Number and size of buttons should be designed while carefully examining abilities of 6-9 year old child's operational skill. Buttons with icons are preferred over letter and should be limited with call, end, select menu,

			and number button (includes emergency button)
	-	9-12 year old	Number and size of buttons should be designed while carefully examining ability of 6-9 year old child's operational skill. Uses numeric keys and should be limited with call, end, select menu, and number button (includes emergency button)
	Size of buttons	-	Size and shape of buttons should consider one hand and two hand operation separately
	Shape of buttons	General	Should have convex design for easy operation of frequently used buttons
		emergency	Should be differentiated with general button and minimize unintended operation
	Arrangement of buttons	-	General and emergency buttons should be separated to minimize unintended operation, but should not hide it
	Type of buttons	Hot key	Specified key type makes for easy operation for a child under the age of 9. However, cannot make calls to many people
		10 key	Able to make phone calls to many people, but losses rapidness and is easy to operate for a child over age of 9
		Emergency key or strap	Can use specified key in addition to keypad to supplement weakness of 10-key type
		Track me	Unlike emergency button or strap, it has general button and different operational strategies
	Color of buttons	Achromatic color	-
		Low /high chroma	Change of chrome can visually alert people to cognize threat
	Text of buttons	-	-
Emergency function	Emergency buttons	Button type	Separate button can activate emergency button. It is easy to locate but has high risk of malfunctioning and is easily exposed to criminals
		Projected type	Projected type looks as if part of a mobile phone but activates when broken. Once it is broken, it is hard to restore. It is not easily exposed to criminals and may be hard for a child to break under certain circumstances
Emergency function	Emergency strap		Has a strap with hook. The hook may lead into malfunctioning; however, it has the advantage that a child can operate quickly compares to a button in any case
	Track me button		Child can inform guardians of his/her location when it is hard to make phone call or cognize great danger (unlike emergency button, it is used with general button and transmits signal with special operational method in emergency)
	Lighting	Lamp	-During night time phone calls -Notifying self location through flickering -Used as lantern in dark areas
	Sound	Speaker	Informs a child what he/she should do through sound
		siren	Ask for help through sound
Battery	Battery cover	Enclosed type (integrated)	Main body has integrated battery and powering off should not be easy

		Screw down type	Stops criminals from forcible powering off of a child's mobile phone. There will be an interval time to power off
	Battery charging	Use solar power	Should be sustained to enable communication with a child under any circumstances
		Self charged kit	Install portable or integrated self charger
	Latent battery		Has enough power to transmits signal of one's position for a certain length of time even after the battery is removed
Ubiquitous	camera	General phone call	Video telephone
		Emergency	Remotely collects data about the environment
	Mic.	General phone call	Telephone
		Emergency	Remotely collects data about the environment
	sound	Siren	Third party can remotely sound the alarm
Optional device	Watch, ring, necklace		Report the threat automatically once child's mobile phone is removed by criminals
	waterproof		Should operate under any circumstances

Table 14. Guideline for figure design

4.2. Guideline for application design

Categories	Features	Characteristics
Screen layout	Selective layout is possible.	Cognition and operational skill of 6-9 and 9-11 year olds should be considered, respectively, for age-specific design.
		Using illustration is suggested over text for UI.
Text	Font size can be adjusted.	Suggests using 16 font of computer monitor and could be modified, if necessary.
	Font type can be adjusted.	Suggests using Gothic type, but may choose other types.
	Maximum number of characters within screen.	Should be able to give information with minimum number of letters; Korean 4-6, English 9 letters, and should be legible instantly (e.g., emergency)
Electronic Tagging	-Receives signal from Electronic Tag. -Informs preregistered guardians about the signal.	Receives signal once Electronic Tag and a child falls within certain distance.
Emergency service	Informs when child breaks out of route.	Warns guardians when child breaks time-based activity pattern.
	Informs when detects change of moving speed.	When detecting dramatic change of speed; from 2-3km/h (normal walking speed) to 30-60km/h or stop moving for long period.

	Guardians can remotely control child's camera and microphone of mobile phone.	With prior consent, guardians who received warning message may access and control child's camera, microphone, and siren, which are installed in child's mobile phone.
SMS	Able to transmits short texts	
	Transmits preregistered message in case of emergency.	Child can transmit text message to his/her guardians with one touch.

Table 15. Guideline for application design

5. Example

5.1. Device specification

The chapter introduces an example of a selective application of guidelines for a crime-prevention device for children.

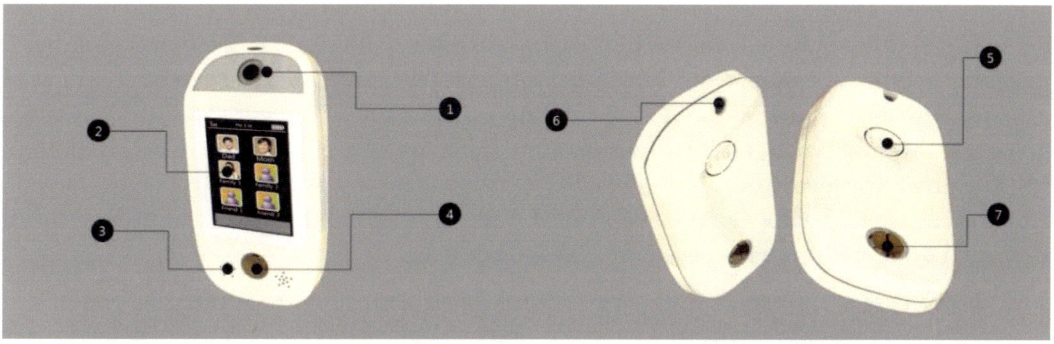

1 Remote Control Camera - Parents/Guardian can check up the child's surrounding using the child's mobile phone
2 Full Touch Screen - The layout can be made to suit one's taste. If the child is too young, parents/guardian can set it up.
3 Emergency Speaker - In emergency situation where child needs help, siren blows to inform their location; parents /guardian can also remotely activate blow the siren
4 Power Button
5 Emergency Button - If the button is pressed in an emergency where a child needs help, pre-set dial is activated to seek help.
6 LED Lamp / Emergency Light - Acts as a lamp and is automatically turned on when a child is isolated in the dark or will blinks to draw attention in the face of danger.
7 Battery Cover - If the power is turned off or battery is removed deliberately, it reports to a preset number.
Has a function that reports the location if the batter is removed.

Figure 9. Example of Device Specification

5.2. Age specified set-up

It is possible to set up the screen by age or taste. As users are aged 6 to 12, it has been divided into hotkey method and 10-key method based on children aged 9; however, can be set up in consideration of cognitive ability and manipulability.

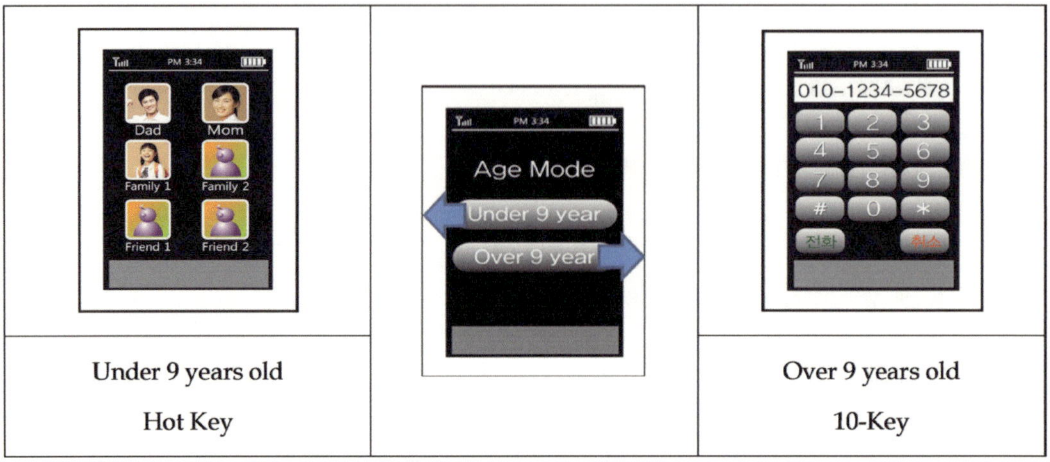

Figure 10. Example of Age Specified Set-up

5.3. Initial route set-up

Because it is difficult for a child to conduct an initial setup for oneself, it can be set up with the help of parents as seen below. The initial setup is conducted based on synchronization of a device with a computer. Figure 11 provides an explanation for the initial setup. First, if the home address and school address (destination) are entered, movement section is indicated, and if a private academy or friends are added, destinations are additionally entered as well. At that time, a child enters all possible routes. Although all routings have not been entered, they can be added during the period of collection of data.

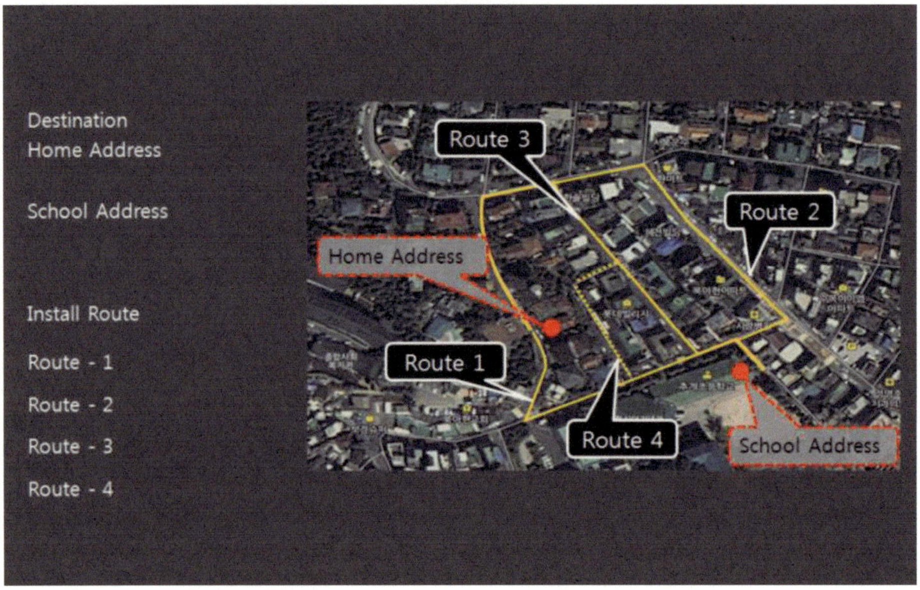

Figure 11. Example of Computer-Based Initial Setup Screen

After the setup, the device collects and records the routing of a child during a certain period. At that time, the direction and speed of movement are recorded by time and routes. The minimum unit of time is a week during a certain period and considerations are given for time of end of the class and after-school activities by day; learning schedule is designated by the week. Figure 12 below shows an example of recording changes in the daily movement of a child.

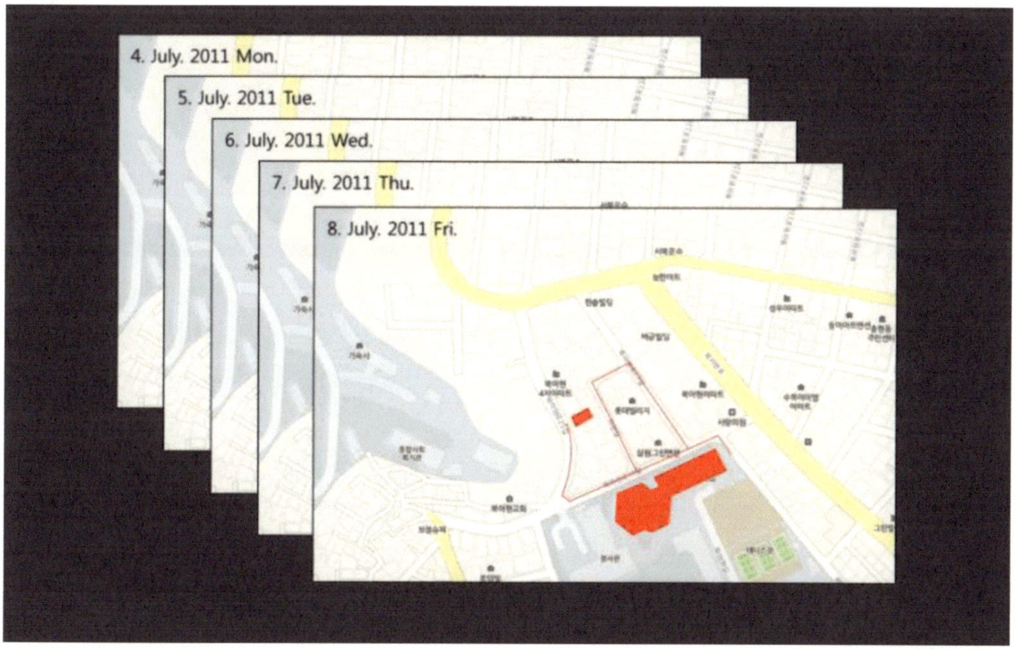

Figure 12. Example of Collection of Routing Data by Time and Day

Information collected for a week is recorded and the longer the period of data collection, more accurate patterns are displayed. The frequency of a child's movements are indicated as the thickness of a line and a private academy and a friend's house that have not been initially set up are recognized as abnormal routes to be reported to a protector for confirmation before the addition of the new destination and route. Figure 13 exhibits patternization of collected information.

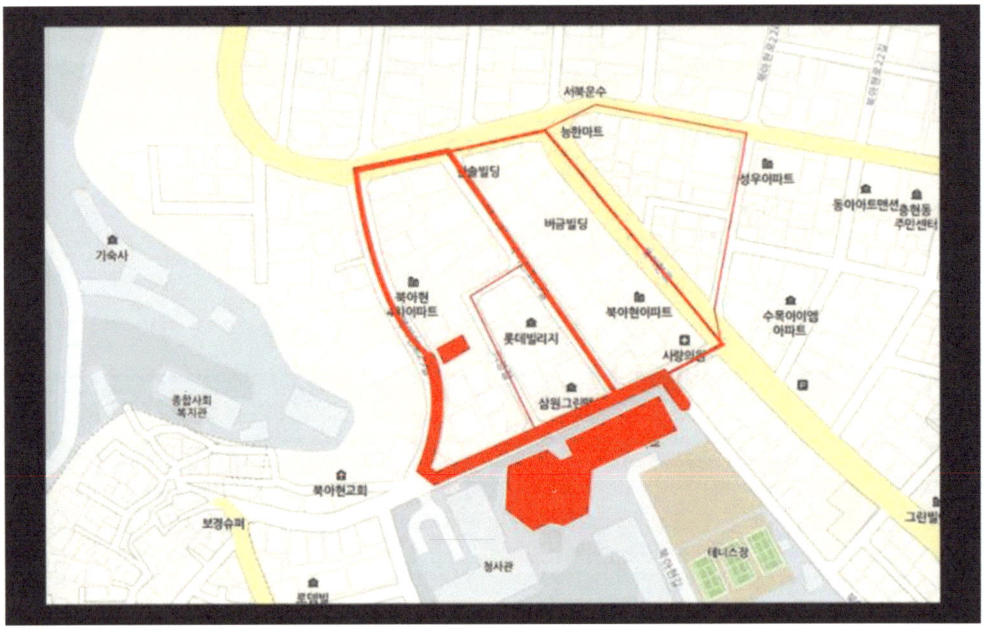

Figure 13. Example of Patternization Based on Collected Information

This figure refers to collecting routing and speed and direction of movement by unit time in addition to frequency of routing.

It senses abnormal changes in speed, long-time stoppage, and reverse-directional movement on the part of a child to report them to a protector for interaction.

6. Conclusion and limitations of the study

6.1. Conclusion

Theoretical examination and statistical research have helped understand serious problems in crimes against children who cannot protect themselves because of physical differences between when children perceive imminent danger. Such research has led to understanding that it is necessary for a third party to intervene for the sake of children. In the process of conducting research on including a third party, finding suggest that effective prevention can be realized when three factors exist (e.g., a child, society (the government or a private company), and a protector) and cooperate with one another. To facilitate such cooperation, a device enabling interaction is required to act as a link among the three factors. Among commercial products that are equipped with such functions, smart phones have been deemed appropriate; however, children are expected to have difficulties using existing smart phones as they are. In this regard, guidelines have been suggested through the application of available technologies and functions based on collected information.

With regard to the effectiveness of the study, it seems desirable that the government, rather than private companies, take the initiative for the welfare of children. This is because more children from low income families could benefit from measures taken by the government as it incurs costs of purchasing and maintaining such devices.

6.2. Limitation of the study

In the process of conducting interviews at welfare facilities, it was found that more sexual assaults are committed by acquaintances than by strangers and unofficial small crimes are frequently committed by relatives, which has not been accurately reported to protect children.

According to the study, it is impossible to protect many children from acquaintances committing a crime; however, it is difficult to prevent ex-con acquaintances from accessing children as they are acquainted with children.

In the process of conducting interviews with experts, other circumstances than usual situations were discussed with regard to evaluation of scenarios, which has been excluded as it appears difficult to consider each circumstance.

The longer the period for collecting data, the more sophisticated patterns; however, it might result in difficulties in preventing crimes that occur in the process of collecting data. Additionally, if it is difficult for parents to use a computer, it might be tricky to get help immediately.

Author details

Euichul Jung and Joonbin Im
Yonsei University, South Korea

7. References

The Legal Research and Training Institute, (2005-2008) *White Paper on Crime,* Ministry of Justice Republic of Korea, Korea(South)

Laura e. Berk(translated by Nang J. Park) (2007) *Infants & Children*(5thedition), Jungmin-sa, ISBN-139788958090687;ISBN-108958090685, Seoul

Sung Sim Han, Joo Mi Song, (2003),*Child Welfare,* Chang Ji-sa, ISBN-139788942602728, ISBN-10894260272X, Seoul

Chul Ok Cho (2009), *General Studies crime rhetoric,* ISBN-139788984683266;ISBN-108984683264, 21seiki, Seoul

Shin Ah Jo, (2007), *Research on Designing Customized Menu for Users in Mobile Phone,* Dept. of Digital Design, Kyung Sung Univ., Pusan

Han Il Lee, (2008), *A Study on Countermeasures of Child-target Sexual Assault Crime,* Graduate School of Public Administration, Soon Chun Hyang Univ., Chungnam

2007 23 ruling source: www.lownb.com

94 1306 ruling source: www.lownb.com

'Suspect Arrested for Murder of Yong San Elementary Schoolchild' YTN 2006. 2. 20 news